T0299052

Economic Openness and Territorial Politics in China

Why and how has the Chinese central government so far managed to fend off the centrifugal forces under rising globalization that are predicted to undermine national-level political authority everywhere? When institutionally empowered by centralized governing political parties as in China, national politicians confronting the menace of economic openness will resort to exercising tighter political control over the subnational governments of the "winner" regions in the global markets. Although its goals are to facilitate revenue extraction, redress domestic economic disparity, and prolong the rule of national leaders, regionally targeted central political control could engender mixed economic consequences at the subnational level. Yumin Sheng examines the political response of the Chinese central government, via the ruling Chinese Communist Party, to the territorial challenges of the country's embrace of the world markets and the impact of the regionally selective exercise of political control on central fiscal extraction and provincial economic growth during the 1978–2005 period.

Yumin Sheng is Assistant Professor of Political Science at Wayne State University. His research interests include globalization and domestic politics, federalism and decentralization, and regional political representation and resource redistribution under authoritarianism, with a focus on contemporary China. His recent work has also appeared in *British Journal of Political Science*, *China Quarterly*, *Comparative Political Studies*, *Journal of Contemporary China*, and *Studies in Comparative International Development*. He was a Visiting Research Fellow at the East Asian Institute of the National University of Singapore in 2008.

Economic Openness and Territorial Politics in China

YUMIN SHENG
Wayne State University

CAMBRIDGE
UNIVERSITY PRESS

CAMBRIDGE
UNIVERSITY PRESS

32 Avenue of the Americas, New York NY 10013-2473, USA

Cambridge University Press is part of the University of Cambridge.

It furthers the University's mission by disseminating knowledge in the pursuit of
education, learning and research at the highest international levels of excellence.

www.cambridge.org
Information on this title: www.cambridge.org/9781107507425

© Yumin Sheng 2010

First published 2010
First paperback edition 2015

A catalogue record for this publication is available from the British Library

Library of Congress Cataloguing in Publication data
Sheng, Yumin.
Economic openness and territorial politics in China / Yumin Sheng.
p. cm.
Includes bibliographical references and index.
ISBN 978-0-521-19538-6 (hardback)
1. China – Economic policy. 2. China – Politics and government – 21st century.
3. China – Foreign economic relations. I. Title.
HC427.95.S5325 2010
330.951–dc22   2010023937

ISBN 978-0-521-19538-6 Hardback
ISBN 978-1-107-50742-5 Paperback

To my grandmother Yuan Juxiu, *my mother* Gao Huijuan,
my father Sheng Jinpan, *and the memory of*
my grandfather Gao Xianwen, *with love and gratitude.*

Contents

Tables

Figures

Acknowledgments

This book grew out of my doctoral dissertation completed in 2005 at Yale University. My most profound gratitude first goes to the three finest scholars I was fortunate to have on my dissertation committee as co-directors. Professors Susan Rose-Ackerman, Frances McCall Rosenbluth, and Pierre François Landry are simply the best teachers and mentors one could ever dream of having. I thank them all for their guidance, support, and help in every possible way, and above all, the inspiration of their own examples.

A world-renowned scholar with influential work in many fields of law, economics, and political science, Susan has been one of the first to call for the rethinking of federalism and decentralization. For all her own busy schedule, she read and commented on multiple iterations of the book manuscript as well as the dissertation. A preeminent comparative political economist as well as Japan scholar, Frances lent both her expertise on Asia and sharp, critical thinking on how to conceptualize politics and the (potentially predatory) nature of the state. Both Susan and Frances have been unfailing sources of support and encouragement throughout the book publication process. Intent upon bridging the gap dividing the social sciences and China studies in his own work, Pierre showed me the ropes of conducting systematic empirical research on China. He also magnanimously shared with me many of his own Chinese provincial economic and political data as well as sources that formed the basis of the dataset first for my dissertation and, later, for this book. Professor José Antonio Cheibub deserves a special "thank you" for his insights and comments as an extra-committee reader of my dissertation.

My foremost intellectual debt is due to two other prominent scholars. Professor Geoffrey Garrett, my advisor during my first two years of graduate school at Yale, kindled my interest in studying economic globalization through his own prolific scholarship on domestic politics under global market integration. As the following pages will amply attest, Professor Yasheng Huang has shaped my understanding of the nature of the political ties binding Beijing and the provinces through his own pioneering work. In a way, my book builds on and seeks to extend an approach to the study of central-provincial relations in reform-era China he first advocated. I am also especially grateful to him for his generous support in so many ways over the years.

Through the munificent giving of their time, many other teachers, colleagues, and friends have helped improve the final product immeasurably. I am utterly thankful to them all. Bruce J. Dickson, Andrew Mertha, Susan Shirk, Dali L. Yang, Andrew Wedeman, Suisheng Zhao, Yongnian Zheng, and four anonymous reviewers for Cambridge University Press all carefully read the various versions of the entire book manuscript, offered critical and constructive comments, and saved me from many potential pitfalls in the logic of the argument, evidence, or presentation. Lei Guang, Yoshiko Herrera, Margaret Levi, Edmund Malesky, Akos Rona-Tas, Brad Roth, Tim Carter, Kevin Deegan-Krause, and Larry Scaff read and commented insightfully on chapters or materials related to the project. Daniel Ho, Takeshi Ito, Matthew Light, Xiaobo Lü, David Nickerson, John Roemer, Jun Saito, Jason Sorens, Endre Tvinnereim, (the late) Michael Wallerstein, Shaoguang Wang, Joseph Wright, Chenggang Xu, David Dahua Yang, Zaifu Yang, David Yoon, Chuanjie Zhang, and Lu Zheng all made excellent suggestions on many aspects of the project during discussions. Very helpful comments also came from fellow participants at the Workshop on Globalization and the State at Syracuse University in May 2008, especially Hongying Wang, Greg Chin, Robert W. Cox, and Kurt Weyland. Of course, any remaining errors are solely mine.

For methodological advice, I want to thank Donald Green, Kenneth Scheve, Nick Cox, Xiangyang Li, Joroen Wessie, and especially Yixiao Sun, whose friendship and expertise I have shamelessly exploited since we met in graduate school in New Haven. I am also indebted to Roy W. Bahl, Maria Cecilia Escobar-Lemmon, Robert Harmel, Hehui Jin, Kenneth Janda, Justin Yifu Lin, Zhiqiang Liu, Edmund Malesky, Yingyi Qian, Lori Thorlakson, Pieter van Houten, and Xiaobo Zhang for generously sharing their published and unpublished work and/or data, and patiently answering many of my questions. Data collection assistance came from Latoyra Weston at the Wayne State University Libraries, who handled numerous interlibrary loan requests with patience and efficiency, and from Jean Hung and the staff of the Universities Service Centre at the Chinese University of Hong Kong – especially Ms. Kwok Siu Yuk (Ruth).

Ming Xia generously shared many contacts and field research tips that greatly facilitated my field trips to China during the summers of 2002 and 2004. I am truly appreciative of the help and hospitality from Cao Xiaolin, Chen Feng, Chen Xian, Chen Xiaoyuan, Deng Guosheng, Hu Ming, Li Yongfang, Li Yu, Liu Desheng, Liu Yufei, Ni Huili, Pan Dawei, Pu Xingzu, Shen Liren, Shi Shijun, Wang Guosheng, Wang Yiwei, Yan Yinglong, Zhang Jianrong, Zhang Shu, Zhao Guobin, Zhong Yongyi, Zhu Guofu, Zou Yimin, and especially Ligang Feng while I was in China.

Research on the project at the dissertation stage was made possible through generous financial support from the Yale Graduate School, the Leitner Political Economy Program, and the Yale East Asian Studies Council. At Wayne State University, the 2005–2006 University Research Grant and the research stimulation grants from the Offices of the Provost of the Dean of the College of Liberal Arts and Sciences, and especially of the Vice President for Research under Professor Hilary Ratner, funded my work to transform the dissertation into a book.

The East Asian Institute of the National University of Singapore, where I was a Visiting Research Fellow during my sabbatical leave from Wayne State (June to December of 2008), provided the ideal environment for me to complete much writing and revision of the book manuscript. For their hospitality during my stay in Singapore, I am thankful to Professors Wang Gungwu, John Wong, and especially Dali L. Yang and Yongnian Zheng. During my visit, I also enjoyed friendly and enlightening conversations (and many a weekly expedition to the "Great Wall Canteen" for most) with a stimulating group of colleagues that also included Tom Bernstein, Zhiyue Bo, Chen Gang, Jing Huang, Huang Langhui, Yanzhong Huang, Kong Qingjiang, Hongyi Lai, He Li, Lin Zhiqing, Hong Lu, Sixin Sheng, Dorothy Solinger, Sarah Tong, Fubing Su, Fei-Ling Wang, Tianfu Wang, Yuqing Xing, Guobin Yang (who also kindly helped me with the collection of some of the latest Chinese fiscal data during his visit to Hong Kong), Lijun Yang, and You Ji.

At the nadir of the book proposal stage, Kurt Weyland and Andrew Murphy offered invaluable suggestions and encouragement, while the enthusiasm, support, and persistence of Dorothy Solinger meant and made a world of difference! At Cambridge University Press, I am above all most deeply grateful to Scott Parris, Senior Editor for Economics and Finance and undoubtedly the best editor any author could have, for his interest and faith in the project, his skillful hands shepherding me through the manuscript reviewing and book production processes, and his most astute advice along the way. I also want to thank Lewis Bateman for his generous support, Adam Levine for his able assistance throughout, Lisa McCoy for her excellent and meticulous copyediting, and Bindu Vinod for cheerfully coordinating all the work at the book's production stage. In addition, I am grateful to the superb editorial assistance from Nancy Hearst of Harvard University, who did a marvelous job of getting rid of many excessively long sentences from an earlier version and proofreading the final book, among other things, and to Anne Holmes and Rob Rudnick for preparing a preliminary index.

Over the years, many dedicated educators in China have quietly provided the most caring teaching and guidance. Among many others, I want to express my most heartfelt thanks to, roughly in the order I was lucky enough to have met them along the way, Hua Zuyi, Wang Yingru, Shao Shijin, Pat Bower (as well as her friend Mrs. Lee H. Robertson, who generously sent news magazines, books, and other English reading materials all the way from California), (the late) Gao Si, Christy Housel, Maxine Lindell, Xuelin Liu, Debbie Mar, Mei Renyi, and Yang Limin.

Likewise, heavy debts of gratitude have also been accumulated to many teachers in the United States. Even though I had little prior formal training in political science, Joseph Schwartz was willing to help admit me into the political science graduate program at Temple University with a generous university fellowship so that I could come to study in America. For me, his graduate seminar provided the best and most badly needed ontological overview of the discipline of political science. Benedict Stavis picked me up at the Philadelphia International Airport on an August afternoon in 1997 and put me up at his beautiful suburban house during my first week in America while helping me with apartment hunting. More important, he sought to maximize my exposure to the real-world policy debates concerning China by taking me to the Inter-University Study Group on China organized by the Foreign Policy Research Institute as its only regular student member. In the classroom, Richard Deeg, Lloyd Jensen, and Lynn Miller introduced me to the study of comparative politics and international relations. They also selflessly supported my later application to other graduate programs with more resources, and have remained invaluable sources of professional guidance and mentoring ever since. Outside the classroom, the friendship of and patient coaching by

Ming Xia was undoubtedly crucial in helping me survive my initial induction and immersion into political science at Temple.

Despite the awkwardness in my addressing him as "Professor Rogers" during application e-mail inquiries, Rogers Smith was instrumental in admitting me into the Yale graduate program he directed at the time. For their classroom teaching at Yale, I am grateful to Joseph Chang, Hanming Fang, Geoffrey Garrett, Alan Gerber, Donald Green, Martin Gilens, Anna M. Grzymala-Busse, Pierre François Landry, John Lapinski, (the late) Fiona McGillivray, John Roemer, Susan Rose-Ackerman, Bruce Russett, Kenneth Scheve, Ian Shapiro, and Alastair Smith.

During my years at Wayne State, invaluable support and encouragement has come from Dean Robert Thomas of the College of Liberal Arts and Sciences, the veteran "China hand" of the university whose unbounded enthusiasm about the country has never failed to inspire so many of us here. I have been particularly fortunate to work with Dan Geller, the most fair-minded and supportive department chair one could ever have. For their wonderful friendship and collegiality, I am also thankful to Phil Abbot, John Strate, Larry Scaff, Jered Carr, Tim Carter, Kevin Deegan-Krause, Sue Fino (the official department connoisseur of Chinese tea), Brad Roth, Ron Brown, Jim Chalmers, Charlie Elder, Rich Elling, Ewa Golebiowska, Kyu-Nahm Jun, Sharon Lean, Jodi Nachtwey, Charlie Parrish, Fred Pearson, Marjorie Sarbaugh-Thompson, Lyke Thompson, Mary Herring, Tim Bledsoe, and especially Bin Li and Haiyong Liu. My deepest gratitude also goes to Patti Abbot, Sheré Davis, Patricia Robinson, and above all Delinda Neal for their kindhearted, patient, and cheerful assistance in numerous ways.

I dedicate this book to the memory of my grandfather, to my grandmother, and to my parents. I thank them all for their unconditional love and support all along. By example, they have taught me the value of hard work in life. I also want to express my special gratitude to my mother-in-law He Yulan and my father-in-law Zhang Guanlin, who traveled thousands of miles away from their home in China to Michigan to lend us their helping hands during a most difficult period in the writing of this book. My wife Ying has been another true blessing in my life. I want to thank her for everything. Writing and completing the book must have also been made much easier by the arrival of our son Benjamin, with all the delightful distractions from work he has managed to bring so far.

Abbreviations

CC	Central Committee (of the Chinese Communist Party)
CCP	Chinese Communist Party
DPI	Database of Political Institutions (World Bank)
FDI	foreign direct investment
FFE	foreign-funded enterprise
FIE	foreign-invested enterprise
FTC	foreign trade company
GDP	gross domestic product
GIOV	gross industrial output value
GNP	gross national product
MPF	market-preserving federalism
NMP	net material product
PAN	Partido Acción Nacional (National Action Party of Mexico)
PLA	People's Liberation Army
PRC	People's Republic of China
PRI	Partido Revolucionario Institucional (Institutional Revolutionary Party of Mexico)
SEZ	Special Economic Zone
SOE	state-owned enterprise
TFP	total factor productivity
TVE	township and village enterprise

UN   United Nations
USSR   Union of Soviet Socialist Republics
VND   Vietnam dong
WTO   World Trade Organization

The Territorial Politics of Economic Openness in China

1.1 INTRODUCTION

It could be the best of times; it could be the worst of times. Far away from Dickensian England or France, the tale of this book is set about two hundred years later in China. After a tumultuous century of foreign domination, dynastic cessation, Japanese occupation, Communist ascension, socialist transformation, and the Cultural Revolution, the ancient Middle Kingdom was finally on a path to economic modernization. In the late 1970s, the country's reformist leaders began to revamp an economy defined by rigid central planning. Shunning decades of self-imposed autarky, they also opened up to the international markets in a belated quest for foreign trade, investment, and advanced technology from the West.

Soon, the Chinese economy was booming, catapulting the country into the ranks of the world's fastest-growing club, where it has stayed for more than three decades. As living standards were rapidly soaring, the economic success might have breathed new life and legitimacy into the rule by the Chinese Communist Party (CCP). Not all, however, was going well. The litany of domestic troubles was long; by the late 1990s, some problems had reached crisis proportions. Periodic inflation and rampant official corruption fueled urban protests and eroded public faith in the government (Stavis 1989; Walder 1991). Hefty agricultural burdens led to mounting rural unrest (Bernstein and Lü 2003). The emergence and flourishing of pseudoreligious sects and a nationwide criminal underworld posed new problems of governance (Chung et al. 2006). An insolvent state sector threatened to drag down the entire economy in a financial meltdown (Lardy 1998). In the meantime, an equally potent menace to CCP national rule was arising along the territorial dimension.

The challenge was by no means new. Through the millennia, maintaining political and territorial unity had always been a daunting task for the national rulers presiding over a continent-sized country (Solinger 1977, 18–21). Since the late 1970s, however, the problem had been exacerbated by the downward devolution of economic policy-making powers. Despite constant central policy injunctions, public investment urges on the part of the economically empowered local governments fanned a cyclical economic overheating (Huang 1996).[1] For a time, regional blockades pursued by the provinces against each other threatened to fragment the domestic market the reformers had sought to build from scratch (Wedeman 2003). Above all, the CCP-led central government confronted growing difficulties in extracting revenues from the localities amid a general decline of government revenues at all levels (Wang Shaoguang and Hu Angang 1993).

The need for central government fiscal transfers, however, was only heightened as economic disparity among the provinces deteriorated with the opening to the world markets. Provinces fared differently in the global markets by virtue of their geography and natural resource endowments. Those provinces faring less well griped about inadequate assistance from the central government. The winner provinces, in contrast, grew increasingly assertive in demanding fiscal autonomy and in resisting fiscal centralization. Before long, the "waning" of central fiscal capacity worsened regional fissiparous tendencies and prompted a rising cacophony among pundits, journalists, and even scholars who prophesized China's imminent disintegration (for example, M. H. Chang 1992; G. G. Chang 2001; Friedman 1993; Goldstone 1995; Waldron 1990).

There was little solace abroad for the Chinese national leadership. Communist rule was fast crumbling in Eastern Europe and the Soviet Union (Bunce 1999). Market reform, at least for a time, tended to aggravate the debts and deficits of local governments and undermined national macroeconomic stability in the developing world (Wibbels 2005). Most important, the centrifugal forces unleashed by ongoing economic globalization contributed to the recent "authority migration" away from central governments (Kahler and Lake 2003b). As global market integration

---

[1] Unless otherwise noted, in this book I follow the convention to use "local governments" generally to refer to both the provincial (subnational) and lower (subprovincial) levels of government in China.

reduced the minimal size required for viable state survival, intergovernmental fiscal conflicts could brew in face of rising interregional inequality, and separatist movements would agitate for ever-greater fiscal and ultimately political autonomy. Indeed, along these lines, some prominent economists (for example, Alesina and Spolaore 2003) have predicted surging secessionism and the breakup of nation-states around the world.

In short, domestic economic reform; opening to the global markets; and the worldwide trends of democratization, market transition, and globalization all boded ill for continued Communist national rule in China. By the early 1990s, indeed, the very ability to keep the country's territory intact had been called into question. As Goodman (1994, 1) aptly summarizes such sentiments of the time in his introduction to a volume exploring whether China has already "deconstructed," "the capacity of the People's Republic of China (PRC) to remain united has become a matter of considerable concern and debate." However, for all the unpropitious odds, the CCP-led Chinese central government seems to have ushered in the twenty-first century while presiding over a rapidly expanding economy projected by many to become the world's largest by mid-century, if not earlier.[2] Despite popular, ominous predictions to the contrary, so far it has managed to "hold the country together" and oversee a relatively tranquil territorial front at home (Landry 2008; Naughton and Yang 2004b). The wildest fears of intransigent provincial governments along the rich coast rebelling *en masse* have yet to materialize.

Social scientists have not been particularly successful in predicting state or regime collapse; any attempt to prognosticate their perpetual longevity surely will turn out to be no less futile. The goal of this book is more modest. In the broadest terms, I seek to explain the resilience of CCP national rule through the turbulence of economic reform and opening to the global markets during the period of 1978–2005.[3] I tackle one specific slice of this complex puzzle by focusing on the territorial dimension of the

---

[2] For example, in 2003 the investment bank Goldman Sachs estimated that the size of China's economy could outgrow that of the United States by 2041, but its revised estimation in 2008 suggests that the overtaking may occur as early as 2028 (cited in Layne 2009, 163).

[3] In this book, I broadly define the political center (or simply "the center") as the top leaders of the executive branch of the central government and their affiliated political party (or parties). In China, the political center refers to the top national leaders of the central government and the ruling CCP. Sometimes, unless otherwise noted, I follow the convention to use simply Beijing, the capital city, and itself a provincial unit, to refer to the Chinese political center, as Moscow is often referred to as the Russian political center.

tenacity of authoritarian single-party rule in China under rising economic globalization. Indeed, this territorial angle has mostly been neglected in a prominent literature that deals with the crucial question of the survival of CCP rule in China so far, largely through the lens of a state-society dichotomy (for recent important examples, see Dickson 2003, 2008; Tsai 2007). Why and how has the CCP-led central government in China so far managed to fend off the centrifugal forces from below predicted to undermine national-level political authority everywhere in the age of global market integration? Under what conditions are national political leaders better able to stave off the domestic territorial menace posed by economic globalization?

I argue that where they are institutionally empowered by centralized governing political parties, national politicians confronting the fissiparous challenge of economic openness will resort to exercising tighter political control over the subnational governments of the winner regions in the global markets in order to extract revenue, redress regional disparity, and prolong their national rule. The thrust of this logic is especially applicable to post-1978 China under the rule of one single political party, the most centralized party system that affords its national leadership the requisite political predominance and institutional wherewithal to wield territorially targeted political control. This book thus highlights the incentives of and the institutional resources available to national political leaders. In sharp contrast, prevailing economic theories on domestic territorial politics under economic globalization often privilege the demands for, above all, fiscal and, ultimately, political autonomy from subnational regions thriving in the global markets. They tend to predict sweeping national-level political decline and inevitable territorial disintegration (Alesina and Spolaore 1997, 2003; Alesina et al. 2000; Bolton et al. 1996; Bolton and Roland 1997).

Regionally targeted exercise of central political control, however, may engender mixed economic outcomes at the subnational level. In efforts to ensure greater policy compliance from below, tighter political control via the ruling CCP might facilitate central fiscal extraction from the provinces for interregional redistribution. It might also help remedy provincial-level "collective action" problems in providing national-level public goods such as macroeconomic stability. However, it could equally attenuate the center's commitment to protecting local property rights, harm economic incentives, and dampen economic growth in those very provinces targeted for greater political control and fiscal extraction. The remainder of this chapter outlines my argument, introduces the research design and data used in the book, summarizes the broader implications, and previews the chapters to follow.

I.2 THE ARGUMENT

I.2.I Terminology and Scope

The term "globalization" has become a linguistic cliché of our era. The phenomenon itself is not entirely new. A previous incarnation appeared between the 1870s and the eve of World War I, if not earlier (Bordo et al. 1999; Rothschild 1999). Its latest manifestation generally refers to "the rapid increase in cross-border economic, social, technological, and cultural exchange" facilitated by the "exogenous easing" of such enabling factors as advances in modern transportation and communications since the latter half of the twentieth century (Keohane and Milner 1996).[4] For the purposes of this study, I focus on economic globalization, broadly defined as the recent surges in trade and capital flows across national borders. I also use the terms "economic openness," "global market integration," and "economic integration" synonymously and interchangeably with "economic globalization" or simply "globalization."[5]

To be sure, government policies liberalizing international trade and capital flows are fundamental to any aspect of the politics of globalization, as I demonstrate in Chapter 3 in the case of China. In this book, however, I am primarily concerned with understanding the *political* consequences of the more exogenous aspect of economic globalization. I focus on how differential success in competing in the global markets by different subnational regions, largely dictated by geography and their respective natural resource endowments that are not easily amenable to the short-term influence of government policies, might affect their political relations with the national-level political authority.

Conventional scholarship on the politics of domestic intergovernmental conflicts under rising economic openness is usually based in the settings of advanced industrial democracies. It tends to emphasize the demands for greater fiscal and political autonomy from the subnational

---

[4] Keohane and Nye (2000), for instance, also include the military and environmental aspects of globalization in their discussion.

[5] For Berger (2000), "globalization" denotes the unstoppable global market forces. Keohane and Milner (1996) favor the term "internationalization," which implies how lingering state power still largely defines the boundaries of market penetration.

regions thriving in the global markets. The prevailing economic theories thus predict irreversible national political decline and territorial disintegration of nation-states, as noted earlier.[6] Although parsimonious, these theories have confronted a largely equivocal empirical record, as I discuss in Chapter 2. More important, the preferences of national-level political actors as well as those of actors in subnational regions that are faring less well in international commerce and investment, and the specific institutional arrangements binding governments at the national and subnational levels, are seldom taken into account in these lopsided studies.

In some sense, the persistent lack of serious scholarly efforts, even from political scientists, to tackle such glaring neglect of the political center in the existing accounts seems almost a puzzle in itself. In the rest of Chapter 2, therefore, I proceed to develop an argument that privileges the preferences of national-level politicians. Particularly in institutional settings imparting them the requisite political power, I argue, national political leaders have incentives to exert tighter political control over the subnational governments of the winner regions in the global markets. The primary goal would be to exact greater subnational compliance with central revenue extraction, to mitigate regional economic disparity through interregional redistribution, and, above all, to help maintain their national rule.

Throughout, I highlight the pivotal role played by centralized governing political parties in enabling such regionally targeted central political control. Following Riker (1964), I conceptualize the degree of centralization of a ruling political party along two dimensions. The first dimension revolves around the extent to which one governing political party rules both the national and subnational tiers of government. This, in essence, captures the ability of the central government to coordinate policy making with the subnational governments. The second dimension concerns the degree to which the national office of the political party of the national chief executive wields political control, for instance via personnel authority over its copartisans governing the subnational governments. It seeks to gauge the ability of the central government to elicit policy compliance from the subnational governments via the national governing political party.

---

[6] If this is any indication of their popularity or influence (and hence their "prevailing" nature), Alesina and Spolaore (1997) had already been cited 142 times in the Social Science Citation Index as of September 12, 2009. A Google Scholar search on the same day yields a citation count of 842 for the article and 501 for the book version of their argument (Alesina and Spolaore 2003).

Along these lines, in general, authoritarian single-party rule would epitomize the most centralized political party system. Countries under effective single-party rule should boast the most centralized political system where ideally one single political party capable of exerting considerable political power at the subnational level rules both the central government and all subnational governments. During the post-1978 era under study in this book, the CCP has been the sole national governing party in China, with a largely collective civilian leadership at the center. Chinese national leaders, via the ruling CCP, have been able to exercise substantial political control over the provincial governments through their exclusive personnel powers over the top provincial-level cadres. Amid deteriorating regional disparity and heightened needs for interregional fiscal transfers since its opening to international markets in the late 1970s, China has also witnessed growing fiscal intransigence from some of the wealthy coastal provinces. In short, reform-era China provides an ideal empirical setting for studying issues of domestic intergovernmental conflicts and central political control in the age of globalization.

1.2.2 Economic Globalization and Central Political Control

Much prominent research on China's political economy since 1978 has focused on economic decentralization – the devolution of economic policy-making authority from Beijing to lower-tier governments (for instance, Huang 1996; Landry 2008; Shirk 1993). However, the embrace of the global markets, an equally potent driver of China's impressive economic growth in this period, has been no less integral to the process of reform and opening. A small number of book-length studies have shed light on the importance of a linkage to the global markets in the dynamics of contemporary Chinese politics. For instance, Pearson (1991) has examined state control over the jointly owned enterprises in perhaps the first study of foreign direct investment (FDI) in China in the field of comparative politics. Zheng (2004a) argues that the new exposure to the world markets has actually helped the national leaders transform and rebuild the Chinese regulatory state. Gallagher (2005) notes how inflows of FDI have delayed political liberalization in China. Zweig (2002) has shown what the actual process of the Chinese localities opening up to the global markets could look like "on the ground."[7]

---

[7] Still others are primarily interested in understanding why there has been so much economic globalization in China in recent years in the first place. For example, both Huang (2003) and Wang (2001) investigate the political and institutional determinants of China's huge inflows of FDI during the reform era.

By tackling the territorial dimension, in contrast, this book probes how economic globalization has shaped intergovernmental political relations in post-1978 China. As such, I only briefly survey the phases of the country's opening to the world markets. I am more interested in understanding how the embrace of the global markets (largely assumed as an exogenous policy move initiated by the center) and the different provincial resource endowments for competing in international commerce (essentially exogenous, geographically determined attributes of the provinces) have contoured the political ties binding the central and individual provincial governments (endogenous political consequences) in China. Throughout, I focus on the role played by the Chinese political center – their incentives, institutional resources, and how they responded to the regional challenges in the age of economic openness.[8]

As I elaborate in Chapter 3, the striking provincial-level variation in the ability to participate gainfully in the global markets was partly responsible for a growing gap in provincial economic growth and wealth over the years. Consistent with the predictions of the prevailing economic theories, fiscal intransigence from provinces thriving in the global markets toward the central government had been on the rise. With more resources to spare, these winner provinces along the coast were seeking greater fiscal autonomy from the central government. In contrast, provinces faring less well grew more vociferous in their discontent over the worsening regional disparity and in their clamor for more assistance from the central government. For a time, the center confronted mounting strains on its capacity to raise adequate revenues and to perform interregional fiscal transfers. In the face of all these fissiparous pressures unleashed by the country's widening door to the outside, how did China's national leaders manage, for the most part, to preside over calmness and stability along the domestic territorial front in this period?

---

[8] Some scholars, such as Shirk (1994, 1996) and Yang (1991), do adopt a territorial angle, but they also mostly focus on the process of opening to the global markets, rather than the impact of a window to the international markets on the political ties between the Chinese central and provincial governments. There are some exceptions. An earlier study by Zheng (1994) examines how provincial participation in the global markets might enhance the de facto autonomy of the provincial governments. A few chapters in a volume edited by Goodman and Segal (1994) may also be pertinent. For example, Womack and Zhao (1994) briefly speculate on the implications for central-provincial political ties after surveying provincial-level variation in exposure to the world markets for the year 1990; Goodman and Feng Chongyi (1994) and Long (1994) discuss the possible consequences of a global economic linkage for regionalism in Guangdong and Fujian, respectively. None of these studies, however, explicitly or systematically addresses the political response of the Chinese political center, the focus of this book.

Two avenues of action seemed open. Since exposure to the global markets is endogenous to the adoption of an opening policy, an obvious remedy would be to reverse gears and close the door again. As the country scales back its participation in the international markets, regional inequality might abate and the need for fiscal transfers would lessen. Disgruntlement by the loser provinces would also quiet down. The central government would not have to increase its fiscal extractions from the richer provinces that might become less fiscally assertive. The centrifugal pressures unleashed by economic globalization consequently would fade. The option of a policy reversal, however, seemed to have long been foreclosed. After all, it was the rising "opportunity costs of closure" – continuing economic stagnation and the threat to the legitimacy of Communist rule under pre-reform autarky versus the potential efficiency gains from an alternative strategy – that could have prompted the turn to the international markets in the first place. Despite setbacks at times, indeed, the Chinese central government had unswervingly pursued economic opening, culminating in the country's accession to the World Trade Organization (WTO) in 2001 (Sheng 2002).[9]

A more appealing option might be for the Chinese national leadership, like central governments similarly confronting the centrifugal forces of globalization elsewhere, to engage in more active fiscal extraction (from the winner provinces) and redistribution (to the loser provinces), as I suggest in Chapter 2. This seemed to be what the Chinese political center pursued in the period under study. As I discuss at length in Chapter 3, the fiscal capacity of the Chinese central government in this era might have been generally underestimated. Furthermore, interprovincial fiscal redistribution in favor of the inland provinces faring less well in global markets was being implemented by the center throughout this period. The extractive and redistributive capability of the central government in this era, however, cannot be understood in isolation from the resilient political strength of the Chinese national leadership imparted by the ruling CCP. In this book, I study how the Chinese political center took

---

[9] In retrospect, such "opportunity costs of closure" could indeed have been quite high, as the chastening comparison with North Korea that has so far persistently refused to open up amply attests. A recent assessment of North Korea's economic performance during 1950–89 by Kim et al. (2007) links the dismal record of the country's basic economic indicators since the 1960s to its low or even negative total factor productivity (TFP). In contrast, opening to the global markets seems to have been a major driver of China's TFP gains and economic growth in the post-1978 era (Hu and Khan 1997).

advantage of the institutions within the ruling CCP to exercise regionally differential political control over the provincial governments in the age of economic globalization.

I focus on the nomenklatura system whereby the national leaders wield the authority to appoint, transfer, and dismiss top provincial officials (Manion 1985). Specifically, I examine their deliberate choice of different types of leading provincial officials who are predisposed to varying likelihoods of compliance with central government policy preferences to exercise varying degrees of political control over the provincial governments. In Chapter 4, I sketch the workings of China's CCP-dominated political system and the related institutions within the single ruling party that endow the center with political predominance over the provincial governments. I conjecture that the Chinese national leaders would seek to exert tighter political control over the subnational governments in the winner regions in the global markets in order to extract their fiscal resources for redistribution, pursue balanced regional development, and prolong their own national rule. I systematically assess this hypothesis with provincial-level data in Chapter 5.

To be sure, the integrative role of the central nomenklatura powers imparted by the ruling CCP has been noted in a number of astute studies on reform-era China that question the "imminent disintegration and collapse" thesis. Debunking the notion that China was already drifting toward "regionalism" and "deconstruction" under reform and opening, for instance, both Goodman (1994, 4) and Yang (1994, 86) pinpoint such personnel authority as a key institutional mainstay of CCP national rule. Likewise, in explaining "why China will not collapse," Huang (1995b, 1996) attributes the country's overall macroeconomic and political stability to the center's monopoly personnel powers over the provincial governments. For Naughton and Yang (2004a, 11), the "very existence" of central nomenklatura powers has contributed to China's "national unity" in this period. Studying the promotion patterns of cadres below the provincial level, Landry (2008), likewise, argues that China's brand of "decentralized authoritarianism" has so far been held together precisely by the CCP's nomenklatura powers at the local levels even though the center exercises mostly indirect personnel authority beyond the provinces. Nevertheless, none of these scholars has shown exactly *how* the Chinese political center utilized such personnel powers to exercise direct but regionally selective political control over the different provincial governments, the primary task of this book.

1.2.3 Political Control, Fiscal Extraction, and Economic Growth

Existing research tends to highlight the potentially benevolent role of the regionally selective exercise of central political control in reform-era China. Tighter central political control over provincial governments could help suppress provincial public investment urges (Huang 1996) and maintain lower provincial inflation (Huang and Sheng 2009) by enticing provincial sympathy with the central policy aversion to economic overheating. It can thus help provincial governments overcome the "collective action" curse (Olson 1971) in the provision of national-level public goods such as macroeconomic stability. For the purposes of this study, the regionally calibrated exercise of central political control could aim at facilitating compliance with the center's revenue demands from those provinces thriving in the global markets. Conceivably, therefore, it might ease central resource extraction and interregional redistribution, helping contribute to more balanced regional economic development in China, even though "intentions" do not always guarantee "results."

The effect of the territorially targeted central political control, however, is not all benign. Exertion of tighter political control via a centralized ruling political party to ensure greater provincial compliance with revenue extraction might also invite unwarranted central fiscal predation. This line of reasoning echoes a prominent strand of the political economy argument better known under the rubric of "market-preserving federalism" (MPF) in research on reform-era China (see, for instance, Montinola et al. 1995; Qian and Weingast 1997; Weingast 1995). In particular, the MPF adherents build on the insights of North and Weingast (1989) to highlight the growth-enhancing role of a "credible" and "politically durable" commitment by national leaders to protecting local property rights. Because provincial governments under a more tenacious central political grip are more likely to comply with the central government fiscal policy preferences, they are more susceptible to central revenue extraction and perhaps even predation. This could undermine the protection of property rights for the local economic actors, distort their incentives for economic expansion, and hamper economic growth in the very jurisdictions presided over by these more compliant provincial governments.

Accordingly, I hypothesize that, other things being equal, Chinese provinces ruled by the more tightly controlled subnational governments are subject to greater central fiscal extraction than other provinces, and the exercise of tighter central political control has a dampening effect on provincial economic growth.[10] In Chapter 6, I investigate how the regionally selective exercise of central political control affected provincial revenue remittances to the central government and provincial economic growth in the post-1978 period. Although it is inherently in keeping with the notions of "credible commitment" and "property rights protection" in the political economy research on economic development, my argument is also different. In this book, I focus on the *provincial-level* variation in central-provincial *political* ties.

By contrast, conventional applications of MPF tend to dwell on the national level in discussing "political decentralization" in post-1978 China. They also overemphasize the primacy of fiscal contracts with the provincial governments as a credible commitment device used by the central government (for instance, Jin et al. 2005; Lin and Liu 2000; Montinola et al. 1995; Oi 1999). Due to the political predominance of the Chinese political center in a most centralized political system, however, the overall credibility of fiscal contracts and the related central commitment to protecting local property rights should be questionable. Reneging on fiscal contracts and "forced borrowings" from below by the central government in contravention of formal contractual terms were common. This has been extensively documented in existing research on the post-1978 Chinese political economy, as I will review in Chapter 3. Applying the logic of MPF to study economic growth in reform-era China at the national aggregate level with a focus on nominal fiscal contracts is thus misleading. An approach emphasizing the provincial-level variation in the degree of central political control exercised over the different provincial governments, as pursued in this book, is more apropos and fruitful, and still consistent with the underlying thrust of MPF's original logic.

1.3 RESEARCH DESIGN AND DATA

1.3.1 A Subnational Research Design

This book focuses on the political relations between the national-level political authority and governments at the subnational level – the provinces

---

[10] This line of reasoning is also consistent with observations based on careful case studies by White (1989) and Whiting (2001) that the Chinese central government's heavy fiscal burdens on Shanghai could have stunted the metropolis's economic dynamism in the post-1978 era. However, these studies often neglect the possibility that the exercise of tighter central political control can make certain provincial units such as Shanghai particularly vulnerable to fiscal extraction by the central government in the first place.

in China in our case – for the following reasons. First, because in China provinces constitute the largest administrative and territorial units below the center, with direct fiscal relations with the central government during the post-1978 era, a subnational design focusing on the provinces permits the most logical level of analysis for examining possible centrifugal forces and territorial conflicts unleashed by economic globalization from within a state. Second, for our purposes, the monopoly personnel powers directly wielded by the political center over the leading provincial officials via the sole governing CCP throughout this period is essential to our study of the regionally targeted central political control over the provincial governments.

Third, employing the provinces within one country as the basic unit of analysis provides methodological advantages over a cross-country research design. In contrast to studies comparing a small number of countries, a subnational research design increases the number of observations, allowing us to obtain higher confidence in the findings of our analysis (King et al. 1994, Chapter 8). Unlike large-N cross-country comparative studies drawing on diverse data sources from many countries that often maintain different statistical standards, analysis based on subnational units within one country utilizes relatively homogenous data, implicitly controls for many unobservable but important factors, and thus can improve the overall validity of comparative research. Given these strengths, it is no wonder that the approach has been gaining rapid popularity in political science (Snyder 2001). Thus, although I briefly examine the relevant national-level policies, institutions, and trends, this book primarily relies on provincial-level data.

1.3.2 Data and Possible Endogeneity

As I will review in Chapter 3, many empirical studies have found that the Chinese provinces more exposed to the international markets tended to grow faster and to enjoy higher levels of wealth in the post-1978 period. In other words, provinces that trade and export more are more likely to benefit from a linkage to the global markets. Therefore, throughout this study, I proxy the degree to which a province thrives under economic openness through the extent of its exposure to the global markets. More concretely, the degree of economic globalization of a province is operationalized as the share of provincial exports in provincial gross domestic product (GDP), and, alternatively, the share of total foreign trade (exports plus imports) in provincial GDP. The data on these and other economic variables come from the official publications of China's national and provincial statistical agencies.[11]

I specifically examine the exercise of political control over the provincial governments by the national leaders with regard to the latter's management of the provincial party secretaries, the top-ranking officials in the provinces. Although I also survey the temporal trends and regional patterns exhibited by some other indicators, I mainly follow the seminal work of Huang (1996) and use the measure of "bureaucratic integration" of the provincial party secretaries to gauge the degree of central political control exercised over the provincial governments. The notion of "bureaucratic integration" seeks to capture the inclination of the leading provincial officials to comply with central policy directives by virtue of their career trajectories. The political data used for the analysis are culled from various compilations of official material on top provincial personnel.[12]

As noted, I treat the variation in the provincial degree of exposure to the global markets as largely exogenous, reflecting for the most part the differences in relatively unchanging provincial natural resource endowments, such as their geographic proximity to the coast. Such variation could be potentially endogenous in that the preferential policies in the foreign economic sector from the central government had been regionally tilted, favoring in particular the coastal provinces at the outset of the reform and opening era. Nonetheless, a strong case can be made that these regions received preferential policy treatment precisely because they enjoyed favorable geographic locations and were initially perceived by the political center as being better endowed to compete in the global markets. As noted, meanwhile, our indicator of the degree of central political control exercised over the provincial governments is based on the career patterns of leading provincial cadres. A related issue could be that the measure might capture the personal connections of the provincial officials with the top central leadership and the provincial abilities to lobby for policy pork from the center in the first place. Such concerns do not appear to be empirically warranted, however. I discuss at length these issues of endogeneity in Chapter 3, and systematically tackle them in Chapter 5.

---

[11] In the Appendix to Chapter 3, I provide details on the sources of, and possible issues related to the use of, Chinese official economic data.

[12] Together with the coding details, the sources of the political data are discussed in the Appendix to Chapter 4.

1.4 BROADER IMPLICATIONS

This book is primarily concerned with the causes and consequences of the evolving political ties that bind the national-level political authorities and their subnational units under growing economic openness, with an empirical focus on post-1978 China. As such, it is broadly lodged at the intersection of four subfields in the study of comparative political economy: domestic territorial politics under economic globalization, political decentralization, authoritarian resilience under single-party rule, and China's central-provincial relations during the country's transitions.

First, the book highlights the linchpin role played by centralized political parties in helping national political leaders ward off the centrifugal pressures from within national borders induced by integration with the global markets. I take issue with popular economic theories that privilege the autonomy demands of the winner subnational regions in the global markets and that predict the inevitable demise of national-level political authorities. I focus on the incentives of national political leaders, especially those in countries governed by centralized political parties, to exercise tighter political control over the subnational governments in the winner regions in order to extract fiscal resources with which to compensate the loser regions, and more importantly, to keep the country together and maintain themselves in power. In the case of China, I argue that the political center, in response to the fissiparous forces of the global markets, has resorted to the nomenklatura tools imparted by the sole governing CCP to exercise regionally selective political control over the provincial governments.[13]

Second, this book contributes to efforts to construct a more meaningful subnational measure of political decentralization. My main emphasis on the role of centralized governing political parties echoes Riker's (1964) exhortation to conceptualize political decentralization as governing political party decentralization. Although pioneering research with a Rikerian approach has been largely cross-national in scope (see, for instance, Wibbels 2005), I capitalize on the advantages of a subnational research design, drawing on provincial-level data from one country under single-party rule. Indeed, all ruled by one political party but under varying

[13] As I discuss later in Chapters 3 and 4, China's national leaders of this period, conservatives (such as Chen Yun and Li Peng) or reformers (such as Deng Xiaoping and Jiang Zemin) alike, have expressed similar concerns over the centrifugal consequences of rising regional economic disparity and the need for fiscal centralization and interregional redistribution.

degrees of political control exercised by the center, different Chinese provincial governments essentially enjoy varying degrees of de facto political decentralization. Thus, the case of post-1978 China under single-party rule furnishes an ideal subnational empirical setting for studying political decentralization.

Third, the story of the regionally selective exercise of central political control over the subnational governments in a resilient single-party regime illuminates a possible political mechanism along the territorial dimension behind the relative durability of single-party authoritarianism. Much recent work in the broader study of comparative politics has noted that authoritarian single-party rule tends to last longer than dictatorships led by military juntas or individual autocrats (Geddes 1999b; Magaloni 2008). Most existing studies have emphasized how authoritarian leaders in single-party regimes tend to co-opt and control the political opposition in the civil society (Huntington and Moore 1970)[14] or rival autocrats from within the ruling regime (Brownlee 2007; Gandhi 2008). Research focusing on either the state-society dichotomy or internal elite rivalry, however, neglects the territorial dimension of challenges to authoritarian rule that are especially salient under rising global market integration. My focus on how the Chinese national leaders exercised regionally targeted political control via the sole governing CCP in this book, in contrast, will help highlight the territorial aspects of authoritarian political co-optation and control under single-party rule.

Finally, this book will advance the study of central-provincial relations amidst China's domestic transitions. Above all, I pinpoint economic globalization as a key determinant of the regionally selective exercise of political power by the center over the provincial governments. My study casts doubt over assertions linking the country's reform and opening with the gradual withering of central political authority and imminent disintegration of China. Regional variation in the degree of central political control exercised over the different provincial governments implies that the center's ability to secure provincial policy compliance could vary across the provinces. By exploiting a subnational research design, my book also echoes a small number of existing studies that highlight provincial-level variation in central state capacity to secure local policy implementation in post-1978 China (for example, Chung 2000; Huang 1996; Whiting

---

[14] For recent seminal work on how the CCP has tried to co-opt the most vibrant entrepreneurial class into its ranks in order to sustain its rule in China, see Dickson (2003, 2008).

2001). It thus departs from scholarship that focuses predominantly on the national aggregate level and that highlights the possible decline in the center's overall political strength over the years (for instance, Oi 1999; Walder 1995b; Zhao 1990).

Furthermore, my book suggests the possibly mixed consequences of regionally targeted political control by the center under CCP single-party rule for China's economic and political transitions. Exercise of tighter central political control might help provide a more stable macroeconomic and political environment for the country's ongoing economic transition. However, it might also hurt local economic incentives in those provinces that bear the brunt of a firmer central political grip. Central political predominance via the monopoly personnel powers upon which the effective exercise of central political control over all provincial governments hinges, however, could be undermined by the prospect of the country's democratization that will end CCP single-party rule. This, in turn, might deter national-level politicians from initiating the advent of political democracy in China in the first place.

I will further discuss these broader themes in Chapter 7, but it is also important to clarify here what this book is *not.* Privileging the incentives of and institutional resources available to the national-level political actors in no way endorses the often-untenable assumption of a benevolent political center. Rather, I assume Chinese national leaders are primarily animated by the desire to stay in power, much like their counterparts elsewhere, democratically elected or otherwise (Mayhew 1974). Compared with officials working at the subnational level, they are more likely to be concerned about national-level issues such as the fiscal capacity of the central government, macroeconomic stability, or overall balanced regional development, things that are all vital to their paramount goal of political survival. Nor does this book advocate the idea that the ability to exert central political control over the subnational governments via a single governing political party is a panacea for the multitude of challenges in territorial governance of our era. As already noted, the overall effects of regionally selective exercise of central political control at the regional level seem far from clear-cut.

1.5 PRÉCIS

After this brief overview in Chapter 1, I take issue with the prevailing economic theories that forecast inexorable national-level political decline and national political disintegration under globalization in Chapter 2.

Where the center is institutionally empowered to exert political control at the subnational level via Rikerian centralized political parties, I argue, national politicians will seek a tighter political grip over the subnational governments of the winner regions to extract fiscal resources, pursue interregional redistribution, and maintain their own national rule. I also suggest the mixed economic consequences of the regionally targeted central political control at the subnational level. Tighter control may help alleviate subnational "collective action" problems, but could also facilitate central fiscal extraction and predation, and hurt local economic incentives.

In the following chapters, I turn to the story of China during the post-1978 period. Chapter 3 provides a synoptic account of the country's opening to the global markets. I highlight the issues of growing economic disparity between the thriving coastal provinces and the inland provinces that were faring less well, and the rising imperative for interregional fiscal redistribution by the center. Indeed, the strength of central fiscal capacity has often been underestimated. Interprovincial fiscal transfers performed by the central government seemed quite alive and well throughout this period. To understand the center's political prowess underpinning its fiscal capacity, in Chapter 4 I highlight the role of party primacy and central political predominance under CCP single-party rule. I also discuss the workings of the CCP nomenklatura system that endows the center with monopoly personnel powers over the top provincial cadres and enables the national political leadership to exert selective political control over the provincial governments. Our broad-gauge assessment of temporal trends and regional patterns via employing various indicators detects no clear signs of weakening political control by the Chinese central government over the provincial governments in general during these years. Preliminary evidence also suggests that the center exercised (increasingly) tighter control over the coastal provincial governments, in particular by installing in their top leadership posts the more "bureaucratically integrated" provincial party secretaries.

Chapter 5 tests, in a more systematic and rigorous fashion, the hypothesis that the Chinese political center exercised more stringent political control, via the appointment of the more loyal top provincial officials, over the provincial governments in subnational regions that benefited more from a linkage to the global markets. Provincial-level time-series cross-section evidence for the 1978–2005 period shows robustly that pro-center provincial party secretaries – more predisposed toward compliance with the center's policy directives by virtue of their career backgrounds – were more likely to be assigned to govern the provinces conducting more exports and foreign trade. Investigation of possible endogeneity reveals little support for the notion that the more loyal agents of Beijing took advantage of their closer career ties with the center to secure generous policy pork from the central government regarding the establishment of economic development zones. That is, tighter central political control did not appear to have made the jurisdictions overseen by these more loyal officials become more exposed to the global markets in the first place.

I examine the consequences of the regionally targeted political control by the center in Chapter 6. I first show aggregate trends of tighter central political control over the provincial governments closely associated with greater fiscal centralization in China throughout the post-1978 period. Moreover, those provinces ruled by pro-center agents tended to remit more budgetary revenues to the central government after the 1994 fiscal reform, implying their greater susceptibility to fiscal extraction by Beijing. There is also strong evidence that tighter central political control was negatively correlated with provincial economic growth in post-1978 China. Taken together, these empirical results are consistent with the notion that tighter central political control over the provincial governments could not only facilitate central resource extraction but also dampen economic growth in those targeted provinces.

By way of conclusion, I elaborate on the broader implications of the book in Chapter 7. I first call for greater attention to the incentives and institutional resources of national-level political authorities in research on domestic territorial conflicts under rising economic openness. I then point to other possible cases – specifically Vietnam and the former Soviet Union – where similar arguments can be tested in future research. I also stress the often-underappreciated advantages offered by subnational-level data in studying the macroeconomic consequences of political decentralization. Finally, I assess how the regionally selective exercise of central political control under CCP single-party rule has affected China's ongoing economic transition and speculate what this implies for the country's prospect of political transition to democracy.

Globalization, Institutions, and Domestic Territorial Politics: A Theoretical Framework

2.1 INTRODUCTION

Burgeoning political economy research has probed the dynamics between global market integration and national political disintegration. In particular, prevailing economic theories forecast rising secessionism and inevitable state breakups, but they confront an ambivalent empirical record. Indeed, our replication exercise based on a large cross-national sample and reported later in this chapter furnishes little evidence that economic globalization is unambiguously linked to decline of national-level political authority. In this chapter, I highlight the utility of an approach privileging the national rulers. I argue that national political leaders who rule with the help of centralized political parties will resort to exerting tighter political control over the subnational governments in the winner regions of the global markets in order to facilitate resource extraction, mitigate regional disparity, and prolong their national rule.

Centralized political parties governing at both the national and subnational levels impart to the national political leadership the institutional wherewithal to wield regionally selective political control – for instance, via personnel powers over copartisans staffing the subnational governments. Appointing agents who are more likely to comply with the policy preferences of their national superiors enables the center to exercise a greater degree of political control over the regional governments that these agents lead. Thus, national leaders who rule with the help of centralized political parties can exercise varying degrees of political control over the different subnational governments through appointing different types of officials to the regional government leadership positions. They should be particularly interested in exerting tighter political control over the subnational governments in the winner regions of the global markets. This aims at ensuring their greater compliance with central resource extraction and dampening their intransigence in demands for greater regional fiscal and ultimately political autonomy.

The logic of the argument is most applicable to reform-era China that has rapidly embraced the global markets. Via a most centralized national governing party – the single ruling CCP – the national leadership enjoys political predominance over and monopolizes personnel management of the top provincial officials. This allows the political center to engage in regionally selective political control. Tighter political control exercised over the subnational governments helps solicit greater policy compliance from below, remedy provincial "collective action" problems in contributing to national macroeconomic stability, and ease central fiscal extraction for interprovincial transfers. However, it may also tempt central fiscal predation, undermine the credibility of the central commitment to protecting local property rights, and harm the incentives of local actors for economic expansion in the targeted provinces.

The remaining sections of the chapter are organized as follows. I first review the economic theories on globalization and national political decline that have emphasized the demands from the winner subnational regions for ever-greater regional autonomy. I then proceed to sketch the main elements of an approach highlighting the incentives of national political leaders, especially in polities governed by centralized political parties. However, I note the mixed consequences at the subnational level of the regionally targeted central political control. Along the way, I briefly discuss the applicability of the argument to post-1978 China.

2.2 GLOBAL MARKET INTEGRATION AND DOMESTIC POLITICAL CONFLICTS

2.2.1 Economic Openness and National Political Decline

Conventional measures of trade and investment flows have unmistakably painted a picture of rapid strides toward global market integration, both in the developing and developed countries since the early 1980s (Guillén 2001, 238–239).[1] Paralleling the controversy over the causes

---

[1] Some authors (for instance, Horowitz 2004) identify the end of World War II as the start of the latest phase of economic globalization. Others (Frieden and Rogowski 1996; Garrett 2000), however, tend to pinpoint the 1970s. Both camps seem to agree on the existence of an earlier phase of global market integration during the 1870–1914 period that was interrupted by World War I (Bordo et al. 1999).

of the current phase of economic globalization (Garrett 2000) has been the dispute over its *consequences*. On the economic side, one manifestation of the divide has been captured by the sometimes violent antiglobalization protests against the yawning gap between the world's haves and have-nots outside the conference halls of international institutions in favor of further opening of the markets worldwide (Levi and Olson 2000). Meanwhile, academic debates have mainly revolved around the effects of international trade and capital flows on economic growth and inequality both within and across countries.[2]

On the political side, the most celebrated "big questions" concern the possible constraints on government policy autonomy, the relevance of government in compensation and redistribution, and the shifting domestic political fault lines in the age of economic globalization.[3] One body of scholarship in particular has focused on the territorial dimension of domestic political conflicts under global market integration (for instance, Alesina and Spolaore 1997, 2003). It puzzles over the relationship between rising economic openness and the probability of disintegration of nation-states when subnational regions benefiting from exposure to the global markets begin to seek greater fiscal and ultimately political autonomy.

One primary source of domestic intergovernmental discord fanning fissiparous tendencies from below involves fiscal matters. Openness breeds schisms in wealth levels among subnational regions that are differentially endowed for the global markets (Hiscox 2003). Thriving on their comparative advantage in international commerce, the winner regions are tempted to exit the preexisting political union. For them, the potential losses from policies made by a distant central government less cognizant of local preferences (the costs of "preference heterogeneity") begin to outweigh the benefits of a unified domestic market in more efficient provision of public goods (the gains from "scale economy"). Above all, the winner regions seek greater fiscal autonomy in terms of how to dispose of revenues from their own jurisdictions (Bolton and Roland 1997).

This seems to be taking place at a time of surging needs for interregional redistribution, usually via the central government, perhaps to

---

[2] See, for instance, Frankel and Romer (1999), Freeman (1995), Richardson (1995), Rivera-Batiz and Romer (1991), Sachs and Warner (1995), and Wade (2004).
[3] Examples include Adserà and Boix (2002), Cameron (1978), Frieden (1991b), Garrett (1998b), Hays (2009), Hiscox (2002), Iversen and Cusack (2000), Kaufman and Segura-Ubiergo (2001), Rogowski (1989), and Solinger (2009).

compensate the less well-endowed but growingly discontented regions for agreeing to open up the country to outside market competition (Garrett 1998a). Fiscal conflicts and eventually national political disintegration seem inevitable. Against the backdrop of recent real-world developments, Alesina and Spolaore (1997, 1042) conclude:

[P]olitical separatism should go hand in hand with economic integration. We feel that the current European experience, the idea of a Europe of regions, and the separatism of Quebec in the context of NAFTA yield some support for this implication. Furthermore, the incentives for the states of the former Soviet Union, Yugoslavia, and Czechoslovakia to break away would have been much lower if they had expected to be economically isolated instead of integrated with the rest of the world, in particular, with Western Europe.... [T]he benefit of country size on economic performance should decrease with the increase of international economic integration and removal of trade barriers.

These economic theories have furnished powerful insights into some of the most important political dynamics under economic globalization in recent decades, with some empirical evidence in their support. For example, in a cross-sectional analysis based on around sixty nations during the period of 1980–97, Hiscox (2003) shows that rising globalization can induce some form of downward devolution of political power. In a sample of fifteen provincial units from mostly democracies during 1980–2000, Sorens (2004) likewise finds that global market integration is associated with vote gains for separatist regional political parties. Above all, as seen in Figure 2.1, the striking positive correlation between the world average foreign trade over gross domestic product (GDP) share and the number of countries worldwide – measured as the size of United Nations (UN) membership – is also often cited as prima facie evidence that smaller states become more viable in more globalized markets (Alesina and Spolaore 2003, 1).[4]

There are also causes for caution here, however. A closer look at Figure 2.1 suggests that the relationship is far less than straightforward. To be sure, across this period both the world's average degree of economic openness and the number of UN member states rose, from about 25 percent and 99 in 1960 to 57 percent and 189 in 2001, respectively. However, it can be difficult to disentangle the effect of globalization from that of the end of the Cold War and the collapse of the Soviet Union on the sudden increase of about 20 states between 1990 and 1992. Indeed,

---

[4] The correlation coefficient for the period of 1960–2001 is as high as 0.93 ($p = 0.000$).

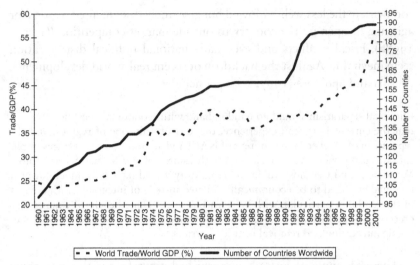

FIGURE 2.1. Economic globalization and the number of countries worldwide,
1960–2001.
Source: Appendix to Chapter 2.

the number of states remained quite steady during most of the 1990s
even as globalization continued to surge. Of course, by definition, a larger number of countries increases the value of world trade/GDP share
because trade previously treated as domestic is now counted as foreign
trade conducted across national borders. Presenting such aggregate data
raises issues of possible endogeneity. A sweeping causal claim of growing
globalization necessarily leading to the disintegration (hence the larger
number) of nation-states could be misleading.

Aside from the breakup of a few former Soviet bloc countries induced
by the end of the Cold War, the vast majority of states seem to have
survived the current phase of globalization.[5] Evidence questioning the
predictions of surging local demands for political autonomy and inevitable central political decline and collapse has also appeared in systematic empirical research. In a more homogeneous sample of Western
European states, two studies find the effect of globalization on the devolution of political power and the demand for regional political autonomy
largely ambiguous during the post-1950 era (Camões 2003; van Houten
2003). Moreover, no secession has succeeded among the industrialized

---

[5]   The end of the Cold War also witnessed the merger/reunification of countries such as East
and West Germany and South and North Yemen.

democracies, arguably the most globalized part of the world, despite the occasional threats (Meadwell and Martin 1996, 70).

2.2.2 A Quasireplication

To be fair, the mixed picture presented earlier can be due to our reliance on inherently incomparable studies using different dependent variables from different datasets. To get a clearer sense of the ambivalent empirical findings regarding the dismal predictions of the prevailing economic theories, I broadly replicate here the study of Hiscox (2003) by employing the most commonly available data for a large sample of countries. Hiscox contends that rising economic openness could spawn regional income disparity and lead to fiscal discontent and ultimately demands for greater political autonomy from the winner subnational regions that are thriving in the global markets, hence the greater downward movements of political authority. His two alternative dependent variables come from the World Bank's *Database of Political Institutions* (DPI).

State measures whether "state/province governments are locally elected" (Keefer 2005, 20). It takes on a value of 0 if neither the provincial executive nor the legislature is locally elected, a value of 1 if the legislature is elected but not the executive, and a value of 2 if both are locally elected.[6] *Municipal* applies to the lower municipal level. It is coded separately but according to the same rules. Rather than directly using these "level" data, Hiscox derives his dependent variables by taking the difference of their values between 1980 (his baseline year for *State*) and 1985 (his starting year for *Municipal*), and those in 1997 (perhaps the last year for which the data were available at the time of his study). A higher value thus indicates the more drastic downward devolution of political power, most probably a consequence of the demands for greater political autonomy by the winner subnational regions.

Instead of using conventional measures such as total foreign trade/ GDP share or export/GDP share, Hiscox (2003, 80) notes that agricultural exports and ore/mineral exports data better capture the degree of economic globalization leading to regional income disparity and local demands for fiscal and political autonomy in many countries.[7] He also

---

[6] The code book (Keefer 2005) does not specify a value if the local executive is elected but the local legislature is not.

[7] They are measured by the "agricultural raw materials exports as percentage share of merchandise exports" and "ores and metals exports as percentage share of merchandise exports" in World Bank (2003).

controls for a country's regime type – *Democracy* (from the *Polity III* dataset); its level of economic development – *Income*, measured by the natural log of per capita GDP; its population – *Population*, measured by the log of national population; and its territorial size – *Size*, measured by the log of land surface area. All independent variables are period-average values. We expect them to be positively correlated with the dependent variables as higher levels of democracy and income, and larger population and territorial sizes might induce greater downward movements of political power. He estimates his cross-sectional data for slightly fewer than sixty countries with an ordered logit model.

My replication uses the same dependent and independent variables in an ordered logit model for data starting in 1980,[8] but with a few minor modifications. First, rather than arbitrarily picking two years to calculate the differences in the values of the dependent variables for cross-sectional analysis, I use the annual first-difference values of *State* and *Municipal* as my dependent variables and estimate the data with a time-series cross-section setup. In this way, I maximize the number of observations for analysis and minimize the unnecessary loss of information. A higher value of the dependent variable thus denotes greater downward devolution of political power. Second, rather than the "level" data, all independent variables have been similarly first-differenced. They are also lagged by one year to mitigate mutual causality.

Third, I use the DPI data for the years up to 2003 because our data for the independent variables end in 2002 (World Bank 2003).[9] Fourth, I also test the effect of a more conventional measure of globalization – *Export/GDP* (the percentage share of total exports in national GDP). Finally, I use the *Democracy* data from the more recent *Polity IV* dataset.[10] Convergence during estimation, however, is no longer achievable when country-specific fixed effects are included. As a partial remedy, I follow the UN classification to add twenty region dummy variables to control for region-specific effects.[11] Annual year dummy variables are included to control for the year-specific effects, and to correct the

---

[8] The DPI data on political decentralization start in 1975 for many countries, but following Hiscox, I use data from 1980 onward. Including data from the pre-1980 years does not affect the replication results reported next.

[9] The results remain unchanged if 1997 is used as the endpoint, as in Hiscox (2003).

[10] Using the dichotomous measure of democracy in Przeworski et al (2000), updated by Cheibub and Gandhi (2004), will not change the major results to be reported here. I thank Professor Cheibub for making their data available for my analysis.

[11] See the Appendix to Chapter 2 for the definitions of the regions included here.

temporal autocorrelation in such models (Beck et al. 1998). Alternatively, I replace the year dummy variables with a lagged dependent variable to account for serial correlation in the dependent variable. The results are reported in Table 2.1.

Models 1–3 use annual differences in *State* (availability of elections for state/provincial executives and legislatures) as the dependent variable; Models 4–7 use annual changes in *Municipal* (presence of elections for municipal governments). Models 1, 2, and 4–6 follow Hiscox's original specifications; the rest replace his measures of globalization with the conventional measure of *Export/GDP*. Most important for our purposes, most openness variables turn out to be *not* significantly related to either dependent variable, except in Model 5, where *ΔAgricultural Export* is positive and statistically significant (at 0.05) when I replace the year dummy variables with a lagged dependent variable.[12] For the most part, therefore, changes in the role of agricultural exports, ore/mineral exports, or total exports in the national economies do not appear to have induced downward movements of political authority. Broadly similar results have been obtained in alternative specifications using levels of the dependent and independent variables, or first-differenced dependent variables but "level" values of the independent variables.

In short, our replication exercise provides little straightforward evidence to support the argument that greater economic openness is associated with trends toward greater devolution of political power from the central government. It casts doubt on the sweeping predictions of inevitable central political decline and national political disintegration under rising economic globalization in theories that focus solely on the demands for greater local autonomy by those subnational regions thriving in the global markets .

2.3 POLITICAL PARTIES AND CENTRAL POLITICAL CONTROL

2.3.1 Actors, Incentives, and Institutions

A major weakness of the prevailing economic theories is that under economic openness, the demands of the subnational regions alone should yield indeterminate predictions. Globalization and rising regional disparity

---

[12] Table 2.1 omits the results from other specifications that replace the year dummy variables with a lagged dependent variable. None of the globalization variables was statistically significant in those models.

TABLE 2.1. *The Effect of Globalization on the Devolution of Political Power: Cross-national Analysis*

	ΔState			ΔMunicipal			
	1	2	3	4	5	6	7
ΔDemocracy	0.15	0.18	0.10	−0.25**	−0.19*	−0.25**	−0.20
	(0.16)	(0.17)	(0.12)	(0.12)	(0.10)	(0.11)	(0.18)
ΔIncome	4.70	3.72	2.16	22.56***	17.88***	18.45**	10.61**
	(9.40)	(7.58)	(4.54)	(6.54)	(6.23)	(7.77)	(4.44)
ΔPopulation	−53.80*	−34.89***	−16.73***	71.40***	71.51***	14.78	−0.89
	(28.92)	(13.11)	(5.69)	(27.19)	(18.95)	(18.42)	(6.07)
ΔSize	19.91	4.54	−74.38	−836.3***	249.8***	−744.8***	−823.9***
	(33.28)	(11.53)	(48.93)	(180.89)	(70.78)	(193.65)	(279.63)
ΔAgricultural Export	0.06	0.05		0.15	0.22**	0.08	
	(0.05)	(0.04)		(0.11)	(0.09)	(0.10)	
ΔOre and Minerals Export	0.03	0.00		−0.07	0.001	−0.05	
	(0.07)	(0.05)		(0.15)	(0.17)	(0.16)	
ΔExport/GDP			0.02				0.01
			(0.03)				(0.03)
ΔMunicipal $_{i,t-1}$					−1.57		
					(1.12)		
Cut 1	−11.62	−11.09	−6.59	−5.91	−5.76	−6.22	−3.15
	(2.29)	(2.65)	(1.06)	(3.05)	(0.77)	(0.90)	(1.39)

28

	Model 1	Model 2	Model 3	Model 4	Model 5	Model 6	Model 7
Cut 2	-10.93	-10.40	-5.89	11.01	8.51	7.69	-2.61
	(2.13)	(2.17)	(0.56)	(2.89)	(0.78)	(1.02)	(1.22)
Cut 3	5.03	3.25	7.42	12.01	9.46	8.63	11.60
	(1.51)	(1.13)	(1.05)	(2.84)	(1.11)	(1.37)	(1.94)
Cut 4	6.65	4.83	9.30				13.03
	(1.86)	(1.46)	(1.18)				(2.21)
Region dummy	Yes	No	Yes	Yes	Yes	No	Yes
Year dummy	Yes	Yes	Yes	Yes	No	Yes	Yes
Log pseudolikelihood	-80.01	-89.50	-117.69	-31.35	-37.78	-38.30	-69.05
Countries included	101	101	110	73	72	73	84
Observations	1443	1443	1983	884	850	884	1301
Wald X^2	176.59	130.36	307.13	196.02	236.65	148.89	285.85
Probability $>X^2$	0.00	0.00	0.00	0.00	0.00	0.00	0.00
Pseudo R^2	0.22	0.13	0.11	0.35	0.21	0.21	0.23

Note: The dependent variables are the annual differences of *State* (Models 1–3) and *Municipal* (Models 4–7) indicating whether there are local elections for provincial- and municipal-level executives and legislatures, respectively. They cover the 1980–2003 period and are estimated with ordered logit regressions. All independent variables are annual differences and lagged by one year; they cover the 1979–2002 period. $\Delta Municipal_{it-1}$ is the dependent variable lagged by one year in Model 5. Results for the region and year dummy variables are omitted to economize on space. Robust standard errors are in parentheses.

***: p < 0.01; **: p < 0.05; *: p < 0.1 (two-tailed tests).

Source: See the Appendix to Chapter 2.

may also trigger demands for interregional redistribution and compensation from regions faring less well in the global markets. Unfortunately, the need for interregional transfers, usually carried out by the central government,[13] is conspicuously absent from these models (Alesina and Spolaore 1997, 1029). Satisfaction of such demands requires a more robust redistributive role by the political center, not its retreat. We thus also need to take into account the national political leaders in the age of rising economic globalization, growing interregional disparity, and conflicting regional demands.

For simplicity in exposition, I assume there are three (groups of) actors in a country with imperfect factor mobility opening itself to the global markets – the winner regions, the loser regions, and the political center.[14] By region, I refer to both the government and dominant economic interests (firms, sectors, groups, etc.) in a subnational geographic unit. To be sure, the economic interests might be quite diverse even within one single region. I assume that the dominant firms and sectors have relatively homogenous preferences due to their specific natural resource endowments that are dictated by their geographic locations and to their positions in the international markets. Other things being equal, a regional government tends to be sympathetic with the dominant economic interests in its jurisdiction because of the latter's vital role in the regional economy. These firms contribute to a variety of goals valued by subnational politicians, such as regional revenue, employment, economic prosperity, and the related political benefits – facilitating reelection by the electorate from below or continued nomination, appointment, and promotion by political superiors from above.[15] They thus should enjoy a more "privileged" political status in the regions, just like the investors and capital owners in any state under modern capitalism (Lindblom 1977).

The winner regions have figured prominently in the prevailing economic theories surveyed earlier. More dependent upon the global markets, they are less attracted by the benefits of scale economy promised by

---

[13] For evidence on how the federal government in the United States engages in interregional transfer payments through tax reductions to help states adversely affected by region-specific shocks, see Sachs and Sala-i-Martin (1992).

[14] With perfect mobility in an ideal world (hardly obtained in reality), the fiscal conflicts under economic openness to be discussed next would simply disappear (Bolton and Roland 1997).

[15] During the period under study, local government fiscal considerations were mainly behind the close ties that the local firms often enjoyed with the local governments in China, as I further discuss in Chapter 3.

a unified domestic market. They favor a less redistributive tax scheme, resist demands for greater contributions to fiscal transfers to the rest of the country, and clamor for greater fiscal autonomy, or perhaps ultimate secession, as predicted in these economic theories. The loser regions, in contrast, might experience deteriorating welfare (even if only relative to that of the winner regions) in the global markets. Like other adversely affected domestic groups, they might have agreed to embrace external trade liberalization only after being promised fiscal compensation (Garrett 1998a). If regional economic disparity worsens, we might expect the loser regions to demand more fiscal assistance from the center.

As already noted in Chapter 1, I broadly define the political center as composed of the leadership of the executive branch of the central government, together with the national leaders of their affiliated political party (or parties). The role of the political center remains much undertheorized in the existing scholarship on global market integration and national political disintegration. Assuming the simple majority rule in democracies, most economic theories treat the political center as automatic aggregations of the preferences of economic actors at the subnational level and below. However, such simplification might be problematic, especially when it comes to matters involving the possible fate of the political union. Above all, the political center is most interested in its continued existence. In other words, the political survival of national-level politicians depends upon the ongoing viability of the national political union.

Amidst increasing domestic territorial conflicts under rising globalization, I follow Garman et al. (2001, 209–210) to argue that the center will seek to expand its fiscal capacity and will implement interregional redistribution in order to keep itself in power.[16] It will accommodate the redistributive demands from the loser regions, but it will take a less conciliatory stance toward the autonomy-seeking winner regions. Such preferences for fiscal centralization are consistent with the predictions of the compensation thesis in the study of globalization and domestic politics (Cameron 1978; Garrett 1998b; Rodrik 1998). This school predicts

---

[16] It is conceivable that a Reagan-type national leader might be more pro-state rights than is the average national chief executive envisioned here, even though Reagan also presided over, so far, the largest peacetime federal deficit (as a share of GDP) in U.S. history, a result of a huge expansion of federal government defense spending as well as tax cuts. The assumption that national political leaders are more likely to be concerned about the interests of the central government and favor fiscal centralization than are local political leaders, however, is meant to be a probabilistic, rather than deterministic statement. I thank one anonymous reviewer for reminding me of the possible example of Reagan here.

mounting pressures for national governments to cushion the shocks from the more volatile world markets and to assist domestic groups adversely affected by rising world competition. Domestic groups targeted for fiscal transfers naturally extend to include the loser subnational regions in the global markets.

Fiscal centralization provides the center with the resources to implement interregional redistribution. An enlarged redistributive presence by the center essentially pacifies the loser regions that are demanding compensation. If such assistance helps reduce the income gap between the winner and loser regions, it also mitigates one root cause fueling the autonomy-seeking intransigence of the winner regions in the first place (Bolton and Roland 1997). Greater fiscal powers by the center also justify the center's legitimacy and raison d'être that are threatened by those regions demanding greater fiscal and ultimately political autonomy. In contrast, the winner regions' demands for greater autonomy can be gratified only at the expense of the center's political power and authority. Even worse, at the extreme, they might lead to regional secession and breakup of the country, directly imperiling the very existence of the center. Therefore, we expect the center to resist such demands from the winner regions.

Indeed, the notion that the center has incentives to centralize fiscal resources in its own hands under rising global market integration is consistent with recent cross-national empirical evidence that links more globalized economies with more centralized government fiscal structures (Diaz-Cayeros 2005; Garrett and Rodden 2003). Preferences for fiscal centralization alone, however, do not suffice. Political institutions often help filter the political consequences of economic globalization (Garrett and Lange 1996). Unfortunately, the prevailing economic theories are too institutionally sparse (Kahler and Lake 2003a, 18). The rich institutional varieties even among the democratic states often have to be assumed away in formal models that accommodate no more than the bare-bones assumptions of the simple majority rule.

Above all, the center's ability to pursue fiscal centralization and to rein in the restive regions could vary with the existing institutional ties linking the political center and the subnational regions. It is easier for the center to expand its fiscal resources and fend off regional demands for fiscal and political autonomy in the more centralized political systems where the center marshals greater political powers vis-à-vis the subnational units. For instance, regional separatist demands are more easily contained in a more politically centralized, unitary country than in a more decentralized, federal system. Indeed, Meadwell and Martin (1996) attribute the relative strength of the separatist movement in Quebec to the federal structure of the Canadian state. Similarly, cross-national evidence indicates that government finances tend to be more decentralized in constitutionally federal countries (Diaz-Cayeros 2005; Garrett and Rodden 2003).

However, notions such as federalism and political decentralization are often fraught with conceptual and measurement complexities (Rodden 2004). Conventional definitions of federalism, for instance, tend to revolve around the formal provisions set forth in a national constitution (Castles 1999; Elazar 1995; Treisman 2000).[17] As Rodden (2004, 491) has recently pointed out, such measures can be too "blunt" in "lumping together" countries that differ substantially in terms of the extent of political decentralization into one single crude analytical category. For example, countries as different as Pakistan, with its much greater de facto political centralization, and Switzerland, which is more decentralized, are often both coded as "federal" if we use such a constitutional litmus test.

2.3.2 Centralized Political Parties

An alternative conceptualization of political decentralization focuses on the role of the ruling political parties. That is, a key determinant of political decentralization can be the degree of decentralization of the governing political party. For Riker (1964, 131), this can be defined as "(1) the degree to which one party controls both [the national and subnational] levels of government; and (2) the degree to which each potential governing party at the national level controls its partisan associates at the level of constituent governments." Political decentralization and intergovernmental power division promised by a federalist constitution are less meaningful – it is easier for the national government to recentralize all political powers – in countries governed by the more centralized political parties. Thus, a political system is more centralized if the political party of the national chief executive governs a larger share of the regional governments – via holding more governorships (Rodden and Wibbels 2002) – and exercises greater power – for instance, regarding personnel appointment or candidate nomination – over its subnational copartisans (Willis et al. 1999).

Cross-nationally, we could examine a country's degree of political decentralization along these two partisan dimensions. It is straightforward

---

[17] Others (for example, Keefer 2005) focus on the locus of the power to elect subnational governments, which is also often constitutionally prescribed.

to calculate the share of subnational governments ruled by the political party of the national chief executive (the horizontal axis in Figure 2.2). For example, we can easily determine the share of the fifty states in the United States whose governors share the president's party label in any single year. The higher the share of subnational governments ruled by the copartisans of the national chief executive, the easier it would be to negotiate revenue divisions for the two levels of government, other things being equal. For instance, regional governments in democracies might be more sympathetic to the revenue preferences of a central government whose chief executive shares the same partisan label in hope that they can gainfully ride the "electoral coattails" generated by the latter's national-level policy success later on (Rodden and Wibbels 2002). Thus, Riker's first partisan dimension of political decentralization in essence gauges the ease of intergovernmental policy *coordination* via the national governing political party.

The second partisan dimension of political decentralization concerns the degree of political control exercised at the subnational level (the vertical axis). It captures the extent to which the central government, via the national office of the political party of the national chief executive, is able to secure policy *compliance* from regional government officials bearing the same party label. One mechanism for exerting such political control involves the authority regarding subnational-level personnel appointment or candidate nomination.[18] In contemporary United States, the national committees of the two major political parties have little effective say over the choice of candidates for state governorships. In contrast, national governing political parties in some Latin American countries may nominate regional candidates with a closed list or may directly appoint regional government leaders (Willis et al. 1999). The Indian National Congress Party led by Prime Minister Indira Gandhi during the 1969–75 period is another example of a governing political party armed with subnational-level personnel authority (Hankla 2008).[19] Compared with their counterparts without these powers, a national party wielding such personnel authority enables the central government to exercise tighter political control over – and lends it a greater ability to extract policy compliance from – subnational governments run by its copartisans.

---

[18] Riker himself did not explicitly spell out the specific channels whereby the central government could exert such political control. Although there are other avenues for exercising control, such as the authority over party finances, means of communications, etc., in this study, I focus on the aspect of personnel authority.

[19] Subnational government leadership is also often "handpicked" by the national governing political party in Pakistan (Rodden and Wibbels 2002, 496).

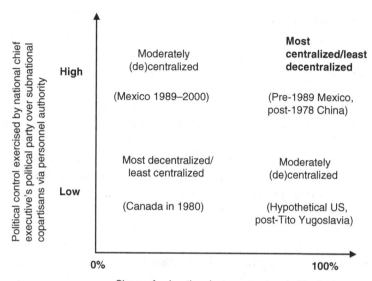

Political control exercised by national chief executive's political party over subnational copartisans via personnel authority

High — Moderately (de)centralized (Mexico 1989–2000) — Most centralized/least decentralized (Pre-1989 Mexico, post-1978 China)

Low — Most decentralized/ least centralized (Canada in 1980) — Moderately (de)centralized (Hypothetical US, post-Tito Yugoslavia)

0% — 100%

Share of subnational governments ruled by the political party of the national chief executive

FIGURE 2.2. Rikerian typologies of political (party) decentralization.
Source: Riker (1964, 131); Rodden and Wibbels (2002); Willis et al. (1999).

In the most centralized type of political system, one single political party capable of exercising personnel authority over its subnational copartisans would rule the executive branch of the government at both the national and subnational levels. This refers to the top-right corner of Figure 2.2, where the ability of the central government to engage in policy coordination with and to solicit policy compliance from the subnational governments is the greatest. Either a functioning authoritarian single-party state or a democracy – if the national chief executive's political party equipped with the requisite personnel powers happens to govern all of the subnational regions via winning all the gubernatorial elections nationwide – could exemplify this type. Along this line of reasoning, we might be able to point to growing political centralization in Russia with the recent emergence of the Putin-led United Russia Party playing an increasing role in nominating candidates for and winning a growing number of gubernatorial elections (Konitzer and Wegren 2006). It is certainly easier for the central government to press revenue demands on the subnational regions in such a political system ruled by a most centralized political party.

At the other extreme, in the bottom-left corner of Figure 2.2, the national governing political party in the least centralized system would rule few or none of the subnational governments and wield little or no personnel authority over its subnational party branches. One example is Canada, where the provincial parties are only loosely connected to the national political parties bearing the same labels (Thorlakson 2009). In 1980, none of Canada's provincial premiers was from the Liberal Party of Prime Minister Pierre Trudeau (Europa Publications Limited 1980). For our purposes, imposition of central revenue demands on the subnational regions is certainly far more difficult, if not impossible, under such a decentralized system.

The ability to exercise political control at the subnational level and to extract policy compliance from below via governing-party-imparted personnel powers is less meaningful if few of the subnational regions are actually ruled by the party of the national chief executive, as is the case in the top-left corner. For instance, in Mexico, the opposition parties began winning the governorship in more states in 1989. Thus, even before the *Partido Revolucionario Institucional* (PRI) lost its seventy-year monopoly hold on the Mexican presidency in 2000, greater de facto political decentralization was already creeping into the erstwhile highly centralized political system under "PRI hegemony" in Mexico.[20] Although local candidate nomination powers still remained with the national office of the PRI (Diaz-Cayeros 2006), the share of regional governments ready to comply with central revenue demands would decline accordingly.

Intergovernmental policy coordination might be weakened if the national governing party exercises little or no political control via personnel authority over its subnational copartisans even though politicians wearing the same party cap rule most or all of the regional governments, as in the bottom-right corner. This could be the case with post-Tito Yugoslavia, where the subnational-level personnel authority of the national party office was already atrophying even though nominally the Communists still ruled all its constituent republics.[21] It could also apply to a hypothetical United States with a Republican president when most

---

[20] The opposition *Partido Acción Nacional* (PAN) first won a governorship in Baja California in 1989 (Hernández-Rodríguez 2003, 107–108). PAN and the other opposition parties had since gradually increased their share of the Mexican governorships. In early 1999, before losing the presidential election for the first time in 2000, the PRI held the governorship in only 21 of Mexico's 32 provincial units (Europa Publications Limited 1999).

[21] After the death of Tito in 1980, the ruling Communist party in Yugoslavia essentially fragmented into a loose confederation of the League of Communists of the constituent republics, which enjoyed substantial political as well as economic autonomy. Not surprisingly, by 1986, the republics promptly achieved "fiscal sovereignty" when they were no longer willing to make revenue contributions to the central coffers (Bunce 1999, 99).

or all of the state governors are Republican. Here, the central government boasts little political muscle to impose its policy preferences from above, although having copartisans run the regional governments might facilitate its efforts to negotiate with the regional governments over fiscal matters.

In both of the previous cases, the political system can be seen as moderately (de)centralized at best. The ability to ensure lower-level government policy compliance by the center can be partial in one case, limited by the number of regions ruled by the copartisans of the national chief executive. In the other case, intergovernmental policy coordination through the national governing party becomes more complicated, absent the ability of national politicians to rein in subnational copartisans politically.

Clearly, these typologies are preliminary and largely illustrative in nature. For our purposes, however, it might be reasonable to posit that with rising globalization and regional disparity, it would be easier to centralize fiscal resources in countries governed at both the national and subnational levels by the more centralized political parties wielding substantial personnel powers over the subnational party branches (countries located in the top-right corner in Figure 2.2). To be sure, regional governments tend to be sympathetic to the preferences of the dominant economic interest groups/sectors in their jurisdictions. Still, cross-nationally, we expect the central government to be better able to secure regional compliance with its fiscal preferences where the political party of the national chief executive rules a larger share of the regional governments and manages the careers of its subnational copartisans, other things being equal.

This is consistent with evidence from Latin America where more centralized political party systems are associated with more centralized state fiscal structures (Garman et al. 2001). It also suggests that political party centralization might have facilitated fiscal centralization in the more open economies (Diaz-Cayeros 2005; Garrett and Rodden 2003). In other words, more centralized state finances in the age of increasing economic globalization, worsening regional disparity, and mounting pressures for interregional redistribution should be more likely in countries governed by the more centralized political parties. The limited nature of the cross-national data collection at the current stage, however, does not yet allow us to test directly the relationship between party centralization and fiscal centralization under growing global market integration in a larger sample.[22]

---

[22] One example of the immense information collection required for coding political party decentralization that bears on candidate selection is the work of Janda (1980), which covers a sample of political parties in 53 countries. Despite its monumental effort, the

2.3.3 Central Political Control at the Subnational Level

Fortunately, the empirical implications of an approach highlighting the incentives and institutional resources of the political center do not have to be observed or tested only with cross-national data. If more center-directed interregional redistribution is called for, a significant and perhaps growing portion must be funded by the regions with more resources to spare. Yet these are the winner regions in the global markets resisting central redistributive demands due to the fading appeal of a domestic scale economy. Existing cross-national studies thus far have rarely delineated how a more centralized political system might make the winner regions in the global markets more pliable and willing to submit their revenues to the center, precisely at a time when they have more reasons to become recalcitrant.

For instance, Garman et al. (2001) argue that state fiscal structures tend to be more centralized in Latin American countries where regional government leaders are appointed by the national presidents. It is plausible that the regional governments in these countries are more likely to be compliant with the president's fiscal preferences than in countries where the national chief executive does not boast such personnel authority at the subnational level. For our purposes, however, it is not clear whether and how the levers of presidential personnel powers can be pulled differently for subnational governments in regions of varying fiscal importance to the center. Two questions immediately follow, especially for countries ruled by a most centralized political party (that is, one single political party, enabling the political center to exert considerable political control over all the regional governments). First, to help extract revenues and finance its growing redistributive needs, how can the center exercise a greater degree of political control over the subnational governments of the winner regions that are attractive for revenue-extraction purposes but assertive in demanding, for instance, fiscal autonomy? Second, what can be the micromechanism whereby the political sway of the center might translate into greater compliance with central revenue preferences by subnational governments in the restive winner regions?

book, with over 1,000 pages, only covers the 1950–62 period and many of the important countries, such as China, Mexico, and Japan, are missing from the dataset. A second example is the 900-page data compilation by Katz and Mair (1992) that includes only 12 Western democracies for the 1960–90 period. Indeed, this has led Rodden and Wibbels (2002, 509) to lament the daunting difficulty of gathering comparative data on internal party personnel control for a large cross-national sample.

Since the top members of the central government leadership – such as the national chief executive – and the leaders of their political party collectively constitute the political center, they should share similar interests and preferences regarding the central government's relations with the subnational units. This does not deny possible internecine power rivalry or factionalism based on differences over personalities or policies among these leaders themselves. Even if their membership is not internally monolithic, however, the political center should be more likely to act together when their common interests as national leaders are challenged from below.[23] In a country governed by a most centralized political party, the political center is the major source of office and political power for top regional government officials due to its personnel authority (direct appointment or candidate nomination) within the single ruling party. The political center thus effectively constitutes the "principal" confronting similar problems of incentive divergence under information asymmetry favoring its "agent" – the regional government leaders.[24]

Hailing from the economics and business research on corporate governance, the principal-agent framework models efforts by the principal (firm owners, for example) to ensure the proper alignment of incentives of the agent (firm managers). Under information asymmetry, the agent knows more and better about the tasks she is assigned to perform and is often tempted to pursue actions counter to the interests of her principal.[25] The problem of securing agent compliance, however, is complicated by the cost of information gathering and monitoring in the real world. This framework has been widely used in the study of American bureaucracies (see, for instance, McCubbins et al. 1989; Moe 1984; Weingast 1984). The bureaucrats often enjoy greater expertise and information about the jobs delegated by their congressional and presidential principals. Instead of faithfully performing these tasks, however, they could be more interested in maximizing their own "organizational slack" – the difference between the true cost of and the actual resources spent by the bureaucrats on the services they provide (Niskanen 1975). The agency framework is

[23] Indeed, even accounts that question the ability of national-level "oligarchs" in nondemocratic systems to solve their internal "collective action" problems readily admit that these leaders have little trouble unifying against their common enemies (Ramseyer and Rosenbluth 1995). As I discuss in Chapter 4, this also seems to be the case in post-1978 China despite the possible prevalence of elite factional politics among the top national leadership.

[24] For instance, van Houten (2009) advocates the agency framework for the study of political parties.

[25] For an excellent review of the literature, see Eggertsson (1990, Chapter 2).

equally pertinent to the study of intergovernmental conflicts under growing globalization in countries governed by the most centralized political parties.

In this study, I have assumed that regional governments tend to share the preferences of the dominant economic interests within their jurisdictions because of the special role the latter play in the regional economies. Even in a centralized political system where one single political party governs at both the national and subnational levels, preferences might still differ for the political center and the copartisans of the national chief executive appointed to lead the subnational governments in the age of globalization, as predicted by the prevailing economic theories.[26] Subnational government preferences in the winner regions are especially likely to diverge from those of the center over matters of fiscal extraction and redistribution.

Although the center is interested in extracting more resources from the winner regions for interregional redistribution in face of growing regional economic disparity, subnational governments in the winner regions might want to keep as much as possible in their own hands. After all, there is no guarantee that the urge of the government to maximize revenues (Levi 1988) is confined to the national level.[27] The imperative to increase their own fiscal resources could be especially pressing for the subnational governments in the winner regions. Greater exposure to the global markets might engender rising economic inequality within these regions that calls for greater internal balancing efforts by the regional governments.[28] These governments might also agitate for greater regional fiscal autonomy favored by the local economic actors who are resentful of the heftier tax obligations entailed in the center's extractive demands toward these regions. The political center, however, lacks adequate information about the true revenue-generating capacity of the regions or the true tax-collecting effort of the local officials, matters that the regional governments know better.

---

[26] The degree of such preference divergence between the central and subnational governments, of course, could be even greater in countries that are not ruled by centralized political parties.

[27] Garman et al. (2001) make similar assumptions about the revenue-maximizing propensities of the regional governments in Latin American countries, as does Malesky (2008) for the provincial governments of Vietnam. For similar assumptions made in the context of post-1978 China, see, for example, Tao and Yang (2008) and Wong (1991).

[28] As noted earlier, this is also consistent with the compensation thesis in the cross-national literature applied to the subnational level within a country. Jeanneney and Hua (2004) provide evidence from China along this line.

Hierarchy, monitoring, incentive alignment, and external checks are commonly used tools for ensuring greater agent compliance with the preferences of the principal. The hierarchical structure of the firm, monitoring by the board of directors, and the presence of watchdog institutions (such as the Securities and Exchange Commission in the United States) serve such purposes in the corporate world (Alchian and Demsetz 1972; Jensen and Meckling 1976). In regulating American bureaucracies, hierarchical agency structures, congressional monitoring ("police controls"), and external checks (through the "fire-alarm" role played by interest groups) constitute similar efforts to seek greater bureaucratic compliance by the United States Congress (McCubbins and Schwartz 1984; Moe 1984).

The most straightforward strategy for the principal seems to be appointing agents who tend to share the principal's policy preferences a priori (Shepsle and Bonchek 1997, 366). Huang's study (1996) on how the appointment of pro-center provincial leaders by the single ruling CCP remedied central-provincial macroeconomic conflicts in China is particularly illuminating for our purposes. He argues that working previously in the national capital or holding a concurrent national office might better orient the policy outlooks of the otherwise unruly regional officials. For the 1977–92 period, indeed, he finds that Chinese provincial governments led by the more "centrally oriented" provincial officials by virtue of their career trajectories were more likely to comply with the central policy injunction against excessive growth in local public investment feeding inflationary pressures.

Because the political center via the single ruling party in China appoints all top provincial cadres, it is capable of wielding substantial political control over all Chinese provincial governments. The ability to assign different types of officials predisposed to varying degrees of compliance with central policy preferences to rule the provincial governments also implies that the center can exert varying degrees of effective political control over the different Chinese provincial governments led by these officials. For instance, appointing loyal, sympathetic officials to rule certain subnational regions might lend the center a greater degree of political control over – and ease compliance with central policy preferences in cases of central-subnational conflicts from – the regional governments led by these officials.[29]

---

[29] Later, in Chapter 4 I discuss in more detail why different types of officials with different career trajectories can be predisposed to varying degrees of compliance with central government policy preferences, and why assignment of different types of officials to lead different

In countries where a most centralized governing party imparts the center the requisite personnel powers over the regional government leadership, we expect the political center to resort to similar strategies to induce regional government compliance with its revenue demands and to remedy its agency problem during the era of globalization. Given their divergent preferences over fiscal matters, the center should be especially interested in appointing pro-center agents to lead the subnational governments in the winner regions whose fiscal compliance is essential to fulfilling the center's redistributive agenda and to keeping the country together and central politicians in power. If the exercise of tighter central political control implies a greater ability of the center to secure policy compliance from lower-level governments, efforts via the personnel powers imparted by the single ruling party to seek greater fiscal compliance from the subnational governments in these economically resourceful but politically restive regions constitute efforts to exercise more stringent central political control.

To empirically assess this argument, we could examine, across different regions and years *within* a centralized political system – governed by one single political party capable of exercising regional-level personnel authority – whether the center has exercised a greater degree of political control over the subnational governments of the winner regions in the global markets. A subnational research design is most appropriate for such research questions (Snyder 2001), but little empirical scholarship along this line has appeared. With its rapid embrace of the global markets since 1978, China under CCP single-party rule provides an ideal empirical setting for our purposes.

2.3.4 Consequences

Through better aligning the incentives of the regional government leaders with those of the national leaders, exercise of a greater degree of political

provinces constitutes the exercise of varying degrees of central political control over the provincial governments in China, along the lines of Huang (1996). Meanwhile, such variation in political control by the political center over provincial governments led by different types of provincial officials seems also present in other centralized systems, such as PRI-controlled Mexico where *cacique* governors in some states were local bosses less sympathetic to central government policy preferences (Diaz-Cayeros 2006, Chapter 3). Presumably, even if it wields the requisite personnel authority, the central government in such systems does not have the luxury of being able to station officials uniformly predisposed to high policy compliance in all subnational regions due to such constraints as lack of a sufficient number of qualified personnel. The need to assign different types of officials to lead different regional governments inevitably results in their varying effective political control by the center.

control might not only help the center extract badly needed resources, carry out interregional redistribution in order to mitigate rising regional disparity, and maintain political stability and territorial unity in the age of growing economic globalization. It might also help the targeted subnational governments better overcome the "collective action" curse (Olson 1971) in contributing to the provision of national-level public goods such as macroeconomic stability that are often more of a concern for the national leadership. The effect of the regionally selective exercise of central political control via a most centralized governing political party imparting national-level political supremacy, however, might not be uniformly benevolent.

I have argued that the exercise of tighter political control by the center via installing trustworthy, pro-center agents into the top government leadership of the rich but unruly winner regions could aim at extracting more resources from these regions to help finance the mounting imperative for fiscal transfers to the loser regions that are faring less well in the global markets. If these regional government officials are conscientious agents of the center who assiduously comply with its extractive demands, they can also make the regional jurisdictions they oversee become especially vulnerable to fiscal extraction and even possible predation by their national principals. This in turn could undermine the protection of the de facto property rights of the local economic actors, distort their incentives, and impede economic growth in these regions ruled by the more tightly controlled subnational governments.

This line of reasoning is inherently consistent with a leading theme in political economy research on economic development that has long cautioned against the excesses of unconstrained political power of the central government. To be sure, the role played by government in general and the central government in particular in promoting economic development is complex, as Weingast (1995, 1), this school's foremost proponent, has readily acknowledged:

[The] fundamental political dilemma of an economic system is this: A government strong enough to protect property rights and enforce contracts is also strong enough to confiscate the wealth of its citizens. Thriving markets require not only the appropriate system of property rights and a law of contracts, but a secure political foundation that limits the ability of the state to confiscate wealth.

Still, scholars of this genre tend to highlight the perils posed by an omnipotent political center. For them, only when the central government is stripped of the ability to overpower lower-level governments easily can it become "credibly committed" (North and Weingast 1989) to protecting the property rights of the local economic actors vital for long-run economic development. Dubbed "market-preserving federalism" (MPF), one set of institutional constraints seems especially effective in preventing the central government from turning into predatory "grabbing hands" that plunder local economic resources, and in helping provide "a secure political foundation" for sustainable economic growth (Montinola et al. 1995; Qian and Weingast 1997). Throughout history, few countries have come up with such "politically durable" commitment devices for solving this "fundamental political dilemma" of economic development. Despite the country's highly centralized political system, as noted earlier, impressive economic growth during the era of reform and opening has somehow made China a favorite example of the growth-friendliness of MPF in these accounts, together with England after the Glorious Revolution and antebellum United States (Weingast 1995).

In particular, the MPF advocates have heralded the use of fiscal contracts by the Chinese central government specifying the above-quota budgetary revenues to be retained by the provinces as a hand-binding commitment device since the early 1980s before they were phased out in 1994 (Jin et al. 2005; Lin and Liu 2000; Montinola et al. 1995; Oi 1999). However, China's centralized political system and the political predominance of the Chinese national leaders throughout this period imparted by a most centralized ruling political party – the sole governing CCP – have made these fiscal contracts not truly binding upon the central government. Hence, these contracts could not have been regarded as "credible" in the eyes of local economic actors in the provinces. As I will review in Chapter 3, arbitrary transgressions of fiscal contracts by the central government were common during this period. Thus, it is *not* appropriate to apply the logic of MPF to discussions of China's political system at the national level or to focus on the use of the oft-breached fiscal contracts.

The subnational implications of the "credible commitment" logic of MPF, when considered in the context of regionally differential exercise of political control by the Chinese center, should be more pertinent for our purposes here. As noted, provincial governments under more stringent political control by the central government are ruled by officials who are more sympathetic to and compliant with the policy preferences of the central government. They should be particularly heedful of the center's fiscal extractive demands. Local economic actors in these jurisdictions hence are subject to greater risks of resource expropriation, enjoy more attenuated protection of their de facto property rights by the central government, and consequently should have fewer incentives to pursue economic expansion, other things being equal. In this book, therefore, I will also probe how the exercise of regionally selective political control by the Chinese political center over the provincial governments affected central fiscal extraction from the provinces and provincial economic growth.

Investigation along these lines of the effect of territorially differential exercise of political control by the Chinese national leaders via the single ruling CCP not only allows us to examine whether such regionally targeted control had actually worked. In testing the observable implications at the subnational level of a leading political economy perspective on economic development, it will also contribute to the emergent but largely cross-national research on the macroeconomic consequences of political decentralization that is conceptualized in terms of Riker's governing political party decentralization (Rodden and Wibbels 2002; Wibbels 2005). With a subnational strategy studying a country under single-party rule – the most centralized political party system located in the top-right corner of Figure 2.2, here I focus on the effect of the cross-region variation in the exercise of central political control and the related ability of the political center to extract policy compliance at the subnational level.

If one single political party rules both the national government (that is, as the party of the national chief executive) and the subnational governments in all regions, we effectively hold constant the first dimension of Riker's measure of political party decentralization bearing on intergovernmental policy coordination. We can then isolate the effect of the varying degrees of political control exercised through the personnel powers of the ruling single party over the different subnational governments. This is the second Rikerian dimension of political decentralization that seeks to gauge the ability of the central government to extract policy compliance from below via the national governing political party (the vertical axis in Figure 2.2). To the extent that the governing political party helps the central government exert varying degrees of political control over different regional governments, these regional governments effectively enjoy varying degrees of de facto political decentralization. Regional governments led by the more compliant agents of the center are under tighter central political control and enjoy a lower degree of political decentralization.

During the 1978–97 period, the more tightly controlled Chinese provincial governments were indeed more likely to overcome the "collective action" curse in helping contribute to a national-level public good – lower inflation and a more stable macroeconomic environment, as was desired by the central government (Huang and Sheng 2009). The central government harbored more "encompassing interests" in macroeconomic stability. The provincial governments, in contrast, tended to regard low inflation as a public good that benefits each locality regardless of whether they pay for its provision. Although the incentive to shirk and free-ride could be high at the subnational level, provincial governments under tighter central political control were less likely to pursue inflation-prone policies. They might be less inclined to overstep their authority to approve public investment projects (Huang 1996, Chapters 2–3), or less likely to exert political pressure on local branches of state banks in their jurisdictions to make bad policy loans to local enterprises (Lardy 1998). In this book, I study the potentially less benign effect of a greater degree of central political control over the provincial governments – that is, a lower degree of political decentralization measured at the subnational level – on central fiscal extraction and provincial economic growth.

2.4 CONCLUSION

For all the dismal predictions of national political disintegration, empirically we have observed few cases of breakup of nation-states because of a growing linkage to the global market. Instead, government fiscal structures tend to be more centralized in the more globalized economies. In this chapter, I take issue with the prevailing economic theories that have privileged the demands for greater fiscal and eventually political autonomy from the winner subnational regions in the global markets. I advocate an approach that emphasizes the incentives of national leaders to exert tighter political control over the government leadership in the winner subnational units, especially in institutional settings where the center wields considerable political power over all the regional governments. In particular, I highlight the pivotal role played by the personnel authority over the regional officials granted by centralized governing political parties to the national political leaders.

As schematized in Figure 2.3, in this study I pinpoint a possible political mechanism whereby the center can manipulate the institutions within the ruling political parties to alleviate central-regional preference divergences engendered in the opening up to the global markets. I also suggest the mixed consequences of the regionally selective exercise of central political control. On the one hand, exercise of tighter political control might facilitate central fiscal extraction, promote interregional redistribution, and contribute to more balanced regional development,

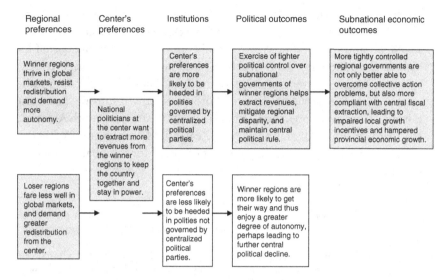

Regional preferences	Center's preferences	Institutions	Political outcomes	Subnational economic outcomes

FIGURE 2.3. The stylized argument.

as well as remedy regional "collective action" problems in the provision of national-level public goods. On the other, it might invite central fiscal predation, undermine the center's credible commitment to local property-rights protection, and harm local incentives for economic growth. In the following chapters, I apply the theoretical framework that privileges the role of national-level political actors to study the territorial politics in China under growing economic globalization. I first examine the regional dimension of China's recent embrace of the global markets.

APPENDIX: CROSS-NATIONAL DATA

Consistent with Alesina and Spolaore (2003, 1), I draw on UN data for information on the number of states in the global system in Figure 2.1.[30] World average trade/GDP data in Figure 2.1 and country-level export-related data, together with other economic variables (except for the *Polity IV* data, see the following) for the analysis reported in Table 2.1

---

[30] The information is available at http://www.un.org/members/growth.shtml, accessed on March 8, 2009. The number of UN member states is slightly smaller than the number of states in the global system according to the Correlates of War 2 Project (2003). The latter also includes political entities that are not UN members, such as Taiwan. The number according to the Correlates of War 2 Project is 107 in 1960 and 201 in 2001.

are from the World Bank (2003).[31] Data on *State* and *Municipal* come
from Beck et al. (2001) and Keefer (2005).[32] *Polity IV* data are from
Marshall and Jaggers (2002).[33] Finally, the region dummy variables
include the following: Eastern Africa, Middle Africa, Northern Africa,
Southern Africa, Western Africa, Eastern Asia, South-central Asia, South-
eastern Asia, Western Asia, Eastern Europe, Northern Europe, Southern
Europe, Western Europe, the Caribbean, Central America, South America,
Northern America, Australia and New Zealand, Melanesia, and Polynesia.
There is no country included in the dataset used for my analysis located
in Micronesia.[34]

---

[31] I thank Professor Nick Cox for valiantly writing the program to "reshape" the original
World Development Indicators digital data into a format usable by the statistical software *STATA*.

[32] Data are available at http://siteresources.worldbank.org/INTRES/Resources/
DPI2004-no_formula_no_macro.xls, accessed on June 5, 2006. For potential issues with
an earlier version of the dataset, however, see Zoco (2004).

[33] Specifically, I use the "Polity2" variable. It "modifies the combined annual *Polity* score
by applying a simple treatment, or "fix," to convert instances of "standardized authority
codes" (that is, –66, –77, and –88) to the conventional polity score (that is, within the
range, –10 to +10)" so as to "facilitate the use of the *Polity* regime measure in time-series
analyses" (Marshall and Jaggers 2002, 8, 16). The *Polity* dataset is available at http://
www.cidcm.umd.edu/inscr/polity, accessed on April 11, 2004.

[34] All the categories come from the "Definition of Areas and Regions" by the United Nations
Population Division, available at http://esa.un.org/unpp/definition.html, accessed on
August 16, 2008.

3

Economic Openness and Its Regional Dimension

3.1 INTRODUCTION

Under growing economic globalization, economic disparity within countries tends to widen as differentially endowed subnational regions fare differently in the world markets. The winner regions become more assertive in clamoring for greater fiscal and even political autonomy, and in resisting central demands for more revenue contributions. The loser regions start crying for more fiscal assistance from the central government. There are mounting strains in the center's ability to pursue fiscal transfers for mitigating the yawning economic gap among the regions. In time, fissiparous tendencies develop and territorial challenges to the national-level political authority start to emerge from below. So goes the storyline of the prevailing economic theories.

How does the story of post-1978 China fit these stylized facts? I start this chapter by reviewing some national-level economic trends and policies related to the country's recent but rapid embrace of the global markets. However, I focus on the regional dimension. Of primary interest are the following questions: What were the central government's foreign economic policies for the provinces? What were the patterns of cross-province variation in the actual degree of participation in economic globalization during this period? How did increasing exposure to the global markets affect the economic schism among the provinces? Did globalization unleash similar centrifugal forces from below? If yes, how did Beijing respond?

To a certain extent, the pursuit of economic efficiency gains under the rising "opportunity costs of closure" prompted the first opening in the late 1970s and has sustained it ever since. Considerations of regional comparative advantage based upon geography and natural resource endowments largely dictated the regional distribution of preferential policies from the central government that had initially favored the coastal provinces more exposed to and faring better in the global markets than their inland counterparts during the post-1978 era. The subsequent rise in regional economic disparity, in fiscal assertiveness from the coastal provinces, and in the strains in central fiscal capacity all highlighted growing central-provincial discord over fiscal matters. Nevertheless, throughout this period, the Chinese central government continued to implement substantial interprovincial fiscal transfers whereby the inland provinces doing less well in the global markets apparently benefited more than did the winner provinces along the coast.

The rest of this chapter proceeds as follows. After surveying the country's growing participation in the global markets since 1978, I turn to examine the regional dimension of economic globalization in China. I pay particular attention to the patterns and nature of preferential policies in the foreign economic sector for the provinces from the central government. I then discuss the economic consequences at the provincial level of the country's opening to the international markets. Following a brief review of the debate on China's state fiscal capacity during this period – especially that of the central government – I provide some preliminary assessments of the extent of interprovincial fiscal redistribution in this era.

3.2 ECONOMIC TRENDS AND GOVERNMENT POLICIES

3.2.1 China's Embrace of the Global Markets

Efforts to characterize China's economic growth since 1978 are often more than enthusiastic. For some scholars (for example, Lin et al. 1996), nothing short of a "miracle" can capture the sheer magnitude of the country's economic achievement wrought in such a short period. According to its official statistics, during the 1978–2004 period, China's GDP and per capita GDP in real terms grew on average at 8.4 and 7.1 percent per annum, respectively.[1] By 2004, China's GDP was

---

[1] See the Appendix to this chapter for sources of Chinese official national-level data cited here. These data cover a longer period and might be more conservative than the figures provided by the World Bank, which, according to Lardy (1992), might inflate China's

TABLE 3.1. *Growth of China's Economy, Foreign Trade, and FDI*

	1953–77	1978–2004
Per capita GDP	3.89	7.17
GDP	6.07	8.43
Exports	4.23	13.91
Total foreign trade (exports+imports)	6.69	18.11
Net FDI inflows	–	46.60

Note: All figures are period averages of annual real growth (in percentages). The constant 1950 RMB (deflated with the general consumer price indices) is used to calculate the growth rates of the real values of GDP and trade figures. Due to data availability, the 2000 constant USD is used for calculating real growth in net FDI inflows, covering the 1981–2004 period.
Source: Appendix to Chapter 3.

more than seven times as large as it was when the reform began; its real per capita GDP more than quintupled from about 262 yuan in 1978 to 1,502 yuan in 2004 (both in constant 1950 Renminbi [RMB]).[2] Still, the economic leap forward pales in comparison with the rapidity of China's embrace of the global markets, as I summarize in Table 3.1.

Although the economy did indeed take off in the post-1978 period, a much larger spurt occurred in foreign trade. Even in the same faster-growing latter period, performance of both exports and foreign trade far surpassed that of the economy as a whole. On average, exports expanded at nearly double the speed of per capita GDP, whereas total foreign trade grew more than twice as fast as GDP. Yet the most striking thing is the annual increase of *net* inflows of foreign direct investments (FDI), on average by as much as 46.6 percent during the 1981–2004 period.[3] Not

GDP size. Based on the World Bank (2008), the average annual real growth rates of GDP and per capita GDP during the 1978–2004 period were 9.7 and 8.4 percent, respectively.

[2] The World Bank (2008) puts the size of the Chinese economy (GDP) as the fourth largest in the world in 2004 at constant 2000 USD, behind the United States, Japan, and Germany among 181 individual economies with available data. In 1978, China ranked the 15th out of 127 individual economies with available data. In constant 2000 USD, China's per capita GDP rose from $165 in 1978 to $1,323 in 2004. The improvement in ranking in terms of per capita GDP, from about 123rd out of 127 in 1978 to about 109th out of 180 in 2004, although significant, might not be as impressive due to China's gigantic population.

[3] Although the FDI growth data from the World Bank (2008) start in 1980, I only include the period of 1981–2004 to avoid overly exaggerating the FDI growth figures due to China's extremely low base of FDI inflows in 1979.

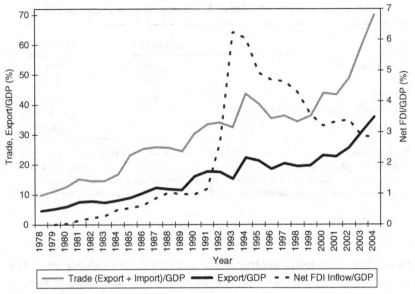

FIGURE 3.1. Economic globalization in China, 1978–2004.
Source: Appendix to Chapter 3.

surprisingly, China's degree of economic globalization, as measured by
the conventional indicators, rose sharply in this period.

As shown in Figure 3.1, China's total foreign trade as a share of GDP
soared from only 9.8 percent in 1978 to nearly 70 percent in 2004; the
export/GDP share jumped from about 4.6 percent to 36 percent. On
average, the trade/GDP share and export/GDP share for the 1978–2004
period were 31.2 and 15.9 percent, respectively; the respective numbers
for the 1953–77 period were only 8.1 and 4.2 percent.[4] The role of FDI
in the national economy also rose rapidly. *Net* FDI inflows, as a share of
China's national GDP, reached a peak of 6.2 percent in 1993, up from
about nil in 1979, according to the World Bank (2008). Although the
importance of FDI seems to have diminished somewhat in more recent
years, it still maintained a considerable presence in the national economy
as late as 2004, at about 2.8 percent of GDP. The average share of net
FDI inflows in GDP for the 1979–2004 period was 2.31 percent, making FDI a significant component of the economy even in a comparative

---

[4] Data for China's foreign trade and GDP in World Bank (2008) start from 1970, with the
average trade/GDP share at 7.9 percent for 1970–77 and 35.7 percent for 1978–2004.
Respective figures for India, a comparable developing country, were 10.2 and 19.6 percent. For the United States, they were 14.3 and 21.1 percent, respectively.

perspective.⁵ Thus, there is little doubt that reform-era China has made great strides in joining the global markets.

3.2.2 National Policy Impetus

China had been under near autarky after decades of pursuing "import substitution." Only sufficient exports to earn foreign exchange to import the heavy machinery and capital goods required for its industrialization drive had been allowed (Lardy 1992, Chapter 1). Reform of the foreign economic sector was ushered in as part of the broader economic restructuring launched in late 1978. As noted earlier, this was taking place against the backdrop of the general "easing" of exogenous enabling factors that sharply reduced the costs of transportation, communications, and commerce across national borders (Frieden and Rogowski 1996). As the "opportunity costs of closure" continued to surge, governments worldwide began to liberalize their foreign trade in this period (Garrett 2000). Most probably, the Chinese central government had jumped aboard the globalization bandwagon in search of similar efficiency gains from foreign trade.

The immediate catalyst behind the country's decision to open its doors, however, might be more complex. One conjecture by Shirk (1994, 1996) attributes liberalization in the foreign and domestic economic sectors to the imperative of succession power struggles at the national level. In this view, the reformist leader Deng Xiaoping advocated the general liberalization package that favored light industry and exports. It provided an alternative to the pro–heavy industry and import substitution program pursued by his political rivals during the leadership contests in the aftermath of Mao's death. This is an important insight, but Deng apparently had already favored opening a link to the outside world even before the onset of these succession struggles, according to Shirk herself (1996, 193). Similarly, Harding (1987, 58–59, 133) notes that Deng might have developed such a policy vision well before Mao's death. Nevertheless, an argument that privileges the importance of leadership succession suggests that the reform policies could only be adopted when a committed national leadership was placed firmly in power.

Perhaps more important could be the stark economic and geostrategic reality that confronted the country's political elites at the time. Regardless of how they had come to power, the national leaders triumphant in the

---

⁵ During the same 1979–2004 period, the average share of net FDI inflows in national GDP was 0.34 percent for India and 1.04 percent for the United States (World Bank 2008).

post-Mao succession struggles believed that China could no longer afford to keep its doors closed. At home, the country was reeling from the turmoil of the devastating decade of the Cultural Revolution that had undermined the legitimacy of Communist rule. Abroad, the ongoing Soviet threat along the Chinese border might have necessitated an economic and strategic shift to the West (Harding 1987, 38–39; 1994). Meanwhile, recent trips abroad also exposed the Chinese leaders to the economic achievements of their East Asian neighbors (Baum 1994, 57–58). The successful experiences of South Korea and Japan could have persuaded the reformist leadership of the real potential in exploiting China's own comparative advantage in abundant and relatively well-educated labor in the international markets through exports and foreign trade (Shirk 1996, 192).[6]

Thus, one ostensible rationale for economic opening was that the country's participation in the "international division of labor" could speed up its modernization drive through the better utilization of its comparative advantage and promotion of overall economic growth (Deng Xiaoping 1993 [1984], 77–80). Given the role of export-driven growth during this period in both China (see the following) and the postwar East Asian economic success stories (for instance, Amsden 1989; Wade 1990), I mainly examine policies designed to promote export incentives, even though imports are clearly an important component of any globalization story.[7] Although measures such as the gradual devaluation of the Chinese currency are also highly pertinent to explaining China's "rise as a trading nation" (Naughton 1996; Zhang 2001), here I focus on the devolution of authority to conduct foreign trade and exports.

3.2.3 Foreign Trade Liberalization and Decentralization

Liberalization first occurred by enlarging the number of actors below the national level that were authorized to conduct foreign trade directly. Before

---

[6] The role of foreign trips noted by other scholars in convincing China's leaders of the vital importance of focusing on national comparative advantage in the global markets based on natural resource endowments is also confirmed in the recent memoir by Zhao Ziyang. As China's premier during 1980–87 and chief of the CCP during 1987–89, Zhao was instrumental in the country's opening policy. During a trip to Europe in 1978 when he was still the provincial party secretary of Sichuan, for example, Zhao Ziyang (2009, 152–153) wondered how farmers in the seemingly "arid" parts of the Mediterranean countries could thrive on growing only grapes and olives for export.

[7] The difference between foreign trade and exports in Figure 3.1 gives a rough sense of the role of imports in the Chinese economy during this period. For details on the evolution of China's post-1978 tariff regime, see Lardy (2002, Chapter 2).

the reform era, foreign trade had been part of the annual planning by the central government and monopolized by the Ministry of Foreign Trade and about a dozen of its national foreign trade companies (FTCs). While reducing the number of goods subject to the national plan and authorizing several other central ministries to engage in foreign trade (Liu Xiangdong 1993), reform devolved foreign trade authority to lower-level governments. The number of FTCs nationwide quickly rose to more than 1,200 in 1986, more than 3,500 by the early 1990s, and about 31,000 by 2001 (Branstetter and Lardy 2008, 635; Shirk 1994, 45; World Bank 1994). Most FTCs were below the national level as provincial and lower-level governments absorbed the local branches of the national FTCs or created their own FTCs. Moreover, local FTCs seemed heavily concentrated along the coast. Their large presence in Guangdong, the showcase province for China's economic opening, is suggestive. By the end of 1987, there were already about 900 such companies in Guangdong alone (Vogel 1989, 377).

Changes also occurred in the rules governing the allocation of foreign exchange earned abroad. Prior to reform, all foreign exchange earnings had to be submitted to the central government before being allotted for use according to a unified import plan. In 1979, new rules allowed export enterprises and their supervising local governments, or the central ministries that managed these enterprises, to retain some of the foreign exchange. From the very beginning, provinces hosting Special Economic Zones (SEZs) such as Guangdong and Fujian, the five autonomous regions for ethnic minorities, and the less-developed Yunnan, Guizhou, and Qinghai provinces all received preferential retention rates (Zhang 2002). Retention schemes with increasingly favorable terms were offered in the later years.

In 1985, a two-track formula for foreign exchange retention went into effect.[8] For exports below a predetermined quota, 75 percent of the earned foreign exchange went to the central government, with the remaining 25 percent equally shared by the overseeing local governments and the export enterprises. For exports above the quota, the local governments and enterprises would equally split 70 percent. In 1988, the above-quota local retention was raised further to 80 percent (Gao Binhuai 1990; Lu Libin 1989; Wu Zesong 1988). As a result, locally retained foreign exchange soared from approximately nil before 1978 to about 42 percent of the total in the mid-1980s. In 1988, when China's

---

[8] For an excellent discussion of the evolution of the foreign exchange retention system, see Lardy (1992, 52–57).

total foreign exchange was $18.5 billion, this amounted to $7.8 billion (Lardy 1992, 57), or 18.3 percent of total budgetary revenues for all local (provincial and below) governments (Guojia Tongji Ju [National Bureau of Statistics] 1999b, Table 8–10).

Furthermore, by 1988, control over the use of 40 percent of the retained foreign exchange was liberalized so that in theory, local governments could access the hard currency "without restrictions" (Lardy 1992, 103). For the remainder, retention conferred not exactly the hard currency, but an entitlement to the use of the foreign exchange that had to be "deposited" at – essentially sold at the going official exchange rate to – designated state banks. The foreign exchange could later be sold back to these entities if it was approved for "legitimate" purposes, such as importing capital goods for expansion of production (Jie Wenxiu 1993). This was designed to check the excessive imports of consumer goods for profitable domestic sales by local governments with access to more hard currency (Zhang 2002).

Still, the retained foreign exchange constituted tangible resources for local governments even in the local currency. With the establishment of nationwide "swap" centers, local governments with surplus foreign exchange (that is, entitlements) could convert it into the domestic currency at higher-than-official rates by selling it to domestic enterprises, other local governments, and foreign enterprises in need of hard currency to import machinery and capital goods, or to repatriate profits (Lardy 1992, 57–58). The increased retention of foreign exchange thus enlarged the resources for the provinces – local governments and exporting enterprises alike, especially those that exported more to the international markets.

Foreign trade reform continued with the adoption of a uniform foreign exchange retention rate in 1991 (Li Lanqing 1991; Zhang 2002), followed by efforts in the late 1990s to prepare China for compatibility with the membership requirements of the WTO (Zhao Yongqing 1998). In short, foreign economic liberalization during this period was characterized by the downward devolution of the trading authority to the local governments and their FTCs. Together with decentralization of economic policymaking in other areas (Naughton 1995), it enhanced the incentives of the provinces to export and earn foreign exchange in the global markets, perhaps through better exploiting their natural resource endowments, as well as expanded their resources. Another key feature of the liberalization was its regional tilt, regarding not only the retention rates of foreign exchange earnings by the provinces, but also the establishment of the various kinds of economic development zones.

3.3 FOREIGN ECONOMIC LIBERALIZATION IN THE PROVINCES

3.3.1 Preferential Policies

All provinces did not uniformly share the benefits from the central government policies liberalizing the foreign economic sector. The dominant view is that the coastal provinces were the main beneficiaries of the regionally slanted policies from Beijing during the reform period, in contrast to the policies of the Mao era favoring the inland provinces (Shirk 1994, 1996; Yang 1990). This seemed to have been especially the case with the policies establishing the various development zones to attract foreign investment (see the following), but it may not have applied to all policy areas. As noted, the provinces did retain foreign exchange earnings at different rates after meeting a predetermined quota. As we can see in Table 3.2, however, in 1984 at least (for which systematic data are available), there is little evidence that the central government particularly favored the coastal provinces with higher foreign exchange retention rates.

Although most provinces obtained a retention rate of only 25 percent, Guangdong and Fujian, the two coastal provinces hosting the four SEZs at the time, were indeed able to retain as much as 30 percent of their earned foreign exchange. Yet the retention rate for provinces designated as autonomous regions for ethnic minorities, such as Guangxi, Inner Mongolia, Ningxia, and Xinjiang, or for poor inland provinces, such as Guizhou and Qinghai, was 50 percent, even higher than that for Guangdong and Fujian. For Tibet, it was 100 percent. In fact, the average retention rate in 1984 was much higher for the inland provinces as a group (37.5 percent) than it was for the coastal provinces (28.2 percent).[9] It is quite another story, however, with respect to the assortment of preferential policies from the central government that established economic development zones to attract inflows of foreign capital and to promote exports and trade.

These policies did largely favor the coastal provinces. As equity investments from foreign parent firms, FDI arrived in China's coastal export-

---

[9] Unfortunately, we do not have systematic data for every province in every year between 1979 when the policy was first introduced and 1991 when it was phased out, even though we know the rates could change over the years. Neither do we have much information about the exact terms of central-provincial foreign trade contracting for each province, for instance, regarding the annual export quota governing foreign exchange earnings. Of course, even higher above-quota retention rates did not necessarily translate into larger absolute retained foreign exchange earnings for the inland provinces due to their lower volumes of foreign trade and exports (more below).

TABLE 3.2. *Preferential Policies in the Foreign Economic Sector for the Provinces*

Provinces	Foreign Exchange Retention (%)	Preferential Policy Index	
	1984*	1978–91***	1992–98***
Beijing	25	0	2
Fujian	30	2.57	3
Guangdong	30	2.79	3
Guangxi	50	0.86	2
Hainan		3	3
Hebei	25	0.86	2
Jiangsu	25	1.14	2
Liaoning	25	0.86	2
Shandong	25	1.14	2
Shanghai	25	1.14	3
Tianjin	25	1.14	2
Zhejiang	25	1.14	2
Anhui	25	0	1.86
Chongqing			
Gansu	25	0	1
Guizhou	50	0	1
Heilongjiang	25	0	2
Henan	25	0	1
Hubei	25	0	1.86
Hunan	25	0	1
Inner Mongolia (Neimenggu)	50	0	2
Jiangxi	25	0	1
Jilin	25	0	2
Ningxia	50	0	1
Qinghai	50	0	1
Shaanxi	25	0	1
Shanxi	25	0	1
Sichuan	25	0	1.86
Tibet (Xizang)	100	0	1
Xinjiang	50	0	2
Yunnan	50	0	2

	Foreign Exchange Retention (%)	Preferential Policy Index	
Provinces	1984*	1978–91***	1992–98***
Coast	28.18	1.28	2.33
Inland	37.50	0	1.42

Note: The coastal provinces are in bold. Beijing is coded as a coastal province by convention. The preferential policy index figures are the provincial averages for the indicated periods, except for the coastal and inland average values reported at the bottom of the table and used in the mean comparison tests, which are the averages for all coastal and inland provinces in those periods, respectively. Due to possible uneven year coverage among the provinces in each period, the coastal and inland averages of the preferential policy index could differ from the mean of the provincial averages for the two groups calculated from the table columns here. Hainan's 1978–91 index is the average of 1988–91, as it only became a provincial unit in 1988. The data in the table do not cover Chongqing, which only became a provincial-level unit in 1997.

***: $p < 0.01$ in two-group mean comparison tests for the coastal and inland provinces (two-tailed tests with unequal variances); **: $p < 0.05$; *: $p < 0.1$.

Source: Data on the foreign exchange retention rates are from Zhang (2002, 104). The preferential policy index data are from Démurger et al. (2002b, 176–177).

processing zones very early during the reform era (Wang 2001). Various FDI-related enterprises have played a pivotal role in the country's overall foreign trade. While foreign-invested enterprises (FIEs) accounted only for 0.8 percent of total foreign trade and 0.2 percent of exports in 1982 (Fu 2000, 4), the numbers exceeded 50 percent in both categories by 2001 (Guojia Tongji Ju [National Bureau of Statistics] 2002, Tables 17–3, 17–12).[10] A major goal pursued by the Chinese central government was to lure FDI, together with the advanced technologies and managerial expertise it embodied, into the coastal provinces through the generous incentives provided in the various development zones.

To be sure, the provincial governments also created many of the development zones themselves, as they were often authorized to do so within their own jurisdictions. For example, by the end of 1990, the provincial government of Shandong had launched around 60 development zones of various types in that province alone (Liu 2008, 480). As of 1995, provincial governments in China were responsible for approving about one-fourth

---

[10] Naughton (1996, 295–308) also discusses at length how foreign capital in China, in the form of FIEs, could promote exports.

of the 2,000 new economic development zones nationwide (Li Lanqing 1995, 295–296). Nevertheless, the bulk of the economic zones imparting the various preferential treatments were set up under the auspices of the State Council (the equivalent of the cabinet) of the central government.

Barely a year after the Chinese central government signaled its desire to tap overseas capital with the passage of its first Joint Venture Law in early 1979, SEZs were established in four cities of coastal Guangdong and Fujian provinces. Greater authority to offer concessionary tax policies toward foreign businesses was granted to the local governments in order to build competitive local export-processing zones. In 1984, the areas granted preferential policies from the central government were expanded to fourteen coastal cities located in Guangdong, Fujian, and eight other provinces. In the following year, three river delta regions along the coast (the Pearl River in Guangdong, the Min River in Fujian, and the Yangtze River spanning across Jiangsu and Shanghai) were designated Coastal Open Economic Zones.

The geographic expansion continued with the then CCP chief Zhao Ziyang's "coastal development strategy" (*yanhai diqu jingji fazhan zhanlüe*) in 1988 making Hainan Island (hitherto part of Guangdong) a new province and a fifth SEZ. It also brought Liaodong Peninsula and Shandong Peninsula along the eastern coast into the "Open Coastal Belt." The political instability of the Tiananmen tragedy and Zhao's fall from grace in 1989 did not prevent the opening in the following year of the Pudong New Area in Shanghai, almost equal in status to the SEZs. However, it was not until 1992, following the "southern tour" by Deng Xiaoping to promote further liberalization of the economy, that such preferential policies went beyond the coastal region. With the opening of all provincial capitals in the inland and the ten "Open River Cities" along the Yangtze River, all provincial units and one-third of the national population began to fall under its coverage (Démurger et al. 2002b; Fu 2000; Li Lanqing 1995; Yang 1991).

Despite the later enlarged geographic coverage, the coastal bias of these policies was unmistakable. A study by Chinese economists finds that by the early 1990s, the coastal provinces had been home to as many as 360 out of a total of 422 development zones established by the State Council nationwide (Guo Kesha and Li Haijian 1995, 67). A similar picture emerges from the annual preferential policy index constructed by Démurger et al. (2002a, 453–454; 2002b, 176–177) for each province during the 1978–98 period. These researchers assign a value of 0 to a province if no development zone of any kind was present, and a value of 1 if a province featured a Coastal Open City, Coastal Open Economic Zone, Open Coastal Belt, major city on the Yangtze, bonded area, or capital city of an inland province or autonomous region. A value of 2 is given to a province with an Economic and Technological Development Zone or Border Economic Cooperation Zone. Finally, a province hosting an SEZ (including the Pudong New Area) receives a value of 3.

In essence, a higher index score indicates greater policy autonomy in the foreign economic sector for the overseeing local governments and more tangible benefits for the provinces where these zones were located. For example, a higher score could denote a greater ability of the local governments to exempt "the establishment of foreign-funded enterprises (FFEs), the profits of FFEs, the international trade transactions of FFEs, and the domestic operations of the FFEs from the restrictive state regulations governing the ... foreign enterprise sector" (Démurger et al. 2002b, 181). This would allow the foreign firms to operate in a more liberalized, flexible business environment and make these localities more attractive in the eyes of foreign investors.[11]

Greater policy leeway for the local governments could thus translate into an assortment of positive externalities for the localities hosting the economic development zones. Above all, the infusion of foreign capital lured by the lower transaction cost could boost foreign trade and exports and help generate more foreign exchange. A better infrastructure and more congenial business environment were also attractive to domestic capital from the localities lacking such privileges; tax benefits intended for foreign firms were often extended to domestic businesses operating in the zones. Entrepreneurial and other human talent tended to swarm into the development zones that offered higher salaries and better working conditions (Zweig 2002, 60–64). All this could help promote local economic development and redound to more local government revenues (Shirk 1993, 182–183).

The averages of the index for 1978–91 and 1992–98 (after expansion to the inland provinces) are presented in the remainder of Table 3.2. During the 1978–91 period, the coastal provinces were the sole beneficiaries of the central government policies to establish the economic development zones, enjoying an average score of 1.28, compared with a flat zero for the inland provinces. The gap between the average coastal and inland

---

[11] Among other things, it could affect the firms' ability to "import intermediate inputs duty-free to produce exports; collaborate with foreign companies in investment, manufacturing, and distribution; hire and fire workers in accordance with their performance and demand conditions; and escape the confiscatory taxation that is needed in a centrally planned economy to finance its vast, complicated system of social subsidies" (Démurger et al. 2002b, 152). For details of the types of development zones and the related policy benefits, see also Fu (2000), Li Lanqing (1995), Zhao Jinping (2001), and Zweig (2002). All development zones, with the exception of the SEZs, came to an end on January 1, 1999 (Démurger 2000).

scores narrowed somewhat during the 1992–98 period due to the expansion of these policies to the inland provinces. Nevertheless, on average, the coastal provinces seemed to have benefited to a greater degree than did their inland counterparts, even in the latter period. The coastal average for 1992–98 was 2.33, while the inland average was only 1.42. Thus, overall, preferential policies in the foreign economic sector from the central government favored the coastal provinces during these years.

3.3.2 Explaining the Regional Tilt

Why did the Chinese central government tend to lavish the coastal provinces with policies to establish the various development zones? One appealing view emphasizes the role of explicit or implicit provincial lobbying. In a rich study of incentives at the level of the cities hosting most of the development zones, Zweig (2002, 18, 20) argues that the benefits for the localities induced all provincial governments to lobby the central government to create more development zones in their own jurisdictions. His interviews with central government officials reveal that provincial officials indeed often made such requests (Zweig 2002, 80–81). If most development zones were located in the coastal provinces, did the provincial governments along the coast just lobby the central government more effectively?

The efficacy of direct provincial lobbying in national policymaking, however, has been generally questioned in the Chinese context. As Shirk (1996, 204) insightfully points out, although "all provinces have lobbying operations in the capital …, there is no evidence that demands from below drove the policies" during the reform era. Instead, Shirk contends that the reformist national leaders in China pulled off their reform program largely as a side-product of their bids to win the succession contests at the highest level. To counterbalance the "[C]ommunist coalition" composed of the inland provinces, heavy industry, and the military that were less enamored of the idea of opening to the global markets, the reformists sought the political support of other important actors in the "Selectorate" formally entrusted with the task of choosing China's top leadership. In particular, they wooed the CCP Central Committee members working in the coastal provinces with foreign economic policy largesse (Shirk 1993, 1996).

Nevertheless, predictions of Shirk's "political logic" do not jibe particularly well with the actual process of China's opening to the global markets (Zhang 2002). In Chapter 5, I will provide systematic evidence to show that membership of provincial officials on the CCP Central Committees did not seem to have helped the provinces secure a greater extent of preferential foreign economic policies. Suffice it to say here that an approach favoring the role of the provinces, either as lobbyists actively pushing the central government for policy pork or as courting targets of the reformist national leaders, does not appear to be very cogent.

A more persuasive perspective privileges the considerations of central leaders in pursuit of an economic development strategy based on the regional comparative advantage dictated by the geographic location, past experiences with industrial production and trading, and preexisting human capital of the provinces. In fact, opening up to the global markets was aimed at transforming the coastal provinces into export-processing zones in the fashion of those in some of China's East Asian neighbors. The attraction of the coastal provinces for such a strategy was obvious. Geographic proximity to the sea cannot be artificially created overnight. Longer experiences with industrialization and international commerce in these regions dated back at least to the era of the "treaty ports" in the late Qing dynasty (Spence 1990).

Data from the early years after the Communist takeover of the Chinese mainland similarly show much higher industrial productivity in the coastal provinces. In 1957, the coastal average of per capita industrial output was about 3.3 times the national average, and the inland average was only 0.69 times the national average (Lardy 1978, 104). The advantages of the coastal provinces in infrastructure and industrial productivity largely persisted through Mao's egalitarian regional development strategy that lopsidedly poured state investment into the inland provinces, though with largely disappointing results. According to Yang (1990, 237), although the inland share of total fixed assets more than doubled from about 28 percent in 1952 to nearly 57 percent in 1983, in the same period their contribution to national industrial output only grew from 30.6 percent to 40.5 percent. The advantages of the coastal provinces seem hardly surprising:

[T]he coastal region enjoyed superior factor endowments compared with the interior. Coastal bases possessed an industrial labour force with long years of experience while the interior had workers who were mostly recent recruits from the peasant population. Coastal industries also accumulated superior managerial skills compared with the interior. Moreover, the coastal region generally had better supporting facilities such as in transport than the interior. (Yang 1990, 238)

Preferential policies that would help the coastal provinces attract foreign capital and build up competitive industrial processing and export platforms in the development zones thus reflected a new willingness on the part of the central leadership to take into account the regional comparative advantage enjoyed by the coastal provinces. As early as 1979, the CCP Central Committee and the State Council had highlighted the proximity of Guangdong and Fujian to Hong Kong and Macao and ties to overseas Chinese to justify favorable foreign exchange retention policies for the two provinces (Zhao Dexin 1989, 784). Gu Mu, state councilor (the equivalent of a vice premier) in charge of foreign economic policies, put it candidly in early 1985: "[T]he coastal regions have easier access to foreign markets, better communications with the outside world, a certain industrial foundation and more specialised a personnel and management experience" (quoted in Howell 1993, 20).

The exact same reasoning was apparently behind the "coastal development strategy" of 1988, an initiative that was first proposed by then–CCP chief Zhao Ziyang and anointed by Deng Xiaoping himself. According to Zhao Ziyang (2009, 164), the coastal regions were given a head start because they "enjoy excellent transportation links and boast better infrastructure than the inland. Their labor force is well educated and technically sophisticated even given China's comparative advantage in abundant labor. Their closer vicinity to the foreign markets and longer experiences with the market economy will also make them easily adaptable to the international marketplace." These were all long-preexisting traits highly valued for foreign trade and exports.

Indeed, the vital role of provincial factor endowments in affecting the regional distribution of preferential policies has also been tacitly acknowledged in research explicitly espousing the provincial lobbying thesis. Before turning to an examination of the incentives of the provincial governments to lobby the central government for preferential policies, for instance, Zweig (2002, 15) faults Shirk's "political logic" for ignoring "the coast's comparative advantage in foreign trade," which for him "is the real explanation why the center favored it over the inland areas." Indeed, Zweig (2002, 54) might easily pass off as an advocate of a regional comparative advantage thesis when he observes:

And because they were more accessible to world markets, were the ancestral home to millions of overseas Chinese whose capital and knowledge were critical for the success of the open policy, and were not home to many state-owned enterprises (SOEs) that could not compete globally, coastal areas in south China were deregulated first [with preferential policies].

It is unfair, however, to accuse Shirk of losing sight of the importance of the comparative advantage of the coastal provinces. Although the "political logic" is the defining contribution of her work, Shirk (1996, 198) admits that the coastal provinces are more competitive in the global markets. After all, these are places "where China's labor force is concentrated; where labor is better educated; where most of the prior light industry was located; and where memories of precommunist era commercial ties with the world still exist." Indeed, the "economic rationale" to locate the SEZs first in South China was the very close links of the region with the capital-rich overseas Chinese in Southeast Asia, ready to be tapped as "sources of international capital" for the country's opening and development drive (Shirk 1996, 201). This view is similarly echoed by Harding (1987, 164–165) in his discussion of the rationale behind the establishment of the SEZs.

Thus, there seems to be an implicit consensus on the crucial role of provincial natural resource endowments in determining the regional distribution of the preferential policies in the foreign economic sector during this period. To be sure, new comparative advantage and momentum could be created once the preferential policies were in place. However, the coastal provinces were lavished with these policies in the first place due to largely "exogenous" factors that cannot be easily molded. This is also corroborated by systematic evidence that being located along the coast was a significant and positive predictor of the extent of preferential policies in the foreign economic sector for the provinces during 1978–98, as I report later in Chapter 5.[12] Indeed, the preferential policies would not have necessarily worked had the requisite resource endowments been lacking, as shown in the failure of the biased Maoist regional policies in favor of the inland provinces (Yang 1990). Nevertheless, regional comparative advantage, preexisting or further reinforced by the preferential policies, also engendered real consequences in the provinces during the period of growing participation in the global markets.

3.4 REGIONAL DISPARITY AND DISCONTENT

If one major goal of China's post-1978 opening was to promote economic growth, to some extent, the record has been a great success. As

---

[12] The most prominent economic theories on comparative advantage in international trade tend to focus on the role of input factors such as labor, land, and capital (for example, Stolper and Samuelson 1941) or the specific sectors where these factors are located and enjoy varying ease of relocating, that is, different degrees of "asset specificity" (for instance, Frieden 1991a). In contrast, the argument here has emphasized the regional comparative advantage of the Chinese provinces based on both geography and preexisting international experiences. This is more akin to the line of research on economic development that stresses the role of geographic locations (Bao et al. 2002; Bloom and Sachs 1998; Radelet et al. 2001) and the dynamic TFP perspective on comparative advantage privileging, among other things, the prior trading contacts abroad of enterprises and firms. For excellent reviews of the various economic approaches to comparative advantage in trade, see Frieden and Rogowski (1996) and Rogowski (1989, Chapter 1).

noted, China during this period witnessed phenomenal economic growth as well as rapid integration with the global markets. Such positive correlations between the two during the reform era have received empirical corroboration from a growing number of econometric studies. At the national aggregate level, foreign trade is found to be positively associated with per capita GDP growth (Lin 2000) and with the size of GNP (Chen et al. 1995; Liu et al. 1997). While exports seem to have increased industrial output (Yu 1998), FDI has been shown to promote GDP growth (Shan et al. 1999). Similar conclusions are reached by studies employing provincial-level data (Chen and Feng 2000; Dacosta and Carroll 2001).

In short, much empirical evidence suggests that the rising exposure to the world markets has been associated with better economic performance in post-1978 China. It might well be via the efficiency gains from trade and exports based on better utilization of the country's comparative advantage (Yue and Hua 2002). It could also be through the assortment of positive externalities generated by FDI inflows (technology, transfer of management expertise, new employment, etc.) that contributed to national TFP gains (Hu and Khan 1997). However, the economic gains from opening to the international markets are far from uniformly distributed at the provincial level. In particular, the coastal regions seem to have benefited disproportionately (Zhang and Kristensen 2001; Sun and Parikh 2001). Differential exposure to the global markets might have led to worsening economic disparity among China's provinces, especially along the coast-inland divide (Dayal-Gulati and Husain 2002; Fujita and Hu 2001; Kanbur and Zhang 2005; Wan et al. 2007).

3.4.1 Provincial Variation in Economic Openness

A good, albeit still preliminary, sense of exactly how the provinces differed from each other in the extent of their participation in the global markets during 1978–2004 can be gauged in the summary provincial-level data on trade/GDP, export/GDP, and FDI/GDP shares (all in percentages) in Table 3.3. I group the provinces into the inland and coastal cohorts. I also divide the data into two periods of 1978–90 and 1991–2004 to capture possible cross-time changes. One clear pattern emerges from our data. The coastal provinces were more integrated with the global markets than their inland counterparts were throughout the post-Mao era. During the periods of 1978–90 and 1991–2004, the average trade/GDP share for the coastal provinces was about 15.7 percent and 46 percent, respectively, whereas the export/GDP share averaged around 12.2 percent and 26.2 percent. By comparison, the

TABLE 3.3. *Economic Globalization Among the Provinces, 1978–2004*

Provinces	Trade/GDP (%)		Export/GDP (%)		FDI/GDP (%)	
	1978–90***	1991–2004***	1978–90***	1991–2004***	1978–90***	1991–2004***
Beijing	10.25	30.76	7.85	14.09	2.27	6.04
Fujian	13.12	50.90	8.51	31.17	0.92	10.04
Guangdong	25.33	130.80	16.90	74.06	2.15	10.53
Guangxi	7.45	11.67	6.04	8.18	0.35	2.70
Hainan	32.76	41.03	16.44	17.43	4.74	12.21
Hebei	7.30	9.78	6.64	7.43	0.08	1.46
Jiangsu	7.53	38.25	6.30	22.52	0.20	6.22
Liaoning	22.35	31.50	20.93	20.74	0.30	4.01
Shandong	11.37	21.98	9.15	14.83	0.15	3.34
Shanghai	30.33	86.12	23.26	44.72	0.79	7.54
Tianjin	27.29	67.02	22.45	35.73	0.46	8.89
Zhejiang	6.47	32.60	5.64	23.23	0.13	2.75
Anhui	2.76	9.33	2.26	6.01	0.05	1.07
Chongqing		8.73		4.73		1.47
Gansu	2.12	6.68	1.78	4.72	0.02	0.50
Guizhou	1.87	6.33	1.25	4.15	0.07	0.42
Heilongjiang	4.23	11.58	3.34	6.44	0.12	1.10
Henan	2.77	5.28	2.48	3.93	0.10	0.90
Hubei	4.62	8.51	3.98	5.65	0.12	1.95
Hunan	4.07	8.62	3.39	5.85	0.05	1.71
Inner Mongolia	2.99	11.09	2.24	5.47	0.05	0.61
Jiangxi	4.09	8.51	3.51	6.47	0.06	2.20

(continued)

TABLE 3.3 (continued)

Provinces	Trade/GDP (%)		Export/GDP (%)		FDI/GDP (%)	
	1978–90***	1991–2004***	1978–90***	1991–2004***	1978–90***	1991–2004***
Jilin	5.39	17.24	4.01	8.57	0.05	1.60
Ningxia	5.09	11.82	4.15	9.44	0.02	0.55
Qinghai	2.61	6.68	1.82	5.31	0.18	0.70
Shaanxi	4.06	11.48	1.88	7.70	0.72	1.76
Shanxi	2.86	9.61	2.24	7.53	0.04	0.87
Sichuan	2.32	7.73	1.72	4.63	0.03	0.97
Tibet	3.57	13.23	1.32	5.15		
Xinjiang	5.51	13.11	3.49	6.91	0.16	0.27
Yunnan	4.27	9.51	3.07	5.97	0.05	0.48
Coast	**15.70**	**46.03**	**12.24**	**26.18**	**0.86**	**6.31**
Inland	**3.61**	**9.76**	**2.66**	**6.06**	**0.11**	**1.06**

Note: The coastal provinces are in bold. Data are the provincial averages for the indicated periods, except for the coastal and inland average values reported at the bottom of the table and used in the mean comparison tests, which are the averages for all coastal and inland provinces in those periods, respectively. Since Hainan only became a province in 1988, its data for the 1978–90 period cover 1988–90. Chongqing's data for the 1991–2004 period cover 1997–2004, as Chongqing became a provincial unit in 1997. Shaanxi's trade/GDP data start in 1984. FDI data are actually utilized, not contracted values. They refer to gross, not net, inflows, as systematic data on provincial outflows are almost nonexistent for these years. Starting years for FDI data vary with the province, ranging from 1980 to 1985. FDI data before 1985 for the provinces are rather sparse. For the years since 1985, FDI data are missing for Inner Mongolia (1985), Guizhou (1987), Gansu (1989), Qinghai (1985–87 and 1989–91), and Xinjiang (1992). FDI data for Tibet are missing throughout.

***: $p < 0.01$ in two-group mean comparison tests for the coastal and inland provinces (two-tailed tests with unequal variances); **: $p < 0.05$; *: $p < 0.1$.

Source: Appendix to Chapter 3.

trade and export measures for the inland provinces were only 3.6 percent and 9.8 percent, and 2.7 percent and 6.1 percent, respectively.

In fact, in terms of their exposure to foreign trade and their ability to export, some coastal provinces in China were comparable to the world's most open economies during these years. The poster child of the era of economic openness, Guangdong has been the most foreign trade–dependent province since 1990, and China's most export-oriented province since 1991. In 2004, for instance, total foreign trade constituted about 184.3 percent of its provincial GDP, making Guangdong potentially the seventh most globalized economy in the world, behind only Singapore, Hong Kong, Luxembourg, Malaysia, Guyana, and Seychelles. In the same year, Shanghai's trade/GDP share registered 177.8 percent, which was higher than that of Macao, the world's eighth most open economy. Moreover, Guangdong and Shanghai were also among the most export-oriented economies in the world. In 2004, exports contributed 98.8 percent and 81.7 percent to the GDP of Guangdong and Shanghai, respectively. Thus, in 2004, Guangdong could rank the sixth most export-oriented economy in the world, and Shanghai the fifteenth.[13]

In sharp contrast, some inland provincial economies could be among the most closed in the world. In 2004, for example, foreign trade and exports constituted only about 6.2 percent and 3.9 percent, respectively, of the GDP of Henan, China's most populous province since 1997 when Chongqing was carved out of Sichuan to become a separate provincial unit. Similarly, trade and exports made up about 7.9 percent and 4.5 percent, respectively, of the GDP of the mountainous, landlocked Guizhou province in the southwest in the same year. In 2004, Henan and Guizhou were much less exposed to the international markets than any of the 175 individual economies for which we have data from the World Bank (2008).

There is a broadly similar picture of huge variation between the coastal and inland provinces in terms of the ability to attract foreign capital. Actually utilized foreign direct investment contributed, on average, around 0.9 percent to the provincial GDP during the 1978–90 period and 6.3 percent during the 1991–2004 period for the coastal provinces, but only 0.1 percent and 1.1 percent, respectively, for their inland counterparts. The island province of Hainan in the south boasted the highest average FDI/GDP share during the 1991–2004 period. In fact, in 1995, FDI made up as much as 24.4 percent of Hainan's GDP, an all-time high among the

---

[13] Data on economic globalization in other countries cited here are from the World Bank (2008).

provinces during the entire 1978–2004 period. By comparison, the role of FDI remained minor in the economies of most inland provinces throughout these years. In 1993, when net FDI inflows constituted the highest share of China's national GDP in this period (Figure 3.1), actually utilized FDI contributed less than 0.2 percent to the GDP of Qinghai, a remote province in the country's inland west. On average, in 1993, the FDI/GDP share for the inland provinces was only 1.1 percent, compared with nearly 7.4 percent for the coastal provinces.

3.4.2 Winners and Losers

Not surprisingly, the more globalized Chinese provinces along the coast fared better economically than the inland provinces during this period. In Table 3.4, I summarize the provincial data for the two provincial cohorts on the levels of wealth in terms of real per capita GDP (constant 1977 RMB), as well as on the pace of economic development in terms of the growth rates (in percentage) of real per capita GDP during the 1978–2004 period. To be sure, both groups gained economically from opening to the global markets in these years. Even the inland provinces registered impressive per capita GDP growth rates of about 6.97 percent and over 9.4 percent during the 1978–90 and 1991–2004 periods, respectively. In terms of absolute numbers, average real per capita GDP in the inland rose from 492 yuan during the 1978–90 period to about 1,261 yuan during the 1991–2004 period.

Nevertheless, the coastal provinces seemed to have benefited to a larger extent from the country's embrace of the global markets. In general, the coastal provinces grew faster in both the 1978–90 and 1991–2004 periods, with average per capita GDP growth rates being around 7 percent and 12 percent, respectively. While the coastal-inland difference in growth rate is not statistically significant at the conventional level for the earlier period in a simple two-group mean comparison test, it turns highly significant (at 0.01) in the latter. This suggests that the gap in economic dynamism between the inland and coastal provinces might have further widened over these years. Moreover, the coastal provinces were much wealthier. Their per capita GDP averaged nearly 991 yuan and 2,989 yuan during the two periods, respectively – more than twice as high as that for the inland provinces. By 2004, for example, coastal Shanghai's real per capita GDP reached 14,478 yuan, followed by that of coastal Tianjin at nearly 9,720 yuan. In contrast, in the same year, real per capita GDP in Guizhou was only about 1,069 yuan, and about 1,631 yuan in Gansu.

TABLE 3.4. *Growth and Wealth Among the Provinces, 1978–2004*

Provinces	Per Capita GDP Growth (%)		Per Capita GDP (1977 Yuan)	
	1978–90	1991–2004***	1978–90***	1991–2004***
Beijing	4.39	10.69	1748.06	4231.02
Fujian	10.05	13.34	481.75	2338.56
Guangdong	9.17	12.30	630.40	2657.21
Guangxi	6.34	9.69	324.58	959.99
Hainan	1.46	9.69	594.19	1348.21
Hebei	6.88	12.32	535.29	1915.29
Jiangsu	8.58	13.22	748.23	2706.88
Liaoning	5.90	9.87	998.56	2645.59
Shandong	9.82	12.94	643.73	2593.29
Shanghai	1.77	13.05	2673.04	7095.80
Tianjin	5.13	13.00	1541.85	4513.29
Zhejiang	10.22	14.41	670.38	2864.33
Anhui	7.52	9.69	445.74	1195.42
Chongqing		12.07		1603.25
Gansu	4.47	8.21	448.00	947.04
Guizhou	8.14	7.64	289.34	633.45
Heilongjiang	4.74	9.93	746.48	1852.11
Henan	8.45	12.17	423.51	1515.86
Hubei	7.77	9.82	554.59	1595.40
Hunan	5.94	9.52	412.92	1060.95
Inner Mongolia	7.63	10.97	537.50	1484.92
Jiangxi	6.46	10.73	409.72	1142.35
Jilin	6.96	9.66	615.05	1618.83
Ningxia	5.29	8.45	523.51	1169.42
Qinghai	5.82	7.59	571.73	1159.92
Shaanxi	6.94	8.97	438.88	1041.45
Shanxi	6.97	9.61	574.74	1334.84
Sichuan	8.26	9.79	390.57	1073.01
Tibet	5.31	8.90	517.90	974.91
Xinjiang	9.04	8.51	581.63	1616.57
Yunnan	9.70	7.97	374.26	1085.00
Coast	7.00	12.04	991.29	2989.12
Inland	6.97	9.43	492.00	1260.95

Note: The coastal provinces are in bold. Data are the provincial averages for the indicated periods, except for the coastal and inland average values reported at the bottom of the table and used in the mean comparison tests, which are the averages for all coastal and inland provinces in those periods, respectively. Since Hainan only became a province in 1988, its data for the 1978–90 period cover 1988–90. Chongqing's data for the 1991–2004 period cover 1997–2004, as Chongqing became a provincial unit in 1997. Data are in constant 1977 RMB, deflated with the provincial general retail price indices.
***: $p < 0.01$ in two-group mean comparison tests for the coastal and inland provinces (two-tailed tests with unequal variances); **: $p < 0.05$; *: $p < 0.1$.
Source: Appendix to Chapter 3.

In fact, the top eight fastest-growing provinces and top ten wealthiest provinces in China during the 1991–2004 period were all highly exposed to the global markets and all located along the coast. The overall coastal-inland divergence in terms of economic openness and economic perform-ance and wealth, especially in the more recent years, is thus unmistakable. The point here is *not* that the degree of economic globalization was the sole determinant of the pace or level of provincial economic development in China. Rather, the more globalized coastal provinces on average tended to fare better economically than their inland counterparts that were less inte-grated with the global markets during the post-1978 era.

The general pattern portrayed by our broad-gauged provincial-level data serves only illustrative purposes here, but it is consistent with the positive correlations between the degree of economic openness and eco-nomic wealth/growth among the Chinese provinces during this period identified in the sizeable empirical literature mentioned earlier. It indi-cates that, overall, during the post-1978 period, the coastal provinces became more exposed to the international markets, and they benefited more economically than the inland provinces. There do appear to have been regional winners and losers, or more precisely, bigger and smaller winners, directly or indirectly based upon a province's geographic loca-tion. More economic resources seemed to have been generated in the coastal provinces that fared better in the global markets.

3.4.3 Centrifugal Tendencies

As regional economic disparity rises, the prevailing economic theories reviewed in Chapter 2 forecast the growing likelihood of fiscal discord, especially between the political center and the subnational regions thriv-ing in the global markets. I have argued that national political leaders have incentives to undertake fiscal redistribution in favor of those regions that are faring less well and demanding greater assistance from the cen-tral government in order to remedy the regional disparity and maintain their national rule. Such fiscal assistance for the loser regions, however, must be funded by increased resource extraction from the winner regions. Conflicts thus seem inevitable if the winner regions have grown more assertive in demanding greater fiscal autonomy for themselves and more resistant toward central extractive demands.

The prospect of a country of differentially developed provinces slipping into regional restiveness and political instability is especially disconcert-ing to the political center whose continued existence and survival depend on, above all, national territorial integrity. The Chinese political center is no exception. Economic efficiency and growth were clearly top priorities of the Chinese national leadership during this period, but regional disparity undermining national political unity would be too high a price to pay. The concerns of CCP General Secretary Jiang Zemin by the mid-1990s were therefore easily understandable: "If we allow polarization of ... regions, then conflict between central government and provinces could burgeon and cause chaos" (quoted in Yang and Wei 1996, 468). If necessary, "one solution" to rising regional disparity, in the words of Deng Xiaoping (1993 [1992], 374), China's paramount leader through much of the post-1978 years until his death in 1997, could be "to have regions that have become rich first submit more revenues to help support the development of the poorer regions."

Such views of the national leadership over the issue of regional economic inequality and interregional fiscal redistribution would certainly be heartening to the inland provinces. Indeed, the leaders of China's inland provinces had already been voicing their disgruntlement over the widening regional economic gap. While systematic evidence is sketchy, two surveys conducted in the mid-1990s suggest that regional disparity was perceived by local officials in the inland provinces to be "excessive" and likely to endanger social stability, absent prompt central government action (Wang and Hu 1999, 69–75). The governor of Guizhou called the need to help the backward regions grow economically "a political problem" (Zheng 1994, 319). Since the preferential policies in the foreign economic sector were seen as partly culpable, the leaders of these provinces argued fiercely for the extension of these policies to the inland.

More important, the inland provinces asked for direct infusion of central funds (Yang and Wei 1996, 465–466). In their annual conference reports to the central government, for example, leaders of the member provinces of the Economic Coordination Association of Southwest China, consisting of inland Guizhou, Yunnan, Sichuan, and Tibet (later joined by coastal but poor Guangxi), called for more "common prosperity" through greater central assistance in the early 1990s. For them, no less than the country's "political stability" and "national unification" could be at stake (Zheng 2007, Chapter 7). In China, such warnings of dangers amidst rising regional economic inequality from the discontented inland provinces could be especially alarming. After all, four out of five provincial units designated as autonomous regions for ethnic minorities and already fraught with ethnic restiveness are in the inland (except coastal Guangxi).

Securing sufficient funds from the coastal provinces with more resources to spare, however, would be no easy task for the central government.

Devolution of spending responsibilities and growing reliance on local self-financing had forced local governments across the board to seek to increase revenues at their own disposal throughout the post-1978 era (Tao and Yang 2008; Wong 1991). The fiscal imperative could be particularly pressing in the provinces more exposed to the volatile global markets; they often experienced rising disparity and growing needs for within-province redistribution in their jurisdictions (Jeanneney and Hua 2004). Increased fiscal contributions to the center naturally dictate dwindling resources available to the provincial governments themselves. Moreover, the prospect of heftier tax burdens entailed by greater central fiscal extraction from the winner provinces would not appeal to the economic actors in these jurisdictions on whom the local governments have relied for their own revenue needs.[14] Sympathy with the local firms could surely dampen possible enthusiasm of the local officials in the winner provinces for the center's redistributive agenda in this age.

Indeed, the provincial governments along the coast had become increasingly assertive toward the center over fiscal matters. Direct challenges to the central government and outright demands for political autonomy by the local governments in the winner regions were still rare in China, to be sure. Central policy directives "[i]n a host of fields, from tax collecting to controlling economic activities" were at least greeted with "feigned compliance," not overt defiance, in "Guangdong, Fujian and other dynamic provinces" along the coast (Pye 1990, 59–60). Provincial governments, especially those in the winner regions, could turn to a variety of covert tactics to maximize revenues in their own hands during this period. They could try to hide local revenues by shifting them to the extrabudgetary category less susceptible to direct central monitoring or regulation.

---

[14] The Chinese local governments tend to enjoy very close ties with local industries. In fact, many of the firms were owned by local governments and managed by local bureaucrats. For the early post-1978 period, active local government involvement in promoting local industrial growth to pursue fiscal revenues is well known (Oi 1999; Wong 1992). Even after the recent waves of privatization, the support from the local governments and the reasons behind it are not lost on the firms themselves. Top managers of a national random sample of firms recently surveyed by Xu and his collaborators "believed that subnational governments were very keen to support firms' development, with an average score 4.1" on a scale of 0–5. The firms also believed that "the reasons for subnational governments doing so were for regional fiscal revenue, for improving their performance, which determines their promotions, and for complying with the central government's policy with scores of 4.0, 3.7 and 3.2 respectively" (cited in Xu 2009, 43). For discussions of the intricate links and "symbiotic" relationship between local enterprises and local governments in China, see also Huang (1990), Solinger (1992), Walder (1992), and Zhang Amei and Zou Gang (1994).

They could also help firms located in their jurisdictions evade taxes by granting them unwarranted tax exemptions and holidays, often at the expense of the center (Oi 1999, 36–37; Wong et al. 1995, 131; World Bank 1990, 84).

Even in a political system where open displays of disobedience from below were almost taboo, however, there were growing signs of fiscal intransigence toward the Chinese central government from the richer, coastal provinces during this period (Jia Hao and Lin Zhimin 1994; Shirk 1993; Wang 1995).[15] Unsurprisingly, during the pre-1994 era of fiscal contracting, provincial governments along the coast were often the most vocal opponents to central government requests to "borrow" loans at the annual national fiscal conferences attended by all the provinces. On the eve of the 1994 fiscal reform to centralize revenue collection and strengthen the redistributive capacity of the central government, moreover, the loud voice of dissidence from these provinces contrasted sharply with the general support from the inland provinces for the new system of tax division proposed by Beijing (Zhao Yining 2003, 20, 27).

The most widely cited is the case of Ye Xuanping, governor and vice-secretary of the provincial party committee of Guangdong. Ye publicly opposed the center-initiated fiscal centralization and insisted upon continued fiscal autonomy for Guangdong in the early 1990s (Baum 1994, 327; Delfs 1991; Shirk 1993, 194).Another high-profile case involved Shen Daren, provincial party secretary of Jiangsu, who openly disagreed with then vice premier Zhu Rongji over the imminent 1994 fiscal reform (Fewsmith 1997, 517; Yang 1994, 86). Amidst popular predictions of a coming collapse of the Chinese state, both academic and journalistic (Chang 2001; Chang 1992; Friedman 1993; Goldstone 1995; Waldron 1990), Toffler and Toffler (1993, 214; quoted in Yang 1994, 81) foresee a dismal future:

[The new elites in the coastal provinces] are already thumbing their collective nose at economic edicts from Beijing's central government. How long before they decide they will no longer tolerate Beijing's political interference and refuse to contribute the funds needed by the central government …? Unless Beijing grants them complete freedom of financial and political action, one can imagine the new elites insisting on independence or some facsimile of it – a step that could tear China apart and trigger civil war.

[15] For a sample of contemporary journalistic coverage of rising local belligerence toward the Chinese central government from these winner provinces in this era, see Delfs (1991), Goldstein (1993), Kaye (1995), and Salem (1988). See also Solinger (1996, 1) for a more extensive list of additional sources of this genre.

Contrary to such wild speculations and predictions, China so far has been spared another separatist civil war in this period. Despite all the regional tensions, things have not grown out of hand for the national leadership. In fact, the Chinese central government has presided over largely relative tranquility on the territorial front during the post-1978 period. Often missing in the discussions of the centrifugal forces unleashed by China's embrace of the global markets, as in the prevailing economic theories, have been the role and possible responses by the national political leadership. Throughout this period, above all, the Chinese central government persistently pursued a strategy of interregional fiscal redistribution in favor of the inland provinces.

3.5   THE CENTER'S RESPONSES

3.5.1 Putative Central Fiscal Decline

Though largely based on considerations of comparative advantage and natural resource endowments, regional preferential policies that had favored the coastal provinces were often seen by the inland provinces as policy favoritism responsible for worsening interprovincial disparity (Wang and Hu 1999). Thus, before their formal phase-out in early 1999, most of the preferential policies regarding the development zones were later extended to all the inland provinces. A more straightforward option appealing to the Chinese political center was simply to provide more fiscal assistance to the subnational units faring less well, as noted. The question is whether the Chinese central government was actually capable of marshalling the requisite fiscal wherewithal to perform such an interregional redistributive task to whose success the fiscal compliance of the increasingly assertive winner provinces was essential.

Some studies have noted the worrisome "decline" in central extractive capacity during this era, an unintended consequence of fiscal decentralization whereby more fiscal resources as well as spending responsibilities were devolved to the local governments (Wang 2006; Wang Shaoguang and Hu Angang 1993). As discussed earlier, the post-1978 era witnessed the gradual use of "fiscal contracting" before the system was discarded during the fiscal reform of 1994. Negotiated with the individual provincial governments, the fiscal contracts specified a revenue quota to be delivered to the central government, but allowed greater provincial retention of the above-quota revenues. Often credited with enticing local governments to expand the local tax base and promote economic growth (Lin and Liu 2000; Montinola et al. 1995), fiscal decentralization and contracting might have also encouraged the siphoning off of resources into local coffers and led to substantial revenue slippage for the central government (Wang 1995).

The most oft-cited evidence is the dwindling share of budgetary revenues collected by the central government in the post-1978 years.[16] To be sure, the central share actually gained some ground for the reform era as a whole, rising from 36.3 percent in the 1953–77 period to 39 percent in the 1978–2004 period, as seen in data that exclude provincial remittances in the second column of Table 3.5. However, for the period of 1978–93, the average central share fell to only 29.9 percent. The drop was especially sharp after fiscal contracting was implemented nationwide in 1988. The central share plunged to merely 22.02 percent in 1993, from an earlier peak of 40.5 percent in 1984. The diminishing central revenue share came at a time when total revenues for all levels of government were shrinking relative to the national economy. As a share of national GDP, total government budgetary revenues shrank quite considerably from 31.2 percent in 1978 to merely 12.6 percent in 1993 before a new round of fiscal reform was launched in 1994. In other words, the central government was collecting a smaller share of general government revenues whose relative size seemed to be rapidly contracting as well.

Another pillar of the purportedly enervated central fiscal edifice lies in the growing importance of extrabudgetary (that is, off the official budget) revenues in China's public finance and the significant portions of such revenues captured by the local governments.[17] As also shown in Table 3.5,

---

[16] The official Chinese sources are often vague in defining the central share of government budgetary revenues. For example, Guojia Tongji Ju [National Bureau of Statistics] (1999b, Table 8-10) reports the budgetary revenues that are "actually collected by" the central government. Because the central government mostly relied on the local agencies to collect its revenues before it created its own nationwide tax collection system in 1994, it is highly unlikely that the figures for the pre-1994 years merely cover revenues *physically* collected by the central government itself. More likely, these numbers could refer to strictly defined "central revenues" (revenues the central government was entitled to, such as those from state enterprises under the ownership of the central government) even though they could have been collected and later turned over by the provincial governments (Wong et al. 1995, 86–90). However, these revenues do not include the postcollection revenue remittances from the local governments fulfilling their formal fiscal obligations to the central government. Indeed, Zhongguo Caizheng Nianjian Bianji Weiyuanhui [Editorial Committee of the *Finance Yearbook of China*] (2006, 396–398) defines the same revenue data as "income from" central government sources and separately lists central revenues due to remittances by the local governments for the years since 1990.

[17] Extrabudgetary funds (*yusuanwai zijin*) consisted of three major categories up to 1992: (1) funds and fees collected by administrative units; (2) tax supplements collected by local governments; and (3) funds retained by enterprises and their supervisory government agencies (Guojia Tongji Ju [National Bureau of Statistics] 2000, Table 8–15).

TABLE 3.5. *State Fiscal Capacity in China, 1978–2004*

Year	Central Government Share of Budgetary Revenues (%)		Share of Government Revenues in GDP (%)		Local Government Extrabudgetary to Budgetary Revenues Ratio
	Collected (Excluding Provincial Remittances)	Available (Including Provincial Remittances)	Budgetary	Extrabudgetary	
1978	15.52		31.24	9.58	
1979	20.18		28.39	11.21	
1980	24.52		25.67	12.34	
1981	26.46		24.18	12.36	
1982	28.61		22.90	15.16	0.61
1983	35.85		23.03	16.31	0.69
1984	40.51		22.91	16.57	0.73
1985	38.39		22.36	17.07	0.72
1986	36.68		20.80	17.03	0.76
1987	33.48		18.39	16.96	0.82
1988	32.87		15.79	15.81	0.92
1989	30.86		15.76	15.72	0.86
1990	33.79	50.21	15.84	14.60	0.84
1991	29.79	45.36	14.57	15.00	0.84
1992	28.12	44.16	13.08	14.47	0.86
1993	22.02	35.82	12.56	4.14	0.35
1994	55.70	66.62	11.16	3.98	0.68
1995	52.17	61.94	10.67	4.12	0.70
1996	49.42	57.57	10.91	5.74	0.79
1997	48.86	55.84	11.62	3.80	0.61

1998	49.53	55.58	12.61	3.93	0.59
1999	51.11	56.34	13.94	4.12	0.56
2000	52.18	56.65	14.97	4.28	0.56
2001	52.38	55.98	16.84	4.42	0.46
2002	54.96	58.33	17.97	4.26	0.47
2003	54.64	57.49	18.50	3.89	0.43
2004	54.94	57.24	19.28	3.43	0.37
1953–77	36.33		28.40	5.07	
1978–2004	39.02	54.34	18.00		
1978–93	29.85	43.89	20.47	14.68	0.79
1994–2004	52.35	58.15	14.41	4.18	0.55

Note: There are two series on the central government budgetary revenue share. One refers to the share of total government budgetary revenues collected by the central government. It excludes provincial revenue remittances to the central government and covers the entire period of 1953–2004. The other refers to the share of total government budgetary revenues available to the central government. It includes provincial revenue remittances, but only covers the years since 1990. Neither series includes foreign and domestic debts or price subsidies. Local government revenues refer to the revenues of provincial governments and lower-level governments. Extrabudgetary revenue data distinguishing between the central and local shares only became available in 1982. Moreover, the scope of extrabudgetary revenues was revised for data in 1993 and again in 1997, making the figures before 1992 inconsistent with those for the later years. In the third column regarding the share of budgetary revenues available to the central governments that includes provincial remittances, the averages of 1978–2004 and of 1978–93 refer to the averages of 1990–2004 and 1990–93, respectively. In the last two columns regarding extrabudgetary revenue data, the averages of 1978–93 and of 1994–2004 refer to the averages of 1978–92 and 1993–2004, respectively.

Source: Guojia Tongji Ju [National Bureau of Statistics] (2000, Tables 8–2, 8–13; 2005, Tables 3–1, 8–1, 8–10); Zhongguo Caizheng Nianjian Bianji Weiyuanhui [Editorial Committee of the *Finance Yearbook of China*] (2006, 367–369, 396–398, 408).

total extrabudgetary revenues as a share of national GDP rose from 9.6 percent in 1978 to 17.1 percent in 1985, and remained at 14.5 percent in 1992. In fact, the share was even higher than that of budgetary revenues during 1988 and 1991–92. Moreover, the bulk of these revenues, still around 56 percent in 1992 and even higher in earlier years, were not in the hands of the central government (Guojia Tongji Ju [National Bureau of Statistics] 2000, Table 8–18). Indeed, extrabudgetary revenues played an increasing role in local public finance during this period as the ratio of extrabudgetary to budgetary revenues for China's local governments rose from about 0.61 to as much as 0.92 in 1988; the ratio was still hovering around 0.86 in 1992. Because nominally such revenues were not subject to sharing with the central government (Wang and Hu 1999, 198), their expansion and concentration below the national level, combined with the relative decline of budgetary revenues, could have left fewer fiscal resources at the disposal of the Chinese central government.

3.5.2 Assessing Central Fiscal Capacity

Such a portrayal of the central fiscal capacity in China may be too bleak. First, both the overall fiscal capacity of the Chinese state (including the central and local governments) and the size of fiscal resources available to the central government might be underrated. Indeed, one should not count only the budgetary revenues as government fiscal resources. Of the three components of the extrabudgetary revenues, funds collected by government-affiliated administrative units and tax supplements collected by local governments were clearly governmental in nature, at least before changes were introduced to their definitions in 1997 (Zhongguo Caizheng Nianjian Bianji Weiyuanhui [Editorial Committee of the *Finance Yearbook of China*] 2006, 408). Funds shared by the enterprises with their supervising government agencies should also be considered partly governmental, as Huang (1996, 47–49) has pointed out. Moreover, the provinces also remitted extrabudgetary revenues to the central government, nearly 13 percent of the total in 1990 alone (Tsui and Wang 2004, 84). Extrabudgetary revenues nominally belonging to local governments below the provincial level have become subject to special levies and surcharges and "forced borrowings" as well as tightening regulations and scrutiny by the Chinese central government over the years (Oi 1999, 53, 162–165; Zhao 1990, 59).

Indeed, even the budgetary portions of the central government revenues could also be underestimated. The much-cited data on the budgetary revenue share collected by the central government, while enjoying the advantage of a longer series, do not include revenues remitted by the provincial governments as part of their formal fiscal obligations to the central government. If we include these revenues in the calculation, as in the third column of Table 3.5, the share of budgetary revenues actually available to the central government may be much higher during the 1990–2004 period for which such data are available. For example, according to this latter series, the central government revenue share might have been 50.2 percent in 1990, compared with only 33.8 percent in the other series excluding remittances from the provinces. Despite the considerable drop in that year, the share might have been 35.8 percent in 1993, rather than merely 22 percent.

Second, studies that have reached such pessimistic conclusions of declining central fiscal capacity in China often neglect the informal aspects of central fiscal extraction from the provinces buttressed by the political strength of the Chinese central government. A fuller treatment of the workings of the political institutions that govern the relations between the central and provincial governments will have to await the next chapter. Suffice it to mention here that China's highly centralized political system ruled by one single political party has imparted the national leadership political powers that can facilitate fiscal resource extraction from below.

Indeed, before the 1994 fiscal reform, the central government often engaged in unwarranted and unrepaid "borrowings" from the provinces despite stipulations for above-quota provincial revenue retention in the fiscal contracts. For instance, although the contracted fiscal remittance by Guangdong for 1988 was about 1.7 percent of the provincial net material product (NMP), its effective contribution reached about 3.7 percent, more than twice the officially contracted amount (Huang 1996, 52–55). During the period of 1980–89, Guangdong's remittance to the center totaled more than 19 billion yuan (current RMB) even though its formal obligations under fiscal contracting in these years should have been less than 13 billion yuan (Cheung 1994, 226). Similar bouts of central fiscal opportunism also occurred in Shanxi province during the 1981–87 period (Wang 2002, 150). [18]

Indeed, "involuntary" loans to the central government from the provinces totaled as much as 7 billion yuan in 1981 and 9 billion yuan in 1987, respectively (quoted in Wong et al. 1995, 94). In terms of current RMB,

[18] See also Chung (1994, 11), Lieberthal and Oksenberg (1988, 348–349), and Tsui and Wang (2004) for similar accounts.

this amounted to roughly 22.5 percent and 12.2 percent, respectively, of the total budgetary revenues collected by the Chinese central government that did not include provincial remittances for those years (Guojia Tongji Ju [National Bureau of Statistics] 2000, Table 8–13). Although they were potentially predatory, forced contributions from the provinces would certainly enlarge the fiscal resources available to a central government that was politically predominant vis-à-vis the provincial governments. In other words, there could have been more fiscal resources for the Chinese central government than met the eye even before the 1994 fiscal reform.

In addition, central political supremacy might also have been behind the all-too-frequent changes in the terms of fiscal contracting that have been extensively documented elsewhere. Contracts set for five-year terms were subject to renegotiation and changes, sometimes long before their original expiration dates, despite provincial complaints (Tsui and Wang 2004, 82; Wang 2002, 150). The terms of the contracts negotiated during the fiscal reform in 1980 were revised for many provinces as early as 1982 (Shirk 1990, 244). According to Oksenberg and Tong (1991, 20–25), additional post-1983 changes were introduced into their 1980–82 fiscal arrangements with the center for about fifteen provinces. Although those for the 1988–93 period did live up to their five-year life expectancy, the 1985–87 regime lasted only three years.[19] By late 1993, fiscal contracting was scrapped altogether as the central government ushered in a new round of fiscal reform, despite resistance from the wealthier coastal provinces.[20] These changes were hardly surprising. After all, national leaders in China are politically equipped to unilaterally "change the 'rules of the game'" (Wang 2002, 142).

Apparently, such monopoly over "the rules of the game" also allowed the Chinese central government to reduce the scope of fiscal resources that formally fell under the category of extrabudgetary revenues. Due to Beijing's "definitional massaging," the size of fiscal resources classified as extrabudgetary revenues that were under less stringent scrutiny of central government fell sharply after 1992. As a share of national GDP, total government extrabudgetary revenues declined from 14.5 percent in 1992 to merely about 3.4 percent in 2004, as shown in Table 3.5. The role of extrabudgetary revenues in local public finance also began to fade. By

[19] This is according to the dataset on provincial marginal revenue retention rates used in Jin et al. (2005).
[20] For excellent summaries of the successive phases of fiscal reforms and the specific schemes for the different provinces, see, for instance, Bahl (1999), Oi (1999, 211–216), and Oksenberg and Tong (1991).

one indicator, the ratio of extrabudgetary to budgetary revenues for local governments dropped from 0.86 in 1992 to only 0.37 in 2004.

Even after the 1994 fiscal reform, in order to introduce changes in its own favor, the center continued to tinker with the new "tax sharing" (*fenshuizhi*) schemes that were originally aimed at institutionalizing central-local fiscal ties, largely because the center still monopolizes the power to set the rate and base for all taxes (Wang 1997, 807). For example, personal income tax – one of the fastest-growing sources of revenue – that was initially assigned to the local governments in 1994 had become a joint revenue source shared with the central government by 2002 (Yang 2004, 80). The central-local sharing ratio was 50:50 for 2002, but was set to change to 60:40 in favor of the center by 2003. The central government has clearly benefited. Indeed, one ostensible goal of these changes was to use all the projected revenue increase for the central government for making general transfer payments to the provinces, especially those in less-developed central and western inland regions of the country (Guowuyuan [State Council] 2002).[21] Another example is the highly lucrative stock trading stamp tax. Although the central and local governments shared this tax equally in 1994, the sharing ratio was revised in 1997 so that effectively 88 percent would go to the central government. Further changes were introduced in 2000 whereby the share for the central government was scheduled to grow to 97 percent in three years (An Xiumei and Yang Yuanwei 2008, 19).

At any rate, despite strong resistance from the rich coastal provinces, the center still managed to pull off the fiscal reform of 1994, largely thanks to its political strength (Yang 1996). It considerably increased the share of budgetary revenues collected by the central government, which grew from 22 percent in 1993 to nearly 56 percent in 1994, and remained 54.9 percent in 2004, as also seen in Table 3.5. While the average central government share for the 1978–93 period was about 29.9 percent, it bounced to almost 52.4 percent during the 1994–2004 period. If provincial remittances are included in the calculation, the share of budgetary revenues available to the central government rose from 35.8 percent in 1993 to

---

[21] Together with personal income tax, enterprise income tax has also become a shared tax between the central and local governments since 2002 under the same sharing scheme. During the period of 1994–2001, the central government taxed the incomes of the state enterprises it owned while the income taxes of the locally owned public and other enterprises went to the local governments. Even then, the central government often tried to redefine the tax base for certain resource-rich provinces in its own favor by changing the ownership of profitable local enterprises (Tsui and Wang 2004, 83–84).

66.6 percent in 1994, and was still about 57.2 percent in 2004. During 1994–2004, the average central share would be about 58 percent.

After a secular slide to a low of 10.7 percent in 1995, the share of total budgetary revenues for all levels of government in the national GDP also made a gradual comeback to nearly 19.3 percent by 2004.[22] Together with the attendant gains in the budgetary revenue share collected by the central government and the relative decline in the role of extrabudgetary revenues in China's general public finance, the overall growth of the budgetary revenues must have yielded more fiscal resources for Beijing since 1994. In short, the Chinese central government could have been less fiscally deprived throughout the post-1978 era than many had thought.

3.5.3 Central Fiscal Redistribution

Interregional redistributive efforts carried out by the central government seemed to have been quite palpable before the onset of the reform era in the late 1970s. Resources tended to flow from the rich provinces, mostly located along the coast, to the poor regions usually in the inland during those years. For instance, Lardy (1978, Table 4.3, 162) identifies rich coastal provinces such as Shanghai, Liaoning, and Jiangsu as net contributors to central coffers, whereas inland provinces like Yunnan, Ningxia, Inner Mongolia, Xinjiang, and Tibet were mostly recipients of central subsidies from the late 1950s to the early 1970s. The "Maoist" development strategy favoring the inland provinces could have driven much of the resource redistribution in this period, but interregional transfers might have subsided with the start of the reform and opening, reflecting the shift in the development focus of the central government toward the coast.

Indeed, the coastal provinces gradually replaced their inland counterparts in absorbing the lion's share of total fixed asset investment, according to Yang's influential study (1990) on the trajectory of China's post-Mao economic development. Yang, however, draws mostly on investment data to make inferences about the regional patterns of resource redistribution

[22] The World Bank (2008) reports a series on total government revenues (excluding grants) as a share of GDP. The figures are generally lower than the data cited here because grants are often considered a source of revenues. According to the World Bank series, China's total revenue/GDP share was around 8.86 percent in 2004. This was not much lower than the share for India, which was nearly 9.8 percent, or the share for the United States, which was 10.1 percent in 2004. The previous low was only around 2.5 percent in 1993. Thus, China seems to have made some strides in recent years even according to these data.

by the center after 1978. It is plausible that those places with greater inflows of central investment capital in fact were receiving more resources from Beijing. The fixed asset investment data used by Yang, however, do not differentiate between the central and local components. Although his data depict broad trends of growing fixed asset investment in the coastal areas, it is not entirely clear how much of the increase actually came from contributions by the central government. During much of the era, more than half of the fixed asset investment already fell under the purview of the local governments.[23] In fact, according to Fujita and Hu (2001, 20–21), there seemed to be little regional bias in the distribution of central investment projects across China during this period. For our purposes, therefore, it is difficult to gauge the exact extent of center-directed resource redistribution by examining fixed asset investment in the provinces.

One alternative, albeit still a largely imperfect one, is to trace the evolving size and composition of the group of provinces that were net subsidy recipients from the central treasury. All else being equal, we might infer larger central redistributive efforts in favor of the inland when more of the inland provinces joined the ranks of those having to subsist upon central fiscal subsidies. During 1980–82, twelve out of China's then total twenty-nine provinces were net recipients of central budgetary subsidies.[24] Of these, only Fujian and Guangxi were coastal provinces. The total climbed to thirteen when Gansu, another inland province, joined in 1983, and to fourteen in 1985 after inland Sichuan and Shaanxi followed suit (even though inland Heilongjiang changed to become a net contributor in the same year). During the 1988–93 period, there were already sixteen such subsidy-receiving provinces. Coastal Hainan, a net recipient, joined as a new province in 1988; Hubei became another inland recipient province, with the "separate listing under the plan" of its capital city Wuhan.[25]

---

[23] For example, the central share of fixed asset investment dropped from 47.3 percent in 1981 to 42.7 percent in 1991 (Huang 1996, 68).

[24] They were Inner Mongolia, Jilin, Heilongjiang, Fujian, Jiangxi, Guangxi, Guizhou, Yunnan, Tibet, Qinghai, Ningxia, and Xinjiang (Bahl 1999, 89, 92–93; Oksenberg and Tong 1991, 24–25).

[25] From 1988 on, both Hubei and Sichuan would have been net contributors had Wuhan and Chongqing, in these two provinces respectively, not become "cites separately listed under the plan" (*jihua danlie chengshi*), which entitled them to direct fiscal dealings with the central government (Zhongguo Caizheng Nianjian Bianji Weiyuanhui [Editorial Committee of the *Finance Yearbook of China*] 1992, 151–152). I discuss issues related to these "separately listed cities" in later chapters. Wedeman (1999, 108–114) lists as many as twenty-one net subsidy recipient provinces in 1992, including also Shanxi, Anhui, Shandong, Henan, and Hunan. Somehow, Hubei is not included on his list.

This is clearly a very crude picture as the exact extent of fiscal redistribution entailed in any given year also depends on the specific amount of transfers for each recipient province. Still, based on the rising number of provinces receiving direct central budgetary subsidies, we can safely conclude that the Chinese central government must still have actively undertaken fiscal redistribution across the provinces throughout the pre-1994 years. In fact, such transfers might have increased in the later years of the period. More important for our purposes, the overwhelming majority of the net recipients of the central fiscal subsidies were inland provinces less exposed to the world markets.

Similar, though still indirect, evidence of lingering central redistribution in favor of the inland provinces in the same period comes from data on provincial marginal revenue retention rates, whereby under fiscal contracting the provinces were allowed to retain budgetary revenues after their contribution quotas were met. Although the two series cover slightly different timespans and do not appear to be fully identical, data on provincial budgetary revenue marginal retention rates collected by both Jin et al. (2005) and Lin and Liu (2000) indicate that the inland provinces were favored throughout the 1980–93 period. This can be readily seen from the summary data presented in Table 3.6. During this period, on average, the inland provinces were allowed to retain budgetary revenues at significantly higher marginal rates regardless of which series we use. At least with regard to postquota budgetary revenue retention, in other words, the central government did appear to have engaged in greater fiscal extraction from the coastal provinces via granting them lower revenue retention rates.

Information on marginal retention rates for budgetary revenues is suggestive, but it is at best an indirect proxy of the actual fiscal transfers between the central government and the provinces. Data on *net* transfers from the central government to the provinces, after subtracting the revenue remittances from the latter to the former, might be more useful. Ideally, we should examine the annual flows of fiscal resources to and from each province for every year. Consistent data, however, are not available before the 1994 fiscal reform. Following existing studies that calculate fiscal transfers on a per capita basis in other settings (for example, Ansolabehere et al. 2002; Horiuchi and Saito 2003; Rodden 2002), I examine such data for post-1994 China.

In the remainder of Table 3.6, I present summary data on net per capita central subsidies to the provinces during the 1995–2004 period for which data are publicly available. There are two series here. One series is

TABLE 3.6. *Fiscal Redistribution in the Post-1978 Era*

Province	Revenue Retention Rate (%)		Net Per Capita Central Fiscal Subsidies	
	1980–92*** (Jin et al. 2005)	1985–93*** (Lin and Liu 2000)	1995–2004*** (With Tax Rebates)	1995–2004*** (No Tax Rebates)
Beijing	42.97	83.18	181.40	2.63
Fujian	100	100	71.66	19.18
Guangdong	100	100	92.82	13.13
Guangxi	100	100	73.60	43.93
Hainan	100		93.94	71.04
Hebei	62.61	89.67	79.39	37.67
Jiangsu	39.34	80	56.51	−12.68
Liaoning	46.22	83.69	158.49	68.01
Shandong	69.02	86.33	70.69	20.63
Shanghai	41.93	74.51	240.11	−151.31
Tianjin	39.27	44.18	194.19	2.50
Zhejiang	51.78	85	88.09	3.69
Anhui	75.08	78.37	72.60	44.98
Chongqing			106.43	71.15
Gansu	91.26	100	132.10	86.05
Guizhou	100	100	92.24	64.20
Heilongjiang	99.69	100	134.69	93.19
Henan	80.35	93.33	72.56	39.37
Hubei	80.96	100	78.30	41.83
Hunan	80.89	96	67.19	38.37
Inner Mongolia	100	100	203.44	161.54

(continued)

TABLE 3.6 continued

Province	Revenue Retention Rate (%)		Net Per Capita Central Fiscal Subsidies	
	1980–92*** (Jin et al. 2005)	1985–93*** (Lin and Liu 2000)	1995–2004*** (With Tax Rebates)	1995–2004*** (No Tax Rebates)
Jiangxi	100	100	87.32	62.73
Jilin	100	100	169.79	117.13
Ningxia	100	100	236.12	200.78
Qinghai	100	100	278.35	243.98
Shaanxi	98.17	100	107.27	76.88
Shanxi	84.37	90.87	105.79	62.89
Sichuan	91.18	100	73.49	47.51
Tibet			705.61	683.70
Xinjiang	100	100	183.02	150.89
Yunnan	100	100	144.18	61.24
Coast	64.26	84.23	116.74	9.87
Inland	93.06	97.56	161.13	124.16

Note: The coastal provinces are in bold. Data are the provincial averages for the indicated periods, except for the coastal and inland average values reported at the bottom of the table and used in the mean comparison tests, which are the averages for all coastal and inland provinces in those periods, respectively. Data on central subsidies for the five "separately listed cities" (*jihua danlie chengshi*) – Shenzhen in Guangdong province, Xiamen in Fujian, Ningbo in Zhejiang, Qingdao in Shandong, and Dalian in Liaoning – are merged into those of their host provinces. Subsidy data are in constant 1977 RMB, deflated with the provincial general retail price indices.

***: $p < 0.01$ in two-group mean comparison tests for the coastal and inland provinces (two-tailed tests with unequal variances); **: $p < 0.05$; *: $p < 0.1$.

Source: Data on marginal budgetary revenue retention rates are from Jin et al. (2005) covering the 1980–92 period, and Lin and Liu (2000, 5) covering the 1985–93 period. Sources for data on provincial fiscal flows to and from the central government used to calculate the net central fiscal subsidies are described in the Appendix to Chapter 3.

constructed simply by subtracting the per capita provincial budgetary transfers (or remittances) to the central government (*shangjie zhongyang*) from the per capita budgetary transfers (or subsidies) to a province from the central government (*zhongyang buzhu*) for each year. The other series excludes "tax rebates" or "returned revenues" (*shuishou fanhuan*) from the data on central fiscal transfers to the provinces in the calculation.

As noted, the fiscal reform of 1994 sought to centralize revenue collection by establishing a system of "tax sharing" or "tax assignment" whereby the central and provincial governments were assigned revenues from their respective tax base. They also share certain other tax categories according to predetermined ratios that often favor the center (Wong 1997, Chapter 1).[26] To compensate the provinces for the revenue losses they have incurred because of the reform, the central government returns to the provincial governments certain revenues as "tax rebates." These tax rebates are determined in part by the levels of provincial revenues as of 1993 and hence the size of their anticipated revenue losses in consequence of the impending fiscal reform (An Xiumei and Yang Yuanwei 2008; Wang 2004). In essence, these tax rebates are a type of provincial "entitlements" that reflect preexisting levels of provincial fiscal strength, rather than actual provincial needs. Unlike the other more discretionary components of central fiscal transfers to the provinces, such as "general transfer payments" (*zhuanyi zhifu*), they are thus not redistributive in nature (Yep 2008, 239–240).[27] Because we are interested in the extent of actual fiscal redistribution pursued by the central government across the provinces, it is more meaningful to examine the second series that excludes the formula-based and less redistributive tax rebates from the central subsidy data in the calculation (Wang 2004).

To be sure, on average, even most of the coastal provinces have become net recipients of central fiscal subsidies since the fiscal reform of 1994, according to this measure of central fiscal redistribution, regardless of whether tax rebates are included in calculating the net subsidies. This

---

[26] Even for taxes going to the provinces, however, the provincial governments do not have the authority to set the tax rates; they are still set by the central government. For a useful summary of the respective taxes for the central and local governments as of 1994, see also Oi (1999, 217).

[27] In order to be consistent with earlier years, data on tax rebates for 2004 do not include export tax rebates, which since that year have been jointly funded by the central (75 percent) and local (25 percent) governments (An Xiumei and Yang Yuanwei 2008). Including them will not affect any of the results reported in this study. I thank Dr. Zhang Licheng of the China Research Institute of Fiscal Science for detailed explanations of the fiscal data in Chinese official sources.

largely reflects the post-1994 centralization of fiscal resources and the growing fiscal strength of the central government as seen in its rising share of budgetary revenues in Table 3.5.[28] Most important for our purposes, central fiscal transfers seemed to have favored the inland provinces throughout this period. Indeed, in any single year between 1995 and 2004, the average net per capita subsidies from the center to the inland provinces were greater than the subsidies to the coastal provinces. The difference between the two groups of provinces is especially pronounced in the series that excludes the more formula-based and less redistributive tax rebates (the last column in the table).

Tibet was the most subsidized provincial unit in China during the period of 1995–2004. Each year, on average, it received 705.6 yuan (constant 1977 RMB) on a net per capita basis from the central government if the tax rebates are included in the calculation and 683.7 yuan if the tax rebates are excluded. In contrast, Jiangsu was the least subsidized province if the tax rebates are included in the calculation of net per capita fiscal subsidies from the central government, receiving on average only 56.5 yuan per annum. If the tax rebates are excluded, Shanghai was the least subsidized province, with an average net per capita remittance to the central coffers of 151.3 yuan each year during this period. This largely confirms the popular perception of Shanghai remaining the largest fiscal contributor to the central government even after the 1994 fiscal reform (Zhao Yining 2003, 27).

Moreover, the gap in net per capita subsidies in favor of the inland provinces has also grown over the years. As seen in Figure 3.2, in real terms, the difference for the two provincial groups rose from about 57 yuan in 1995 (or 9.1 yuan if the tax rebates are included) to as much as 191 yuan in 2004 (or 75 yuan if the tax rebates are included, after dropping slightly from 92.6 yuan in 2002). This is certainly consistent with the launching of the Western Development Program (*xibu dakaifa zhan-lüe*) by the center in the late 1990s aimed at assisting the inland provinces (Naughton 2004).

---

[28] In fact, all provinces became net recipients of central transfers if tax rebates are included in central transfer data in the post-1994 period, reflecting their increasing "fiscal dependence" on the central government. This is largely because the 1994 fiscal reform centralized revenue collection by making the consumption tax a central tax and the value-added tax a shared tax, 75 percent of which would go to the central government. I am indebted to an anonymous reviewer for reminding me of this point. If tax rebates are excluded, however, a few coastal provinces, such as Shanghai, Jiangsu, and Zhejiang, continued to be net contributors for most of this period.

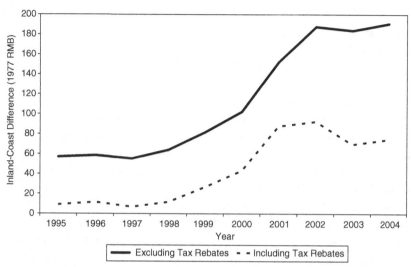

FIGURE 3.2. Difference in net per capita central fiscal subsidies received for inland and coastal provinces, 1995–2004.
Note: The numbers plotted in the figure are obtained by subtracting the average net per capita central subsidies for the coastal provinces from that for the inland provinces (inland subsidies minus coastal subsidies) for each year during this period.
Source: Appendix to Chapter 3.

Because of viable alternative options of fiscal extraction by the central government discussed earlier, our data on central budgetary subsidies remain at best an incomplete measure of the actual central fiscal extraction and redistribution in China during the period. Presumably, the central government can still carry out substantial resource extraction and redistribution without having to secure substantial formal revenue remittances from the provinces. For instance, there is also no guarantee that during the post-1994 period the center is no longer engaging in soliciting "involuntary loans" from the provinces. Meanwhile, of course, it has continued to seek changes in the details of the "tax sharing" schemes with the provincial governments in its own favor, as noted previously.

Nevertheless, the patterns of the regional distribution of central fiscal transfers in post-1994 China suggest continued active fiscal redistribution carried out by the central government across the different provinces. Our evidence from the number and composition of the net recipient provinces of central fiscal subsidies, from the terms of revenue retention in the fiscal contracts until the early 1990s, and from the regional patterns of the post-1994 central fiscal subsidy flows seems quite consistent with each other. Taken together, it indicates that throughout this period the Chinese central government was able to pursue fiscal transfers in favor of the inland provinces faring less well than the coastal provinces in the age of economic globalization.

3.6 CONCLUSION

In order to introduce efficiency into a stagnant economy under the central plan in the aftermath of the Cultural Revolution turmoil, the Chinese national leadership not only sought to restructure the domestic economy but also opted to open the country's doors to the international markets. Capitalizing on their regional comparative advantage, the central government attempted to turn the coastal provinces into competitive export-processing zones by granting them preferential policies that established various development zones to attract foreign capital and technology. As the coastal provinces thrived with greater exposure to the international markets, the rising regional economic disparity pitted these richer, faster-growing coastal provinces against both the central government and the inland provinces, as predicted by the prevailing economic theories reviewed in Chapter 2.

The central government was caught in the middle. The inland provinces faring less well were clamoring for more assistance from Beijing, while the economically more resourceful coastal provinces were growing more assertive in their demands for greater fiscal autonomy. However, the paramount concerns of the center were to check such regional intransigence and prevent regional economic disparity from threatening territorial integrity. Meanwhile, the fiscal capacity of Beijing during this period was generally underestimated. Among other things, the Chinese central government was able to engage in "forced borrowings" from the provinces not warranted by the nominal fiscal contracts, tap into and redefine in its own favor the scope of extrabudgetary funds, and perhaps most important, implement fiscal centralization in 1994 in the face of provincial resistance. Moreover, fiscal transfers favoring the inland provinces persisted throughout this era. The inland provinces were more likely to be net recipients of central subsidies than their coastal counterparts were. They also tended to enjoy more generous terms of budgetary revenue retention during the period of fiscal contracting since the early 1980s and to receive more inward revenue transfers from the central government since the fiscal reform of 1994.

Fiscal ploys by the central government against the provinces that buttressed central fiscal standing and boosted interregional fiscal redistribution were certainly facilitated by the political predominance of the center over the provinces. Above all, the national leaders running the Chinese central government also occupy the top offices within the single ruling CCP. They monopolize the institutional resources within the sole governing party that enable them to manage the careers of the leading provincial officials. As Jiang Zemin, the former CCP chief, put it bluntly during a talk to provincial leaders in the early 1990s, "Don't think because you have money now you can bargain with the center. I tell you, although you have money, your appointments are still controlled in the hand of the center" (quoted in Tao 2001, 90).

Not surprisingly, provincial leaders in Jiangsu and Guangdong who were bold enough to confront the central government over fiscal centralization were promptly removed from their posts (Shirk 1993, 189; Yang 1994, 86). Indeed, Ye Xuanping of Guangdong lost his provincial job despite his reputedly well-entrenched informal connections in China's national political system.[29] A better understanding of the political capacity of the Chinese central government thus requires more sketches of the political institutional arrangements that bind the political center and the provinces, especially those within the ruling CCP. I move to this topic next.

APPENDIX: CHINESE ECONOMIC DATA

The task of constructing a dataset of reasonably consistent (especially provincial-level) economic data for China covering over twenty-five years is daunting. For instance, new provinces were created over the years, thus changing the total number of territorial units at the subnational level to be included in our analysis. More problematic are possible changes in statistical reporting standards and variable definitions, and occasionally, missing data.[30] Throughout, I have tried my best to minimize the number of inevitable judgment calls. In the following, I also make explicit exactly where and why such decisions were made.

---

[29] Ye is a native of Guangdong and the eldest son of the late Marshal Ye Jianying, a crucial figure in helping engineer the downfall of the "Gang of Four" that ended the Cultural Revolution and that brought Deng Xiaoping, China's paramount leader in the reform era, back to power (Baum 1994).

[30] The challenge is not confined to single-country statistical sources. Variable names and definitions in cross-national data volumes such as the *World Development Indicators* (World Bank 2003, 2008) could also evolve over time.

A3.1 Year Coverage and Sources

In this study, I focus on the 1978–2004 period for the Chinese economic data. China's reform and opening program was officially launched in 1978; systematic provincial-level trade and export data were not available for most of the pre-1978 years. I chose the cutoff year of 2004 because in 2006 the Chinese government published adjusted GDP data, starting from 1978 for national-level data and from around 1993 for provincial-level data. GDP data starting from 2005 (published in 2006) for all levels were reported according to the new, adjusted standards and thus are no longer comparable to those from the earlier years. Reasons of consistency aside, in the study I assume, only realistically, that the center decides upon provincial personnel appointments based on the economic information available at the time of decision-making, rather than information from the future (for instance, after adjustment of GDP data years later). Thus, it is crucial for me to use the unadjusted data that are available only up to 2004.[31]

Chinese national-level economic data presented in Table 3.1 and Figure 3.1 are drawn primarily from the various volumes of the *China Statistical Yearbook* (Guojia Tongji Ju [National Bureau of Statistics] 2002, 2005),[32] and the historical series in *Comprehensive Statistical Data and Materials on 50 Years of New China* – hereafter *Comprehensive Statistical Data* (Guojia Tongji Ju [National Bureau of Statistics] 1999a). All published by China's National Bureau of Statistics, an agency of the central government, these volumes include comprehensive historical data for many variables since the 1950s.[33] They are complemented by data on the *net* inflows of foreign direct investment from the World Bank's *World Development Indicators 2008*.

---

[31] As I report elsewhere (Sheng 2009b), patterns of provincial participation in the global markets and provincial economic growth and wealth during the period of 1978–2006 based upon the newly adjusted GDP data are broadly similar to those presented in this chapter. In Chapter 6, where I analyze the determinants of growth of provincial per capita GDP, using adjusted GDP data also yield results that are nearly identical to those reported in this book.

[32] Except for the *China Statistical Yearbook 1981* (Guojia Tongji Ju [National Bureau of Statistics] 1982), the first volume that actually refers to data for the year 1981, all the other volumes of the *Statistical Yearbook* usually cover data for the previous year; the year in the title refers to the year of publication. For instance, *China Statistical Yearbook 2002* contains data for 2001, but it was published in 2002.

[33] The earlier English translation of National Bureau of Statistics was State Statistical Bureau. I use the new translation for consistency.

However, the *China Statistical Yearbook* is not as useful for provincial-level economic data. Its provincial data coverage on variables such as population, national income (*guomin shouru*),[34] and later gross national product (GNP, *guomin shengchan zongzhi*) and GDP (*guonei shengchan zongzhi*), and trade and exports only became systematically available in the early 1990s. For the greatest data availability and consistency, I thus rely on *Comprehensive Statistical Data* (Guojia Tongji Ju [National Bureau of Statistics] 1999a) that contains impressive coverage of many social-economic variables for the 1949–98 period. The dataset has been updated with data for the 1999–2004 period from the provincial statistical yearbooks (Sheng Tongji Ju [Provincial Bureaus of Statistics] 2000–2005) because upon close examination and comparison they are mostly consistent with those in the *Comprehensive Statistical Data*.[35] Whenever there are any inconsistencies between the *Comprehensive Statistical Data* and the provincial statistical yearbooks, I use the data from the latter. As a rule, the data in the more recent issues of the provincial statistical yearbooks are favored in the rare cases of discrepancies between yearbooks published in different years for the same province, under the assumption that the more recent data are more accurate. This is justified because such occasional discrepancies mainly involve typos and printing errors, unlike the systematic adjustment of national and provincial GDP data in 2006 noted earlier.

There are two instances where I do not rely entirely on the data from the *Comprehensive Statistical Data*/provincial statistical yearbooks. The first exception is for the provincial trade and export data used to measure provincial exposure to the global markets. Indeed, different provinces often seem to draw on different sources for the foreign trade data in these statistical volumes. Although all the provincial series begin with data collected by the provincial commissions on foreign trade, the provincial counterparts of the national-level Ministry of Foreign Trade, the provinces often switched to using the customs data in different years. For instance, Shandong began to use customs data for foreign trade in 1984.

---

[34] "National income" is partly based upon the socialist statistical concept of "net material product" (NMP) that refers only to the "productive capacity" of the economy, without including many services-oriented economic activities. NMP is about 20 percent smaller than alternative measures such as GNP, according to Naughton (1995, 327–328).

[35] Economic data for most provinces are published annually in the provincial statistical yearbooks – for instance, the *Beijing Statistical Yearbook*. There are two exceptions. Data for Gansu appear in the *Gansu Yearbook*; data for Hebei are published in the *Hebei Economic Yearbook*.

The *Inner Mongolia Statistical Yearbook 2001* still publishes its provincial foreign trade commission data for 2000.

No explanation is usually provided on the distinction between the customs data and the trade commission data, but possible problems of inconsistency might exist. Moreover, there are also two series of customs statistics on provincial foreign trade, according to the *China Statistical Yearbook*. One refers to foreign trade conducted according to the "location of the managing units." The other refers to trade conducted according to the "source or destination of the goods." That is, the location of the units conducting the trade reported to the customs might not always be identical to the location where the goods are produced and procured for export, or eventually shipped and sold for import. Furthermore, the two customs trade data series in the *China Statistical Yearbook* only began with data from 1992 (Guojia Tongji Ju [National Bureau of Statistics] 1995, Tables 16–9, 16–10); using these data would substantially shorten the time series of our dataset.[36]

An alternative source is the *Almanac of China's Foreign Economic Relations and Trade* (*Almanac* hereafter) published by the China Ministry of Foreign Trade and Economic Cooperation (1987–2003), which has included provincial foreign trade, exports, and foreign direct investment data starting from year 1986. This series enjoys the advantage of being collected by a central government ministry and its provincial counterparts (the provincial commissions on foreign economics and trade). Nevertheless, because it only starts with data from 1986, much information will be lost and many observations for analysis will be excluded if we solely rely on these data. Thus, I use the *Comprehensive Statistical Data*, cross-checked with the provincial statistical yearbooks, for the 1978–85 data and the *Almanac* for the 1986–2002 data. I use the subsequent *China Commerce Yearbook* published by the China Ministry of Commerce (2004–2005) for the 2003–04 data after the Ministry of Commerce was

---

[36] It is often not made clear which customs series is used in the provincial statistical yearbooks when they began to adopt the customs data, or which customs series is more consistent with the data collected by the provincial trade commissions. Fujita and Hu (2001, 34) suggest that data from the provincial trade commissions are consistent with the customs data according to the location of the official managing units that conduct foreign trade. This does not appear to be the case according to the customs data in the *China Statistical Yearbook* (Guojia Tongji Ju [National Bureau of Statistics] 1995, Tables 16–9, 16–10; 1996, Tables 16–10, 16–11; 1999b, Tables 17–10, 17–11; 2002, Tables 17–10, 17–11; 2005, Tables 18–10, 18–11) and those reported by the provincial trade commissions (see below). Indeed, for the 1992–2004 period, the trade commissions data on total provincial foreign trade are correlated with the comparable customs data according to

created to oversee both domestic and foreign trade in March 2003.[37] This is justified by the fact that prior to 1986, the *Comprehensive Statistical Data*/provincial statistical yearbooks mostly report trade data from provincial foreign trade commissions, consistent with the *Almanac*.

Trade data for Beijing covering 2003–04, however, are no longer published in the *China Commerce Yearbook*. Thus, I use the "local portion" of the foreign trade data from the historical series appendix in the *Beijing Statistical Yearbook* 2005 (Beijing Shi Tongji Ju [Beijing Bureau of Statistics] 2005, Table 23–31) because the trade data for 1998–2002 reported in this volume are nearly identical with those reported in the *Almanac*.[38] In Table 3.3 reporting provincial-level FDI data, I use the "actually utilized" (not the "contracted") amount. They are also from the *Comprehensive Statistical Data*/provincial statistical yearbooks (for pre-1986), the *Almanac* (for 1986–2002), and the *China Commerce Yearbook* (for 2003–04).

The second exception is the yearly information on provincial budgetary revenue transfers to the central government and inflows of central budgetary transfers, generally not included in provincial statistical yearbooks. The data used to calculate the net central fiscal subsidies presented in Table 3.6 and Figure 3.2 come from Zhongguo Caizheng Nianjian Bianji Weiyuanhui [Editorial Committee of the *Finance Yearbook of China*] (1996, 1997–2005). Data on tax rebates to the individual provinces from the central government are drawn from Caizhengbu Difangsi [Department of Local Affairs of the China Ministry of Finance] (1996, 1998); Caizhengbu Guokusi [Department of State Treasury of China Ministry of Finance] and Caizhengbu Yusuansi [Department of Budget of the China Ministry of Finance] (2002, 2003, 2005, 2006); and Caizhengbu Yusuansi [Department of Budget of the China Ministry of Finance] (1998, 1999, 2001a, 2001b).

---

the managing units at about 0.65 (p = 0.000). The correlation with the customs data according to origin/destination of goods is 0.995 (p = 0.000). However, this seems less of an issue for data on exports. The respective correlation coefficients are 0.996 (p = 0.000) and 0.998 (p = 0.000). That is, provincial export data from the two customs series and those reported by the provincial trade commissions appear to be quite consistent with each other.

[37] This is according to http://www.mofcom.gov.cn/mofcom_history.shtml, accessed on January 28, 2005.

[38] I use Beijing's actually utilized foreign direct investment data for 2003–04 from the same source. Dropping data for Beijing during 2003–04 from the later statistical analysis does not affect the results reported in the book.

A3.2 Coding of Economic Variables

Despite their comprehensiveness in historical coverage, economic data from the provincial statistical sources are far from perfect. This section discusses some special features of the data in these sources and the steps taken to construct the actual dataset used in this book.

First, Hainan was originally part of Guangdong province before becoming a distinct province in 1988; Chongqing was part of Sichuan province until 1997, when it was designated a provincial-level municipality (together with Beijing, Shanghai, and Tianjin). The *Comprehensive Statistical Data*, published in 1999, reports data according to the internal administrative boundaries of China as of 1998 by listing separately the series for Guangdong, Hainan, Sichuan, and Chongqing. For all the years in which data for Guangdong and Sichuan are available, they exclude respectively those for Hainan and Chongqing. This is unrealistic for Guangdong up to 1987, and for Sichuan up to 1996. Therefore, Guangdong's data covering the 1978–87 period are reconstructed by merging those of Guangdong and Hainan. For Sichuan, since the *Comprehensive Statistical Data* only begins the Chongqing data with 1996, additional data for Sichuan for the 1978–95 period are drawn from the relevant volumes of the *Sichuan Tongji Nianjian* (Sichuan Sheng Tongji Ju [Sichuan Provincial Bureau of Statistics] 1991–1996). For 1996, the data for Sichuan are constructed by merging the data for Sichuan and those for Chongqing from the *Comprehensive Statistical Data*.[39]

Second, due to the merging of data for Sichuan and Guangdong for some years, it is no longer sensible to use the per capita GDP data in the original form from either the *Comprehensive Statistical Data* or the provincial statistical yearbooks. Thus, per capita GDP data are obtained by dividing the GDP figures by the provincial population for all provinces.

---

[39] This procedure could be problematic for aggregate growth figures for the years between 1987 and 1988 for Guangdong, and between 1996 and 1997 for Sichuan. For instance, because of the "loss" of Hainan and the resultant shrinkage in provincial population in 1988, Guangdong's level of employment is likely to witness a substantial decline compared with 1987. Such a drop in the growth rate of provincial employment might be misleading. Therefore, the value of the provincial employment growth variable used in the statistical analysis in Chapter 6 for Guangdong in 1988 and for Sichuan in 1997 is calculated with data from the previous years (1987 for Guangdong and 1996 for Sichuan) that do not include those for Hainan or Chongqing, respectively. The problem is less serious for per capita growth variables that already account for such changes in provincial population (see below).

Third, the statistical yearbooks from some provinces list both data on population with residency registration (*huji renkou*) and another broader series that includes population without such registration (*changzhu renkou*); other provinces only provide data on the former. For instance, Tibet publishes both series for data starting in 1990; Shandong's two population series begin in 1985.[40] As a rule, only data on population with residency registration are used in this study if both series happen to be available.

Fourth, all the original economic data in the *Comprehensive Statistical Data* and the provincial statistical yearbooks are in current prices. The data used in this book are all in constant 1977 RMB, deflated with the provincial general retail price indices. The retail price indices cover more provinces for more years than the series on the provincial general consumer price indices, even though the two price series have a correlation of over 0.96 ($p = 0.000$) with each other.[41] Retail price indices, however, are not available for Tibet (1978–89) or Guangxi (1976–77). For those years, the national averages are used.

Finally, the statistical yearbooks for some provinces such as Yunnan and Tibet have a separate series on "border trade" (*bianjing maoyi*), which might be related to but is often distinct from foreign trade per se. Here I only include the series on foreign trade. Since the original foreign trade data are in U.S. dollars whereas the provincial GDP figures are in RMB, data on the foreign exchange rate (the average annual rate, or the middle rate) are used to calculate the share of foreign trade in provincial GDP and other globalization indicators.[42]

---

[40] Generally, the population with residency registration is estimated with public security records; the other is often through population sampling. Census data is often used for data in 2000 when the census was conducted. Provincial population data from the *China Statistical Yearbook* are not always identical to those from the provincial statistical yearbooks. Using data from the former does not affect the results of our later analysis.

[41] In reporting the national-level economic trends in Table 3.1, I use the 1950 constant price, deflated with the general consumer price indices, in order to obtain a longer time series for these national-level data.

[42] Exchange rate data for 1978–80 are from People's Bank of China Research and Statistics Department (1988, 156–157), as quoted in Lardy (1992, 148–149). Data for 1981–84 are from Guojia Tongji Ju [National Bureau of Statistics] (1999b, Table 17–2), and from Guojia Tongji Ju [National Bureau of Statistics] (2005, Table 18–2) for 1985–2004.

4

Central Political Control via the CCP

4.1 INTRODUCTION

I have argued that the political center has incentives to redress the growing regional economic gap through fiscal transfers in order to maintain its own national rule. However, fiscal resources for interregional redistribution are more likely to come from the richer but more restive subnational regions thriving in the global markets. Following Riker (1964), I suggest that the ability of the center to extract revenues from the winner regions in the era of economic openness should be greater in political systems that are governed by centralized political parties. Other things being equal, central governments in countries ruled by one single political party that wields personnel powers over subnational copartisans (in the most centralized political system) should be more effective in performing such regional balancing tasks via exercise of territorially targeted political control and revenue extraction.

In response to rising regional disparity and discontent as the country opened its doors to the world markets, the Chinese central government seemed able to pursue interprovincial fiscal redistribution slanted toward the loser provinces in the inland all along. Such redistributive capacity of the Chinese central government has to be understood in the context of the political prepotency imparted to the national political leadership by a most centralized governing political party. In this chapter, I first provide more details on the political institutions within the sole-ruling CCP that afford the center the requisite political supremacy and the related ability to engage in regionally selective exercise of political control over the provincial governments.

Indeed, single-party rule under the CCP implies that a most centralized political system has operated in post-1978 China. Under single-party authoritarianism, as opposed to personal dictatorships overshadowed by one dominant individual autocrat or authoritarian regimes led by a military junta (Brooker 2000; Geddes 1999b), the CCP with a mostly collective, civilian national leadership has ruled China throughout this period. In addition, the predominance of the CCP national leaders over party members working at the provincial level was institutionalized in the leadership structure of the ruling party itself – the CCP Central Committee and its Politburo. Most fundamental to our understanding of the nature of central political preponderance vis-à-vis the provincial governments is the monopoly nomenklatura powers wielded by the political center to manage the careers of leading provincial cadres through the single ruling CCP.

Due to the primacy of the CCP at each level of the Chinese government administration throughout this period, I focus on the exercise of central personnel powers with regard to the provincial party secretaries. They are the top-ranking officials (*yibashou*, or number-one officials) who largely have the final say over the implementation of central policy directives or policymaking within their provincial jurisdictions (for instance, Shirk 1993, Chapter 3).[1] Specifically, I examine the cross-province variation as well as the cross-year trends in the center's exercise of political control over the provincial governments as measured by the incidence of new appointments, presence of native sons, and the degree of bureaucratic integration (Huang 1996) of the provincial party secretaries during the 1978–2005 period.

All along, there seemed to be neither straightforward trends nor pronounced distinctions between the coastal and inland provinces in terms of the frequency of new appointments for the provincial party chiefs. Although over time it became much less likely for provinces across the board to be ruled by native sons, the center did not seem to have sought tighter political control over the coastal provincial governments by installing non-native sons in their top provincial party post. Since the early 1990s, the Chinese provinces had been increasingly governed by the more "bureaucratically integrated" provincial party secretaries predisposed to greater compliance with the policy preferences of the

---

[1] Provincial governors, if they are not concurrently provincial party chiefs, are the second-ranking officials in the provinces. Personnel control with regard to the governors seemed to have little independent effect on macroeconomic outcomes. I have discussed the case of the governors during the 1978–2002 period in Sheng (2005b).

central government by virtue of their career trajectories. Most important, provincial governments along the coast were more likely to be led by the more "bureaucratically integrated" party secretaries throughout the 1978–2005 period. Furthermore, increasingly tightening political control by the Chinese national leaders since the early 1990s seemed to have been particularly targeted toward the coastal provincial governments.

The remainder of this chapter consists of the following sections. I first sketch party primacy and central predominance under CCP single-party rule in post-1978 China. I then overview the nomenklatura system related to the center's management of provincial-level officials and recount the reforms introduced in the 1980s and 1990s. This is followed by discussions of the rationale for focusing on management of the provincial party secretaries in studying the exercise of central political control over the provincial governments. After introducing the empirical indicators used in this book to measure the degree of central political control, I present the temporal trends and regional patterns of control captured by these indicators.

4.2   CENTRALIZED SINGLE-PARTY RULE

4.2.1 Party Primacy Under Single-Party Rule

In a strict sense, it is perhaps more apt to characterize China in the post-1978 period, rather than during the entire post-1949 era, as under single-party rule. To be sure, the CCP has dominated Chinese politics ever since it won the Chinese civil war in 1949.[2] After the Seventh Party Congress in 1945, however, Mao Zedong had enjoyed unrivaled personal prestige and power within the CCP and the military. Indeed, Mao might have deliberately sought to maintain his personal charisma and delay political institutionalization in China after the founding of the People's Republic (Shirk 1993, 8). His preeminence in Chinese politics reached its pinnacle during the Cultural Revolution (from 1966 until his death in 1976), effectively silencing any possible challenges from within the party. As the personal influence of Mao peaked, the CCP itself fell into disarray. Party organizations at all levels were severely emaciated. In the provinces,

---

[2] Despite the occasional rise of the influence of the military in Chinese politics (such as during the heyday of Lin Biao), the reins of the supreme power of the party have always been in civilian hands. Efforts by the CCP civilian leadership to retire aging generals and restructure (and reduce the size of) the armed forces in the early post–Cultural Revolution years (Baum 1997, 376–379) and to divest the military of its business operations in later years (Lee 2006) generally met with little resistance.

the regional commanders of the People's Liberation Army (PLA) had to step in to assume top leadership posts and to impose order amidst the local chaos (Godwin 1976; Bennett 1973; Zhongguo Xingzheng Guanli Xuehui [China Society of Public Administration] 2002, 245–247).[3]

At the end of the Cultural Revolution, a less personalist CCP national leadership intent on establishing "a system governed by rules, clear lines of authority, and collective decision-making institutions" began to emerge (Shirk 1993, 9). To be sure, for much of the post-Mao period, Deng Xiaoping remained the "paramount leader" commanding immense prestige and respect. However, Deng's position was different from that of Mao. Until his formal retirement in 1989 (or even up to his death in 1997), Deng still had to deal with a group of powerful CCP elders. They included, among others, Chen Yun,[4] Bo Yibo, and Li Xiannian, who not only challenged his reform policies from time to time but managed to pressure him into sacking Hu Yaobang and Zhao Ziyang, two of his hand-picked successors (Baum 1997). Later "core" leaders such as Jiang Zemin and Hu Jintao could be even less unconstrained in their personal power among the respective leadership cohort over which they formally presided.

The ascendance of a less personalist national leadership has coincided with the gradual return to normalcy of party life for the CCP in the post-1978 era. For one thing, national party congresses are now convened more regularly than during much of the previous period of party history. In fact, since late 1977 beginning with the Eleventh Party Congress, CCP national party congresses have been held every five years, as stipulated in the party constitution, to select a new term of the Central Committee and its Politburo, the collective decision-making organs of the party. In contrast, the Seventh Party Congress was held in 1945 when Mao first consolidated his personal power in the party, and the Eighth through the

---

[3] The drastic weakening of the party at the provincial level during the Cultural Revolution was unmistakable when "only 34 (13.8%) of the 247 provincial party secretaries and 23 (8.7%) of the 266 provincial governors, vice governors, or their equivalents of April 1966 were still politically active two years later," according to one estimate by Goodman (1986, 6). There were a larger number of provincial party secretaries in those years than the number of provinces because at the time the provincial first party secretary was the top provincial party official (see the following) and each province could have more than one provincial party secretary.

[4] Thus, Vogel (2005, 741) characterizes Chen Yun as someone who actually "met Deng as an equal" in many ways during the post-1978 era. However, it is difficult to single out anyone enjoying a similar stature vis-à-vis Mao during the period from the Seventh Party Congress to his death in 1976.

Tenth Congresses were held respectively in 1956, 1969, and 1973 (Sheng 2005a). Term limits and mandatory retirement ages for leading cadres at all levels have also been gradually introduced and institutionalized in recent years (Bo 2007; Manion 1993). Moreover, as I will also discuss in detail later, throughout this period, top-echelon party/government personnel at the provincial level were routinely managed by the party center via the institutional tools imparted by the CCP.

Under single-party rule, the CCP has dominated the government throughout the post-Mao era. Like other Communist countries, China's formal political system during this period has been characterized by the presence of a parallel party/government structure spanning all five administrative levels of the state – center, province, prefecture, county, and township. Through the "cardinal principle" known as "party leadership," the CCP trumps the government at each level (Lieberthal 2003, Chapter 7; Shirk 1993, Chapter 3).[5] At the national level, Rigby's (1982, 3) apt observation that the Soviet central government was merely "an administrative arm of the supreme executive body of the 'Party,' namely the Politburo" is equally pertinent here. The Chinese central government and its cabinet – the State Council – must heed the command of the party center of the CCP over major policy directions. Similarly, the party committees at the provincial levels predominate over the provincial governments.

The subordinate status of the government vis-à-vis the party is also evident in the lower standing of the government chief executive vis-à-vis the party chief at the same administrative level within the party hierarchy if the two positions are not occupied by the same person. The State Council premier – the national chief executive and often a ranking and powerful member of the CCP in his own right – always ranks lower than

---

[5] In this study I do not discuss the legislative bodies – the people's congresses at various levels – because they remained subordinate, if not entirely serving rubber-stamping purposes, to the party during this period. For recent views arguing that local and provincial people's congresses have been used by the CCP as tools of "supervision" to collect information and combat problems such as corruption, see Cho (2009) and Xia (2000, 2008). For an early important discussion of the National People's Congress and its limitations, see O'Brien (1990). Not coincidentally, provincial party secretaries, the focus of this book, have often chaired the standing committees of the provincial people's congresses in recent years. This was the case in twenty out of thirty-one provinces in July 2006 (from http://www.people.com.cn/GB/shizheng/252/9667/9684/20021126/874879.html, accessed on July 14, 2006), and in as many as twenty-two out of thirty-one provinces as of June 2008 (from http://www.xinhuanet.com/local/dfld/bdj.htm, accessed on June 27, 2008). This practice has apparently become regularized since the late 1990s, according to Zhang Quanjing, head of the Department of Organization of the CCP Central Committee from 1994 to 1999 (Zhao Lei and Zheng Yan 2006).

the national party head. During the early post-1978 years, the top party post at the provincial level was still called "first secretary" (*diyi shuji*), a practice that dated back to the years before the Cultural Revolution. They were usually followed in rank by one "second secretary" (*di'er shuji*), one "third secretary" (*disan shuji*), and a number of "secretaries" (*shuji*) and "vice-secretaries" (*fu shuji*). Since the rank of "first secretary" was abolished in early 1984, the provincial party secretary has been the top party official in the provinces (Zhonggong Zhongyang Zuzhibu [Department of Organization of the CCP Central Committee] et al. 2000a, 2000b).[6] If not a concurrent party secretary, the provincial chief executive (governor) has been a vice-secretary or its equivalent on the provincial party committee, ranking lower than the provincial party chief in the provincial-level party hierarchy and power structure. The same holds down the administrative ladder.

To be sure, "interlocking directorates" occasionally exist at the provincial level, as some incumbent party secretaries might serve concurrently as governors (Lieberthal 2003, 239). This was especially common in the early post-Mao years. In 1978, for example, all twenty-nine provinces at the time witnessed the concentration of the top party/government offices in one individual. By 1980, there were only three such provinces. The highest since then was in 1988, when there were four provinces where the governorship and top party post were assumed by one person (Sheng 2005b, 93–95). This phenomenon has become quite rare of late, although it can still occur briefly during transitions. For instance, Han Zheng, mayor of Shanghai, served as its party chief concurrently but temporarily from September 2006 to March 2007. This was during the interregnum after the dismissal of its party chief Chen Liangyu on corruption charges and before the appointment of Xi Jinping as Shanghai's party secretary.

Party primacy over the government is also revealed in the personnel appointment powers wielded by the CCP over major government positions at all levels, known as "the party controlling the cadre" (*dangguan ganbu*) (Zhonggong Zhongyang [Central Committee of the Chinese Communist Party] 1996[1995]; Zhonggong Zhongyang Zuzhibu [Department of Organization of the CCP Central Committee]

---

[6] Some provinces did not have second or third secretaries, while others did not have vice-secretaries when the rank of first secretary was still in use. The actual number of secretaries and vice-secretaries could also vary among the provinces. Unless otherwise noted, in this book, I refer to the top provincial official throughout the post-1978 period as the provincial party secretary for consistency.

1999 [1994]). For example, State Council vice premiers responsible for personnel decisions in the functional areas that they oversee are consulted before candidates are nominated for the top posts in the central government ministries. However, the appointment authority over central government cabinet positions does not lie with the State Council; it is in the hands of the national leaders at the party center (Burns 1994; Huang 1996, 91; Zhonggong Zhongyang Zuzhibu [Department of Organization of the CCP Central Committee] 1984[1980]-b).[7]

4.2.2 Political Predominance by the Center

Although the party dominates the government at each level, the national leadership at the party center prevails within the CCP. The party center broadly encompasses the members of the Politburo, its Standing Committee, and the various CCP national-level standing organs, such as the Secretariat, the Department of Organization, and the Department of Propaganda of the CCP Central Committee. Together with the leadership of the central government that is mostly staffed by its own members,[8] the party center essentially constitutes the political center in China.

China's national leaders, officials working at the national level rather than in any specific province, played the preponderant role at the party center during this period. Above all, they command the military. The supreme military command of the country – the central military commission of the CCP as well as of the state – is effectively led by the Politburo of the CCP Central Committee (Shambaugh 2003, 111–112), in which the national leaders prevail. Furthermore, they dominate the very process of selecting the members of the CCP Central Committee, arguably the only representative institution within the party in charge of formally selecting the national leaders – first called the "Selectorate" by Shirk (1993). They also run the party's daily business via leading such

---

7 Due to its role in handling cadre dossiers, conducting candidate background investigations, making nominations, and exercising effective vetoes over personnel decisions, the Department of Organization of the CCP at all levels plays a prominent role in the personnel system of China (Lee 1991, Chapter 13; Manion 1985; Zhonggong Zhongyang Zuzhibu [Department of Organization of the CCP Central Committee] 1984[1980]-b). For instance, the Department of Organization of the CCP Central Committee at the national level advises the national leadership at the party center on the personnel decisions for all major posts falling under the central nomenklatura (see the following) and formally announces and implements them on the national leaders' behalf.
8 For instance, CCP Politburo members often hold top central government executive positions such as the State Council premiership or vice premiership.

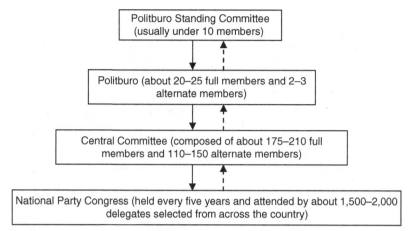

FIGURE 4.1. The party center: CCP Central Committee and Politburo.
Note: Solid arrows refer to the direction of de facto authority; dashed arrows indicate the direction of nominal authority and the fact that membership at the end of the arrow comes from the start of the arrow.
Source: Lieberthal (2003, 174) and Shirk (1993, xi).

national standing organs of the CCP as the Department of Organization. Most important, national leaders have always occupied the overwhelming majority share in the highest collective decision-making organs of the party center – the Politburo and its Standing Committee – as schematized in Figure 4.1. Each year, on average, officials working at the national level took up about 85.8 percent of the Politburo membership share during the 1978–2005 period.[9] Membership in the supreme office of the land – the Politburo Standing Committee – has been exclusively composed of the national leaders.[10]

Not surprisingly, the Politburo of the CCP Central Committee and its Standing Committee are ultimately responsible for all of the most important personnel decisions in the Chinese political system, according to Zhang Quanjing, who directed the central Department of Organization from the

[9] This part draws on Sheng (2005a), which covers the 1978–2002 period. Sources for central Politburo membership shares for the post-2002 years are described in the Appendix to Chapter 4.
[10] To be sure, up to the Fourteenth Central Committee (covering the 1992–97 period), a group of "elders" not holding any formal positions still wielded real power behind the scene. Its members included, among others, Deng Xiaoping, Chen Yun, and Wang Zhen, but these were all leaders at the center. See also the various chapters in Unger and Dittmer (2002).

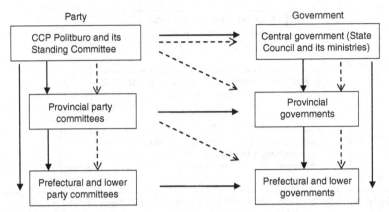

FIGURE 4.2. Party primacy and central predominance since 1983.
Note: The arrows indicate the direction of formal authority. Solid arrows indicate the ability to exercise central policy leadership via direct authority to issue policy directives; dashed arrows indicate the ability to exercise central political control via direct personnel appointment authority.
Source: Zhonggong Zhongyang Zuzhibu [Department of Organization of the CCP Central Committee] (1991[1990]) and Lieberthal (2003, Chapters 6–7).

mid-to late 1990s (Zhao Lei and Zheng Yan 2006). Such personnel powers by the national leaders at the party center are not confined to the national level, but also encompass the leading offices in the provinces (see the following). As shown in Figure 4.2, CCP rule under a predominant party center has helped produce in China a highly centralized system where the political center (the party center and the central government it staffs) predominates over the localities. The political supremacy enjoyed by Chinese national leaders at the party center is indisputable.

Two caveats are in order here. First, from time to time, China's national leaders can be divided among themselves over policy- or personality-based differences. Indeed, for some scholars (for example, Dittmer and Wu 1995; Huang 2000; Nathan 1973; Pye 1992; Shih 2008),[11] factional politics among the ruling elites might have pervaded the entire history of the People's Republic. My point here, however, is simply that these leaders are more likely to see eye to eye with one another regarding such matters as possible conflicts vis-à-vis the provinces, just like the post-Meiji oligarchs in Japan who, though by no means internally monolithic, often stuck together against their common political rivals (Ramseyer

---

[11] For critiques of this school, see Tsou (1976, 1995).

and Rosenbluth 1995). Hence, despite the rumored policy disagreements among themselves, Chinese national leaders tend to take common positions whenever the interests of the center are at stake.

For example, amidst concerns about declining revenue shares for the central government in the early 1990s, the conservative patriarch Chen Yun reportedly told the new CCP chief Jiang Zemin that the "*zhongyang* [the center] should centralise whatever power, in particular financial power – that needs to be centralised." The consequences for failing to do so were also clearly abhorred by the reformist Deng Xiaoping, Chen's archrival, "If the *zhongyang* cannot exercise full authority, the party and nation could disintegrate and nothing can be accomplished" (both quoted in Lam 1999, 214, 220). Similarly, during the height of economic local protectionism among the provinces threatening to fragment China's internal market, the conservative premier Li Peng sought to remind provincial leaders of "the dangers of excessive decentralization" while Deng Xiaoping stressed the need to "bring freewheeling provincial authorities to heel" (Baum 1994, 326–327).

Second, national leaders at the center also boasted a variety of career backgrounds; some had worked earlier in the provinces, as I will further discuss later. Still, even these leaders, once elevated to the highest national offices of the land, are more likely to harbor policy preferences dictated by their current national leadership positions. One revealing example is Zhu Rongji. In the face of Premier Li Peng's attempt to increase central revenues by changing the fiscal contracts with the provinces, Zhu was reportedly trying to defend the fiscal interests of Shanghai, where he held the top party job from the late 1980s to the early 1990s. After he moved to Beijing to become a State Council vice premier, however, it did not take long before Zhu metamorphosed into an ardent advocate on behalf of the central government in the 1994 fiscal reform to centralize revenue collections (Fewsmith 1997, 484, 516–517). Such a drastic about-face in his policy stance is clearly understandable. After all, their new imperative of continued political survival as the supreme leaders of the country hinges on the success of the national policies and their grip over national political power. For our purposes, it is thus justifiable that these national leaders at the center are regarded as a distinct but coherent group in the Chinese political system.

China's national leaders can exert influence over the provincial governments in two major ways – policy leadership and political control. Central policy leadership is exercised when the party center and the State Council (on behalf of the central government), jointly or separately, issue policy directives, of varying degrees of binding power, to the party/government units at the provincial level and below in order to promulgate and implement policy goals deemed important by the national leadership.[12] To facilitate policy compliance by lower-level governments, central political control over provincial governments is exercised via the party center's nomenklatura system of personnel management. Indeed, through the central Department of Organization of the CCP Central Committee, the national leaders dominating the Politburo and its Standing Committee wielded direct appointment, dismissal, and transfer powers over the leading party/government officials at the provincial level throughout this period. Despite the waves of personnel system reform since 1978 that have delegated downward some of its authority in this area, the party center has consistently retained monopoly control over the personnel decisions for the leading offices at the provincial level via its institutionalized nomenklatura power.

4.2.3 Central Nomenklatura Powers

A Russian coinage, nomenklatura is literally "a list of positions, arranged in order of seniority, including a description of the duties of each office" (Harasymiw 1969, 494). In China, it normally refers to a list of job titles (*zhiwu mingcheng biao*) for party/government offices directly managed by the party center, even though CCP organizations at the provincial and lower levels also maintain their own nomenklatura lists. Indeed, the list can be quite long and the task ponderous to manage one of the world's largest bureaucracies. Although it covered about 4,800 personnel in 1950 (soon after the founding of the People's Republic), as many as 14,000 officials were already on the central nomenklatura by the mid-1950s (Landry 2008, 45). Not much is known about the scope or actual workings of the nomenklatura system amidst the turmoil and the organizational atrophy of the CCP during the Cultural Revolution. By late 1977, however, the system must have already been back in operation when Hu Yaobang was made the head of the central Department of Organization (Zhonggong Zhongyang Zuzhibu [Department of Organization of the CCP Central Committee] et al. 2000b, 227).

In 1980, the center began to recentralize the personnel system as part of its overall efforts to strengthen party rule. These moves were also prompted by the need to facilitate the rehabilitation of officials who had

---

[12] These directives range from an order or decree (*mingling*), decision (*jueding*), regulation (*guiding*), instruction (*zhishi*), or circular (*tongzhi*), with decreasing binding force (Lieberthal 1978, 5–19).

been purged during the Cultural Revolution. Central direct involvement was often necessary in the face of possible local opposition by the beneficiaries of the Cultural Revolution, who were threatened by the prospect of working with the people whom they had once purged (Lee 1991, 163–184). The two-level downward cadre management system adopted was officially justified by "work needs" that were inadequately met at the time by managing cadres from one-level below by the center. In contrast, a "three-level" downward system would have been overwhelming and thus not "practical" (Zhonggong Zhongyang Zuzhibu [Department of Organization of the CCP Central Committee] 1984[1980]-a, 160).

In terms of the coverage of local officials, the 1980 system encompassed all major provincial posts occupied by the so-called "Category A" (*jia lei*) officials. These included provincial first party secretaries, provincial party secretaries and vice-secretaries, members of the provincial party standing committees, governors and their deputies, and chairs and vice-chairs of the standing committees of the provincial people's congresses, among others.[13] Direct central personnel powers also reached the leading cadres of the prefectures, with the equivalent rank of provincial departments (*ting*) (Lieberthal and Oksenberg 1988, 143). There was inevitable overlapping under the two-level downward system between the central nomenklatura and the list managed by the provinces, which also covered the prefecture level. In cases of conflicts in terms of personnel decisions, the preferences of the center would prevail (Zhonggong Zhongyang Zuzhibu [Department of Organization of the CCP Central Committee] 1984[1980]-a, 160). By 1980, the center was again directly managing about 13,000 people on its cadre list, almost a return to the level in the mid-1950s (Landry 2008, 45).

The 1980 system, however, did not last long. Most probably, it was no longer needed by 1983 when the large-scale cadre rehabilitation work

---

[13] Category A officials also included (and still include) a long list of party/government officials at the center. I only focus on the officials below the center here. The exact decision-making processes behind the appointment of provincial officials (provincial party secretaries and governors) and their deputies (vice-secretaries and deputy provincial governors) within the same Category A differed slightly. The Politburo Standing Committee (a more exclusive group of members within the Politburo, normally fewer than ten members) decided over the lower-ranking deputy provincial officials after some "collective discussion" among themselves. Decisions regarding provincial party secretaries and governors were made by the entire Politburo membership (normally with around twenty members), even after "collective discussion" within its Standing Committee, according to former central Department of Organization Chief Zhang Quanjing (Zhao Lei and Zheng Yan 2006, A2).

had been completed. It is also likely that the task of effectively managing such a gigantic body of personnel – occasionally complicated by the overlapping of the central nomenklatura and the personnel management lists for the provinces – was becoming too unwieldy for the center. The Department of Organization of the CCP Central Committee, the advising and implementing arm of the center over its personnel decisions, had only housed a staff of about 600 since late 1977 (Zhonggong Zhongyang Zuzhibu [Department of Organization of the CCP Central Committee] et al. 2000b, 227).[14] Too much central meddling in local personnel issues might also have hurt incentives on the ground when the domestic economic reform was already picking up steam.

Thus, a new round of personnel reform was carried out in 1983. The one-level downward system was resurrected whereby only the top provincial leadership, the Category A officials working in the provinces, fell under direct central management (Zhonggong Zhongyang Zuzhibu [Department of Organization of the CCP Central Committee] 1986[1983]-a). This drastically simplified the center's personnel task by reducing the number of nomenklatura-listed officials to about 4,200 in 1984, about one-third of the size under the previous system (Landry 2008, 45). Meanwhile, the staff size of the central Department of Organization grew to nearly 1,000 in the early 1980s (Zhonggong Zhongyang Zuzhibu [Department of Organization of the CCP Central Committee] et al. 2000b, 228). The one-level downward system surely has allowed the center to focus its increased institutional resources on managing more effectively a smaller body of top leaders under the central nomenklatura.

Yet the return to the one-level downward system did not imply the full relinquishment of central control over officials below the provincial level. A system of "reporting for the records" (*bei'an*) was instituted. The provincial-level departments of organization were required to send promptly (in 1986, within 15 days after the decision was made) to the central Department of Organization the materials used for making the personnel decisions for officials falling under their management lists (Zhonggong Zhongyang Zuzhibu [Department of Organization of the

---

[14] Staff size had certainly increased from a nadir of merely fifty-five in 1969 amidst the institutional atrophy of the CCP during the Cultural Revolution (Zhonggong Zhongyang Zuzhibu [Department of Organization of the CCP Central Committee] et al. 2000c, 70–71). The earlier high in 1954 boasted a staff of 841, which after "bureaucratic streamlining," declined to 210 in 1965, the eve of the Cultural Revolution (Zhonggong Zhongyang Zuzhibu [Department of Organization of the CCP Central Committee] et al. 2000a, 61).

CCP Central Committee] 1992[1991]; Huang 1995a, 830). The political instability in 1989 forced the center to tighten its personnel control again (Burns 1994). The "reporting" list of 1990 added a special entry for the fourteen cities "separately listed under the plan" *(jihua danlie chengshi)* to ensure central veto power over the selection of their leadership.

The provincial Departments of Organization only had to report the appointments of party secretaries/mayors for other prefecture-level cities to the center for the records. Members of the party standing committees of these fourteen cities were now also included on the reporting list (Zhonggong Zhongyang Zuzhibu [Department of Organization of the CCP Central Committee] 1991[1990]). The provinces were also required to submit *in advance* written plans for the appointment and dismissal of party secretaries/mayors of these "separately listed cities." Moreover, staff members from the provincial Departments of Organization had to travel to the center to report and discuss such plans *in person* before the planned personnel changes took effect (Zhonggong Zhongyang Zuzhibu [Department of Organization of the CCP Central Committee] 1992[1991], 54).[15]

Centralization of personnel control continued thereafter. By late 1998, all the top leaders of the five "separately listed cities" and ten deputy-provincial cities created since the early 1990s had fallen under the direct, formal purview of the central nomenklatura. They include, among others, party secretaries, mayors, and chairs of the standing committees of the municipal people's congresses and people's political consultative conferences as well as their deputies (Chan 2004, 713, 726). Most important for our purposes, the leading officials at the provincial level were always directly managed by the CCP party center throughout the post-1978 period.

4.3 PROVINCIAL PARTY SECRETARIES AND CENTRAL POLITICAL CONTROL

4.3.1 Provincial Policy Compliance and Provincial Leaders

As noted earlier in Chapter 2, in this study, the degree of central political control exercised over the subnational governments is conceptualized as

---

[15] These municipalities were often major industrial centers. They were carved out of their respective host provinces for establishment of direct fiscal ties with the central government, in essence as "cash cows" subject to direct central revenue extraction. Thus, the tighter watch by the center over these localities is not surprising. See also the Appendix to Chapter 4 for further discussion of the origins and evolution of these "separately listed cities."

the extent to which the political center is able to exact subnational policy compliance via the use of ruling-party-granted personnel appointment authority at the subnational level. Exercise of a tighter degree of central political control over the subnational governments denotes a greater ability of the political center to secure their policy compliance, other things being equal. We can measure the degree of central political control over the subnational governments within a most centralized political system such as post-Mao China along two dimensions. The degree of control can vary across different years over all the subnational governments as a whole (cross-time variation) or over the different subnational governments in any specific period (cross-province variation).

Much conventional research on the capacity of the Chinese political center to ensure local policy implementation tends to focus on the center's evolving overall political strength over time.[16] Scholars writing about the pre-1978 period have painted a largely mixed but static picture. For some (for instance, Barnett 1967; Lewis 1963), China had a highly centralized system with a political center monopolizing most powers of the state and affording little policy leeway to the lower-level governments. Others, however, suggest that the policy influence of the central government beyond Beijing, even under Mao, could be much more limited. Alongside a "cellular" economy composed of semiautarkic and self-sufficient provinces (Donnithorne 1972), for example, Shue (1988) discerns a "honeycomb" polity teeming with local segmentation and prevalent, if often tacit, resistance to central policy edicts.

With the onset of reform and opening that have empowered local governments economically, sophisticated observers of Chinese politics generally shy away from the sweeping predictions of the imminent collapse of CCP national rule noted earlier. Instead, they tend to point to the mounting constraints upon the ability of the political center to seek policy implementation below the national level. For example, Lieberthal (1992) argues that China's brand of one-party authoritarianism has produced largely "fragmented" government authority along both functional and territorial lines. Hence, policy implementation below the center in post-Mao China can be problematic, often a function of, among others, bargaining between the central government and the provinces (Lampton 1987, 1992). Meanwhile, Shirk (1993) has noted Beijing's deteriorating political strength with the growing presence of provincial officials

---

[16] For extensive and insightful reviews of these different approaches in the study of central-provincial relations in China, see Zheng (2007, 7–20) and Whiting (2001, 12–14).

on the CCP Central Committee and the attendant gains of provincial "Selectorate" power in choosing China's supreme national leaders. This could certainly hamper its ability to ensure policy compliance from the provinces.

Likewise, Walder (1995b) has highlighted the "political decline" of China's central state – manifested in the weakening ability of the central government to obtain lower-level policy compliance after economic reform reduced the dependence of local officials on the center for resource inflows, among other things. Oi (1999) similarly argues that Beijing's tight political grip over the localities fortified by its monopoly control of economic resources under Mao has given way to growing local circumvention of and "fake compliance" with central policies since 1978, despite the retention of personnel authority at the provincial level in the hands of the national leadership. For yet still others (for example, Zhao 1990), the capacity of the Chinese political center to enforce its economic policies in the localities has turned outright "feeble" during the post-Mao era, for all the façade of a "strong one-party regime" under the CCP.[17]

Missing in these accounts largely fixated on the national level can be the possible subnational-level variation in the ability of the center to secure policy compliance from the different provincial governments in post-1978 China. Such variation has been documented by several students of China's central-provincial relations during the era of economic reform.[18] For example, Huang (1996) notes that the different provincial governments tended to behave differently in response to the same policy directives from the central government regarding the growth of local public investment. Meanwhile, Chung (2000) examines the patterns of provincial implementation of agricultural decollectivization. In a similar vein, Whiting (2001, Chapter 5) has reported variation in the efforts by the provincial governments of Jiangsu, Shanghai, and Zhejiang to fulfill their fiscal contracts with the center during the 1980s and early 1990s.

At the provincial level, this suggests that the degree of central political control exercised by the Chinese political center and its related ability to seek policy compliance from below can vary for the different provincial

---

[17] These views, of course, contrast sharply with the argument, also mostly focusing on the national level, that the post-1978 political strength of the center has remained resilient, despite economic reform, decentralization, and opening (for example, Huang 1995b; Kim 2002; Naughton and Yang 2004b; Sheng 2005a; Solinger 1996).

[18] Even for the pre-reform era, Goodman (1986) has found that the provincial governments implemented at different paces the agricultural collectivization called for by Mao in the 1950s.

governments as well as across different years. Other things being equal, a Chinese provincial government from which the center boasts a greater ability to secure policy compliance is under a tighter degree of central political control. As already discussed, however, the national leaders wield personnel monopoly authority over *all* provincial governments *throughout* the post-1978 period. Presumably, such personnel powers enable the Chinese political center to exercise tight political control over *all* provincial governments. How can the center exercise regionally differential political control? In other words, how can we account for possible variation in the degree of political control exerted by the national leadership over the different provincial governments within a single-party state and variation in its ability to solicit policy compliance at the provincial level?

A number of scholars have alluded to the importance of the type of provincial government leadership in place in explaining varying provincial compliance with central government policy directives. For example, Lieberthal and Oksenberg (1988, 350) have pinpointed the crucial role of the "characteristics" of top provincial officials actually put in charge of implementing central policies. However, they do not elaborate on or further explore exactly what sorts of provincial leadership traits matter most for our understanding of provincial-level variation in the degree of central political control. For Huang (1996), the various bureaucratic traits – among others, the career trajectories – of the leading provincial officials (more next) best explain variation in provincial compliance with central policy injunctions against excessive public investment growth conducive to economic overheating.

Similarly, Chung (2000, 9–11) conjectures that a critical predictor of provincial implementation of agricultural decollectivization during the post-1978 period could be the "leadership characteristics" in the provinces involved. Conceding that it would be "difficult, if not impossible" to operationalize them in a "systematic and rigorous" fashion, however, he does not spell out in detail the types of characteristics of the provincial leaders that might be especially relevant here. Indeed, such a "leadership traits" variable is absent from the quantitative analysis section of his study (Chung 2000, Chapter 3). Only Huang (1996) has systematically studied the characteristics of the provincial leaders to explain possible provincial-level variation. Nevertheless, much of the existing research has suggested that the type of provincial party secretaries – the top leaders at the provincial level – might be a key determinant of outcome in central efforts to secure policy compliance from the provincial governments.

4.3.2 Role of Provincial Party Secretaries

As the *yibashou* at the provincial level, provincial party secretaries are often seen as "political middlemen" occupying a pivotal position under potentially conflicting demands (Goodman 1984, 1986). On the one hand, provincial party secretaries are all appointed by the center to help implement the policy preferences of the latter as well as to formulate provincial policies in their own jurisdictions (Shirk 1993, Chapter 3). These "central agents" are thus expected to serve as the conduits through which the center's policy preferences can be reflected in the actual policies pursued in the localities. On the other hand, provincial party secretaries and the provincial governments they lead might also have to champion the narrower interests of the jurisdictions they preside over before their national superiors.

Sympathy on the part of provincial party secretaries for the parochial interests of the localities that they rule on behalf of the center is understandable. Even though these officials owe their top provincial job to the center, some measure of local support coming from their identification with or advocacy of provincial interests might help them better perform the primary task they are assigned by the center – implementing the various central policies in the jurisdictions that they oversee (Goodman 1984, 72). As noted, fiscal dependence on industries located within their jurisdictions has grown for local governments at all levels that are now shouldered with vastly increased spending responsibilities (Tao and Yang 2008; Wong 1991). Not surprisingly, local governments in China have often enjoyed "symbiotic" ties with the local industries in this period, as discussed in Chapter 3. Overzealous pursuit of purely central policy goals – for instance, regarding revenue extraction from the provinces – in contrast, might hinder their own ability to govern the provinces. After all, heftier fiscal extraction on behalf of Beijing could alienate the local industries and hurt their incentives to comply with government revenue collection in the future. More revenue contributions to the center by the provincial governments also reduce the fiscal resources available to themselves.

Thus, during the post-1978 period, provincial governments in China often seek to "represent" and help advance the interests of the provinces at national-level policy forums, such as the economic work conferences convened by China's national leaders and attended by provincial officials (Lieberthal and Oksenberg 1988, 344–347). They also try to advocate the policy preferences of the provinces before the relevant central government ministries regarding the establishment of foreign economic development zones (Zweig 2002) or the retention of provincial revenues (Fewsmith 1997, 517; Yang 1994, 86; Zhao Yining 2003). They are indeed tempted to pursue the narrower provincial interests in a range of other policy areas, often contrary to the policy preferences of the national leadership. Tax evasion by the provincial governments can aggravate revenue slippage and undermine the fiscal capacity of the central government (Oi 1999; Wang 1995, 1997; Wong et al. 1995; World Bank 1990). Excessive growth in public investment can contribute to inflationary pressures and endanger national macroeconomic stability (Huang 1996). Erection of trade barriers against other provinces can worsen local economic protectionism and fragment a fledgling domestic market (Wedeman 2003).

Because they are closer to the ground where the central government policies are carried out, the provincial party secretaries know better about how these policies are actually implemented within their jurisdictions than the national leaders based in the distant capital. In fact, the center often has to rely on these agents for exactly such information (Lieberthal and Oksenberg 1988, 345). The provincial party secretaries thus might misrepresent or hide local reality from their national superiors in order to cater to divergent local preferences. Such problems of "preference divergence" under "information asymmetry" favoring the agents engender possible agency costs (Alchian and Demsetz 1972; Jensen and Meckling 1976) for the national principals – the political center in China – when they delegate the task of running the provinces to these officials.

Nevertheless, some provincial party secretaries might be loyal central agents who tend to comply faithfully with the center's policy preferences; others are perhaps more likely to be swayed by the parochial interests of the provinces they rule (Chung 2000; Huang 1996). More important, because the center monopolizes the personnel powers to appoint all provincial party secretaries, the types of incumbent provincial party secretaries that we observe are *endogenous*, subject to the deliberate choice by the national leadership. The selection of provincial officials with certain traits to lead the provincial governments reflects the actual exercise of central political control. In order to lower its agency costs and ensure greater policy compliance, the center can attempt to install in the top provincial post officials with the more "desirable" characteristics, officials in whom it has more confidence a priori.

Indeed, appointing agents of the right types is often a most straightforward strategy for the principal (Shepsle and Bonchek 1997, 366). Along such lines of reasoning, Huang (1996, 185) argues that one key tactic employed by the political center in reform-era China to ensure policy compliance by the provincial governments is to engage in such *"ex ante* monitoring." "[I]nstead of monitoring the specific tasks that local officials perform," the center "carefully monitors political and professional cre- dentials" of the candidates for those officials in making personnel deci- sions. Choosing the "right" officials by the national leaders in the first place can reduce the costs of monitoring and ensure greater policy com- pliance by the provincial governments later on.

For our purposes, a tighter degree of political control is exercised when the center enjoys a greater ability to secure provincial compliance. Across different years, the overall degree of political control exercised by the center should be greater when more of the provincial governments are ruled by party secretaries who are loyal agents of the center and are more compliant with the latter's policy preferences, all else being equal. Likewise, provincial governments led by provincial party secretaries who are conscientious agents of the center and less likely to pursue local inter- ests divergent from those of the national leadership should be under more stringent central political control. The degree of central political control exercised over the provincial governments thus depends on the type of provincial party secretaries at the provincial helm, across the different provincial units as well as over the different years.

Post-Mao China has witnessed the appointment of younger and better-educated provincial party secretaries in pursuit of the "four mod- ernizations" of the cadre corps – recruiting cadres who are "revolution- ary" (*geming hua*), "young" (*nianqing hua*), "knowledgeable" (*zhishi hua*), and "professionally competent" (*zhuanye hua*) (Zhonggong Zhongyang Zuzhibu [Department of Organization of the CCP Central Committee] 1986[1983]-b). In the aftermath of the Cultural Revolution, many of the rehabilitated veteran cadres who had joined the revolution decades earlier were already quite advanced in age. Furthermore, most of them had little formal education. For example, in 1978, the average age of the twenty- nine provincial first party secretaries was about 63; several of them were already in their 70s. Only two had a formal college education or its equiv- alent. By 1986, however, their average age dropped to about 58 years and nearly 45 percent were college-educated. In 2005, the average age of the provincial party secretaries was around 59 years old and almost every provincial party secretary had at least a college degree.[19]

---

[19] Data on provincial party secretaries cited here are described in the Appendix to Chapter 4. College education is defined as graduation from a vocational college (*da zhuan*), university (*da xue*), or graduate school program, including degrees offered by the Party School of the CCP, at the central or provincial level.

The changing demographic traits, such as the age and educational level, of the provincial cadre corps are certainly important. However, younger and better-educated provincial party secretaries by themselves reveal little about whether these officials are more likely to comply with central policy preferences regarding, for instance, central-provincial revenue division or provincial revenue remittance to the center. Thus, other indicators are more appropriate to help us tap the general policy inclinations of the provincial party secretaries and gauge the extent of central political control exercised over the provincial governments that these officials lead.

4.4   MEASURING CENTRAL POLITICAL CONTROL

4.4.1 New Appointments

The first indicator I examine is the incidence of provincial party secretaries who are newly appointed to their current post. A new appointment of a provincial party secretary by the center can take place via the following ways. It can be a "lateral" move without change in an official's bureaucratic rank, essentially "rotating" an official from a top party post in one province to a similar post in another province.[20] For instance, after serving as the provincial party secretary of Guizhou province for about three and a half years, Hu Jintao (CCP general secretary since late 2002) was reassigned, laterally, to work as the party chief of Tibet in 1988. Lateral transfers can also be between the center and the provinces when officials who worked at the national level, such as in the central ministries, were sent, in a horizontal move, to serve at the provincial level. For example, Yu Zhengsheng, party secretary of Shanghai since late 2007, was minister of construction in the central government before he became party secretary of Hubei province in 2001.

A new appointment can also be a "promotion" whereby a sitting governor is appointed as the party secretary of the same province, or is assigned to become the party chief of another province (recall that a party secretary ranks higher than a governor in the provincial power hierarchy). For example, Li Changchun once had worked as the governor of Henan province before he became its party secretary in 1992. Meanwhile, Yue Qifeng

---

[20] Indeed, the regular rotation of leading cadres in the localities has been emphasized as an important feature of the center's personnel policies (Zhonggong Zhongyang Zuzhibu [Department of Organization of the CCP Central Committee] 1999 [1994]; Zhonggong Zhongyang [Central Committee of the Chinese Communist Party] 2002).

moved to become party secretary of Heilongjiang in 1994 after serving as the governor of Liaoning province for nearly four years.

With each new appointment comes a new top provincial leader. It often takes time for newcomers to build close local ties, identify with local interests, succumb to local pressures, or otherwise become more locally entrenched and recalcitrant toward central policy directives perceived to be detrimental to local interests. All else being equal, we expect newly installed provincial party secretaries to be less inclined to pursue local policies that run counter to the preferences of the political center (Huang 1996). Provincial governments overseen by newly appointed provincial party secretaries who are more compliant with central policy preferences, in other words, tend to be subject to a greater degree of central political control.

For any given year, if the party center makes more changes in the top provincial party posts through new appointments in more of the provinces, on the national aggregate level, we expect the Chinese national leaders to exercise a greater degree of political control, on the whole, over the provincial governments in that year than they do in other years. If more replacements in the top provincial party posts have been made for one specific provincial government during a certain period, we similarly expect the national leaders to exert tighter political control over that specific provincial government that has witnessed more leadership changes than it does over other provincial governments during the same period.[21]

---

[21] In this study, I do not include a measure of official tenure length for two main reasons. First, it is not straightforward how we should conceptualize and measure tenure length in a panel dataset with province/year as the basic unit of observation. Should it be merely the total length of time for an official serving in a particular top provincial post or the cumulative tenure length for the official in that post by the time he is observed in a snapshot? For instance, Official A could enjoy a total tenure length of six years as party secretary of Province B, but in any year in our dataset the length could vary, depending on which year we select. Second, there are possible problems of left and right censoring for officials serving at the beginning or end of the period under study if we are focusing on the full tenure length of the officials. For example, if we focus on the post-1978 period, it is not immediately clear how we should account for those years before 1978 served by those officials still in office in 1978. Likewise, if we stop in 2005, it will make it impossible to determine their total tenure length in their provincial post because many incumbent officials were still serving in that year. See Sheng (2005b, 111–114) for discussions of the different ways of measuring tenure length of Chinese provincial officials in this period. Still, given that newly appointed officials tend to have shorter tenure lengths, a variable on new appointments should already capture some of the same underlying dynamics gauged by a tenure-length variable. Indeed, in my annual provincial-level panel dataset covering the period of 1978–2005, a lagged dummy variable on new appointments for provincial party secretaries is negatively correlated at about -0.47 (p = 0.000) with a variable on the cumulative tenure length for these officials.

4.4.2 Native Sons

The second indicator is the presence of native sons. A native son is a provincial party secretary who serves in his native province. In fact, most provincial party secretaries during this period were male. Wan Shaofeng, provincial party secretary of Jiangxi between June 1985 and April 1988, was the only female out of about 186 provincial party secretaries in China during this period. For simplicity, I thus assume the masculine gender for all the Chinese provincial party secretaries. In the official biographies of the provincial party secretaries, a common entry usually begins with the person's name, year of birth (and death if applicable), and native province (" – *ren*," literally "people hailing from – "). By Chinese convention, this often refers to the place where a person's father was born, not necessarily the place where the person was born or raised. For most people, the two will coincide, but this is not always the case.

For instance, although Hu Jintao is believed to have been born in Shanghai (Ewing 2003, 18), his official biography still identifies him as a native of Anhui where, presumably, his father was born. Li Peng, China's premier from late 1987 to early 1998, was also born in Shanghai, but he is officially "from Sichuan."[22] The assumption here is that one might be more likely to strike localistic ties that are pernicious to the center's interests if the official happens to have a network of familial connections, even if he was not necessarily born in that locality. This is a time-honored tradition in the Chinese officialdom going far back in history. The practice of posting officials outside their native provinces in China can be traced to the imperial era when the emperors feared that serving near one's home could breed local favoritism, spawn interests counter to those of the royal court, and pose threats to central imperial rule (Wei Xiumei 1992).

Although similar concerns have surfaced in the official personnel policies for lower-level officials, the party center has not explicitly stressed the importance of this "rule of avoidance" for provincial officials.[23] It can be an empirical question, however, as to whether the center has actually

---

[22] The official biography of Hu can be found at http://news.xinhuanet.com/ziliao/2002–01/16/content_240483.htm, while that for Li can be found at http://news.xinhuanet.com/ziliao/2002–01/15/content_238495.htm. Both were accessed on August 16, 2008. In these cases, I still use the native province information from the official biographies for coding "native sons" here.

[23] Recent documents of the Central Committee require that county-/city-level officials not serve in the places where they grew up (*chengzhangdi*). This seems to be a sensible requirement, although oftentimes no clear definitions are provided (Zhonggong Zhongyang [Central Committee of the Chinese Communist Party] 2002).

sought to apply this in practice. If native sons are indeed more susceptible to local sway, then a greater degree of central political control on the national aggregate level is exercised in those years when native-son provincial party secretaries were leading fewer provincial governments than in other years. Likewise, across different provinces, a provincial government less likely to be ruled by a native son during a period is, on average, under tighter political control by the national leaders than are other provincial governments, all else being equal.

4.4.3 Bureaucratic Integration

The third indicator draws on the notion of the "bureaucratic integration" of the provincial cadres. The measure was first developed by Huang (1996) in his pioneering work that systematically tests the macroeconomic consequences of the selective exercise of central political control at the provincial level during the reform era. The indicator seeks to gauge how "close" a provincial official is to the policy positions of the center by virtue of his career trajectory. In the order of declining tendency of the provincial officials to comply with central policy directives and of diminishing strength of political control exercised by the center over the provincial governments that the officials oversee, there are four types of provincial party secretaries.

The most "bureaucratically integrated" provincial party secretary is a "concurrent centralist" simultaneously holding a top job in a province and occupying a key position at the center – as a member of the Politburo of the CCP Central Committee. There are two ways the center can appoint a concurrent centralist to lead a provincial government. He can be directly dispatched to work in the province by the center as a sitting member of the Politburo who might be working in another province or at the national level before the new provincial appointment. Alternatively, he can be promoted to Politburo membership by the center through its control of the national apparatus of the CCP, when he is already the incumbent party chief of a province. It is thus possible for a sitting provincial party secretary of other types to join the Politburo and become a concurrent centralist in the same province.

In either case, the monopoly personnel powers wielded by the center over the top provincial posts remain the key because even incumbent provincial officials who are promoted to Politburo membership can only retain their top provincial party post for as long as is desired by the national leaders. Take the example of Li Changchun. When in

October 1997 Li was promoted to be a Politburo member and became a concurrent centralist, he had already been working as the party chief of Henan. When in February 1998 he was transferred to Guangdong, he began his tenure in Guangdong as a concurrent centralist. Among all cases of provincial governments ruled by concurrent centralists during the 1978–2005 period in our dataset, the vast majority – over 80 percent – are officials first promoted to Politburo membership from the provinces where they had already been serving as provincial party secretaries. The remainder were transferred to their current top provincial post after they had become Politburo members elsewhere (Sheng 2009a).

In essence national and provincial policymakers at the same time, these cross-posted provincial officials might "calculate that their long-term career prospects lie with the center rather than with the provinces they are assigned to govern" (Huang 1996, 197). They are expected to internalize the center's more "encompassing" interests in maintaining its national rule and have the largest stake in the success of central government policies. Such sympathy with the policy stance of the center is crucial for carrying out its policy objectives such as revenue extraction from the localities, as it might reduce considerably the "transaction costs" for the national leaders (Levi 1988).

Compared with other provincial officials appointed from above, concurrent centralists can also be better monitored by the national leaders. Their smaller size (see the following) and the more frequent Politburo meetings might help remedy the "information asymmetry" problem for the national leaders in a principal-agent relationship with the provincial officials (Huang 2002). For the national leadership, having provincial party secretaries around in the Politburo can mitigate the "noise" and other problems of ensuring accurate information flows confronting the principal (Wedeman 2001). In short, provincial party secretaries sitting in the Politburo should be more compliant with the policy preferences of the political center because they have more incentives to help maintain their own national-level rule or find it harder to shirk in performing the tasks assigned by their national superiors.

Such predisposition to compliance with the center can also be further reinforced through the more ample political rewards at the center later on for Politburo members working in the provinces. Indeed, immediately after completing their provincial stints, provincial party secretaries who were concurrent centralists seemed much more likely to move on to

TABLE 4.1. *Promotions to Central Positions for the Provincial Party Secretaries, 1978–2005*

	Concurrent Centralists	Centralists	Outsiders	Localists
a. Total	29	51	72	34
b. With completed provincial stints	23	43	57	32
c. Substantive promotions to the center	13	9	5	0
c/b (%)	(56.52)	(20.93)	(8.77)	(0)
d. Ceremonial promotions to the center	6	1	1	0
d/b (%)	(26.09)	(2.33)	(1.75)	(0)

Note: Information on the promotion patterns of the officials is based on the next immediate post for the 186 provincial party secretaries in China during the period of 1978–2005 after they completed their tenure in the provinces (some still had not completed their terms at the end of 2005). A substantive promotion takes place when a provincial party secretary is promoted to a higher-ranking post in the central government or national party apparatus with substantive authority. For example, he can become a member of the CCP Politburo Standing Committee, a vice premier, state councilor, a secretary of the CCP Central Secretariat (*zhongyang shujichu*), head or deputy head of the CCP Central Commission for Discipline Inspection (*zhongyang jilu jiancha weiyuanhui*), or chief or deputy chief of the CCP Central Politics and Law Committee (*zhongyang zhengfawei*). A ceremonial promotion occurs when prior to formal retirement, a provincial party secretary is promoted to a nominally higher-ranking position at the national level, such as a vice-chairman of the National People's Congress or a vice-president of the Chinese People's Political Consultative Conference. Information regarding the bureaucratic integration of the party secretaries refers to the year immediately before they completed their provincial stints. The numbers in parentheses refer to the percentage of provincial party secretaries in each of the four categories who already completed their tenure in the provinces.
Source: Appendix to Chapter 4.

higher-ranking positions of greater responsibilities at the national level in the central government or national party apparatus than other types of officials (see the following). As seen from Table 4.1, during the period of 1978–2005, a majority (nearly 57 percent) of the concurrent centralists who had already completed their tenure in the provinces went on to become members of the Politburo Standing Committee, vice premiers, or state councilors.

Compared with other provincial party secretaries, moreover, the concurrent centralists were also much more likely to take up higher-ranking ceremonial positions in the national capital. After departing from their top provincial job, more than a quarter of the concurrent centralists landed national-level honorary posts such as a vice-chairmanship (*fu weiyuanzhang*) of the National People's Congress or a vice-presidency (*fu zhuxi*) of the Chinese People's Political Consultative Conference that nominally rank higher than the office of the provincial party secretary but often impart much less substantive authority. In contrast, only very rarely were other types of provincial party secretaries ever "honorably discharged" into such national-level sinecures in Beijing after exiting their top provincial post.[24]

Cross-posting provincial officials into the highest decision-making body of the single ruling party can be costly and carry its own risks, but does not necessarily compromise the predominance of the political center. To be sure, access to a top national policymaking forum such as the Politburo might provide more potential opportunities for provincial party secretaries to advocate parochial regional interests at the national level. Yet such a scenario is less likely if national leaders prevail in the Politburo, as is the case in China. Above all, national leaders heading the central government and the single ruling party enjoy political supremacy and are always responsible for the most important national policymaking, as noted previously.

Moreover, national leaders have always constituted the overwhelming numerical share the Politburo of the CCP Central Committee and monopolized membership in its supreme Standing Committee (Sheng 2005a). On average, only around 14.2 percent of the Politburo members were incumbent provincial officials in any year during the 1978–2005 period, the highest being 23.5 percent in 1988. Indeed, use of such cross-posting has only been very sparing and selective in China. Incumbent provincial party secretaries from only a selected few provinces have ever been made concurrent centralists with Politburo membership

---

[24] These other officials could still retire into such ceremonial positions at the national level as the chair (*zhuren*) or vice-chair (*fu zhuren*) of the various standing committees of the National People's Congress or the Chinese People's Political Consultative Conference. However, even nominally, these are *lateral* moves, not *promotions* because these ceremonial positions do not rank higher than the office of provincial party secretary. Altogether 18 centralists (about 42 percent of 43 in total with completed provincial terms), 16 (14 percent of 57) outsiders, and 8 (25 percent of 32) localists, but none of the concurrent centralists were transferred laterally to such ceremonial positions at the center during the 1978–2005 period. Regarding the issues of substantive and ceremonial promotions of provincial party secretaries, I have greatly benefited from conversations with Zhiyue Bo and You Ji.

(Sheng 2009a).[25] Not surprisingly, on the rare occasions when provincially based Politburo members did become unruly, their prompt removal from all offices of power (often even their ruling party membership) indicates that the national leaders were ready and able to tame these potential challenges. This was the case with Chen Xitong, party secretary of Beijing, who was sacked in 1995, and Chen Liangyu, party chief of Shanghai, who was expelled from all his official positions in 2006.[26]

Next come the "centralists" who are provincial party secretaries assigned to work in the provinces after significant earlier experiences at the political center.[27] For instance, before he became party secretary of Hubei in 2001, Yu Zhengsheng was minister of construction in the central government for nearly four years, as noted. For our purposes, he was a centralist during his stint in Hubei.[28] One important factor here could be his earlier professional socialization experiences in the national capital. Although less "bureaucratically integrated" than the concurrent centralists, these "centralists" are, in general, not easily swayed by local interests in conflict with those of the center. This is most probably because of the pro-center policy outlooks

[25] Too many provincial officials in the Politburo could certainly challenge the numerical and ultimately political preponderance of the national leaders within the decision-making body. The power and prestige of Politburo membership that elevates its members working in the provinces into the national leadership core and helps make them feel and act more like national leaders also dictates that Politburo membership be small and exclusive. This is probably why cross-posting of provincial party secretaries has not been used more extensively by the center, even though provincial officials who are Politburo members could be most compliant with the political center.

[26] While the official pretext for their downfall was corruption, the purported challenge to the center from both Chens was not necessarily motivated by the desire to defend the interests of the localities they oversaw. Chen Xitong might have been seen as too "disrespectful" by the then-newly installed CCP chief Jiang Zemin (Lam 1999, 31–32; Li 2001, 156–157). A member of the so-called "Shanghai gang" (Li 2002), Chen Liangyu was a protégé of Jiang Zemin when Jiang worked in Shanghai first as its mayor and later as party chief in the mid- to late 1980s. He might have been entangled in an unresolved succession contest between his patron and the new CCP chief Hu Jintao when Chen reportedly tried to buck the macroeconomic policies of Premier Wen Jiabao (Fong 2004). However, his later fall from grace indicates that even Jiang sided with the national leadership of which Jiang was a member. Because of the rare incidence of such cases (only two in the 1978–2005 period) and the effective taming by the center of the possible menaces they posed, the two Chens are treated here as exceptions.

[27] "Significant" here is defined by Huang (1996) as being "at least three years." To avoid possible inconsistencies, I have strictly followed his "three-year" cutoff in defining "significant" work experiences. I give a score of "3" to all secretaries who spent at least three years working at the central ministerial level before their provincial stints.

[28] After he joined the Politburo at the Seventeenth Party Congress in October 2007 (outside the scope of the present study), Yu would be considered a concurrent centralist during his tenure in Shanghai.

they had imbibed while working earlier at the national level in the central government or national party standing organs.

In short, centralist provincial party secretaries tend to harbor sympathy with the center's policy preferences due to their prior professional socialization. More opportunities of upward mobility for the centralists awarded by the national leadership, though to a lesser degree than the concurrent centralists, could also help sustain such a general penchant for compliance among the centralists. After all, many centralists – over one-fifth of those who already completed their provincial stints during the period under study, as shown in Table 4.1 – later ended up working in the national capital in a higher-ranking post of substantive authority in the central government or the national party apparatus. Although lower than that of the concurrent centralists, this is a much higher percentage than that of the remaining two types of provincial party secretaries.

In contrast to the centralists boasting career backgrounds at the national level, an "outsider" usually spent significant periods of his earlier professional life in comparable positions in other provinces before moving into his current provincial leadership position. Due to his longer work experiences in the provinces, an outsider would in general be more sympathetic to a pro-province policy stance than either a concurrent centralist or a centralist. Not surprisingly, an outsider is often not very likely to be rewarded politically by the center through promotion to higher-ranking offices, substantive or ceremonial, at the national level, compared with the concurrent centralists or the centralists. Altogether, only fewer than 11 percent of them ever moved up to higher offices (substantive or ceremonial) in the national capital immediately after completing their tenure as provincial party secretaries, as seen in Table 4.1.

Finally, the least "bureaucratically integrated" provincial party secretary is a "localist" who worked his way up the bureaucratic ladder in the very province that he now leads as its party chief. A localist often has the most extended career experience, and indeed his very power base, is in the province. As Willerton and Reisinger (1991, 348) put it in the context of the former Soviet Union, an official who has made his career in a locality "will most likely have a strong psychological and political attachment to it." In post-1978 China, the policy assertiveness of Guangdong vis-à-vis the center in the 1980s is often attributed to the dominance of leading provincial officials with localistic career backgrounds at the time (Cheung 1994). Thus, a localist party secretary should be the most likely to succumb to the entrenched local interests whenever there are conflicts with the center such as over divisions of fiscal resources, other things being equal. In other words, a localist is even more "localistic" in policy outlook than an outsider, although both types of cadres are more likely to adopt a pro-province perspective than is either a centralist or a concurrent centralist. Indeed, localists are also the least likely to be rewarded with a higher-ranking post at the national level. In fact, throughout the entire 1978–2005 period, none of the localists was ever so promoted immediately after completing his provincial stint.

In sum, among these four types, provincial party secretaries who are concurrent centralists, on average, should be the most compliant with central policy preferences, followed by provincial party secretaries who are centralists. Both of these two groups of officials are more likely to comply than are the outsiders or the localists. Localist party secretaries are the least compliant group. *Ceteris paribus*, the greatest degree of central political control is exercised over a provincial government led by a concurrent centralist, followed in order by one led by a centralist, an outsider, and a localist, respectively. Across different years, at the national aggregate level, we expect tighter central political control over all the provincial governments when the average degree of bureaucratic integration of all provincial party chiefs is higher. Similarly, across different provinces, a greater degree of central political control is exercised over a provincial government that, on average, is headed by the more "bureaucratically integrated" party secretaries.

4.4.4 National Trends and Regional Patterns

As discussed earlier, there have been rising conflicts between the center and the provincial governments, especially those in the winner provinces faring better in the international markets in the post-1978 era. Did the center resort to the exercise of tighter political control over all provincial governments in general and those along the coast in particular to remedy such conflicts? What were the temporal trends and regional patterns in the exercise of central political control over the provincial governments as measured by these indicators during this period?

In Figure 4.3, I present the cross-year trends of the overall degree of central political control exercised over the Chinese provincial governments from 1978 to 2005, as measured by our three main indicators discussed previously. I first examine the average annual share of the provincial governments witnessing new appointments to measure the incidence of newly appointed provincial party secretaries for each year. Again, on average, a higher share of new appointments in any single

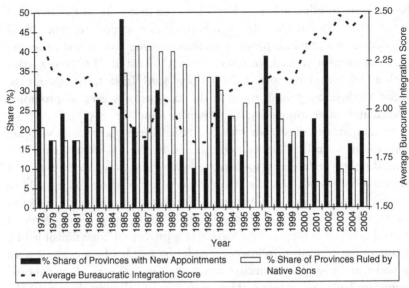

FIGURE 4.3. Trends in new appointments, presence of native sons, and bureaucratic integration among the provincial party secretaries, 1978–2005.
Source: Appendix to Chapter 4.

year when more provinces witnessed the change of their provincial party chiefs implies exercise of tighter political control by the center over the provincial governments.[29] As we can see, although new appointments took place every year, they also tended to occur in waves. In particular, spikes in new appointments of provincial party secretaries seemed mostly to have clustered around (immediately before or after) the convening of a CCP National Party Congress and the selection of a new term of the Central Committee every five years – in 1977, 1982, 1987, 1992, 1997, and 2002 (Sheng 2005a).

The exception was 1985 when the provincial party secretaries in nearly half (48.3 percent) of the provinces changed face due to the retirement of a large number of aged officials at the special national party conference held in September of that year (Pu Xingzu 1990, 464–465). New

---

[29] In a few rare cases – mostly in the early post-1978 years – more than one appointment was made to the top party post of a province in a single year. Even when this was the case, however, it is counted as one case of a province witnessing a new appointment in that year. I use share, rather than the absolute number, of appointments in order to take into account China's rising number of provinces during the years under study here, from twenty-nine in 1978 to thirty in 1988 and thirty-one in 1997.

appointments of provincial party secretaries also tended to take place around the convening of the more recent party congresses, for instance, in 1997 and 2002 with party secretaries in about 39 percent of the provinces replaced. In contrast, 31 percent were replaced in 1978, 28 percent in 1983, 30 percent in 1988, and 33 percent in 1993. This suggests that the degree of central political control might have become tighter of late. The clustering of the new appointments around the convening of national party congresses every five years also points to growing institutionalization of new party norms such as term limits and a mandatory retirement age for leading officials at all levels (Bo 2007; Manion 1993). For the most part, therefore, it is difficult to discern any clear trend in the overall degree of central political control over the provincial governments as measured by the incidence of new appointments of provincial party secretaries.

Such uncertainty in the data at the national aggregate level is also palpable in the provincial-level data assessing possible regional patterns, as in Table 4.2.[30] On average, changes in the top party leadership seemed more frequent in the coastal provinces during the 1979–91 period. However, the difference is not statistically significant at the conventional levels in a simple two-group mean comparison test. Likewise, even though for the 1992–2005 period the inland provinces seemed to be witnessing more changes in their party chiefs than their coastal counterpart, the difference between the two provincial cohorts again fails to achieve any statistical significance. In other words, throughout this period, the Chinese political center did not seem to have differentiated between the provincial governments along the coast and those inland for targeted political control through effecting more changes in their top leadership.

In contrast, the national trend in the degree of central political control measured by the prevalence of native sons as provincial party secretaries is more clear-cut, especially during more recent years. To be sure, the share of Chinese provinces ruled by party chiefs who were native sons rose slightly from around 20 percent in the late 1970s and early 1980s to about 41 percent in 1987 and 1988. This suggests the overall degree

---

[30] In Table 4.2, summary provincial data are divided into the 1978–1991 and 1992–2005 subperiods because 1992 is about the mid-point for the 1978–2005 period. These provincial-level political data are more recent (by one year) than the provincial-level economic data – only consistently available up to 2004 as noted in Chapter 3 – due to the need to lag (by one year) the economic independent variables in the empirical analysis of Chapter 5.

TABLE 4.2. Provincial Patterns in New Appointments, Presence of Native Sons, and Bureaucratic Integration Among the Provincial Party Secretaries, 1978–2005

Province	Appointments (%)		Native Sons (%)		Bureaucratic Integration	
	1978–91	1992–2005	1978–91**	1992–2005*	1978–91***	1992–2005***
Beijing	21.43	28.57	0	0	3.21	4
Fujian	14.29	21.43	71.43	42.86	2.29	1.93
Guangdong	28.57	14.29	42.86	42.86	1.86	3.79
Guangxi	14.29	7.14	0	0	1.64	2.43
Hainan	50	35.71	0	0	2	2.43
Hebei	21.43	28.57	64.29	7.14	2.86	2.43
Jiangsu	14.29	21.43	100	78.57	2.50	1.79
Liaoning	28.57	21.43	50	64.29	1.21	1.43
Shandong	21.43	21.43	50	35.71	1.71	2.79
Shanghai	42.86	14.29	0	0	3.14	3.79
Tianjin	28.57	14.29	14.29	0	2.64	2.36
Zhejiang	21.43	14.29	0	0	1.21	2
Anhui	35.71	21.43	50	50	1.86	1.50
Chongqing		44.44		0		3
Gansu	21.43	21.43	0	0	2.21	1.71
Guizhou	21.43	21.43	0	0	2.50	2.14
Heilongjiang	14.29	28.57	0	0	2.21	2.36
Henan	28.57	35.71	0	0	2.50	2.43
Hubei	21.43	14.29	7.14	0	1.43	2.36
Hunan	7.14	21.43	100	64.29	1	1.36
Inner Mongolia	21.43	14.29	0	0	2.07	2

Jiangxi	21.43	21.43	21.43	42.86	1.64	1.71
Jilin	21.43	14.29	0	0	2	1.21
Ningxia	21.43	14.29	0	0	2	2.29
Qinghai	21.43	28.57	0	0	1.57	1.50
Shaanxi	21.43	14.29	71.43	21.43	1.93	2
Shanxi	21.43	21.43	92.86	35.71	1.71	2.21
Sichuan	14.29	21.43	64.29	57.14	2.50	2.07
Tibet	21.43	28.57	0	0	2.50	2.07
Xinjiang	21.43	7.14	0	0	1.86	2.21
Yunnan	7.14	21.43	42.86	21.43	1.57	2.07
Coast	24.05	20.24	34.81	22.62	2.20	2.60
Inland	20.24	21.46	25	15.71	1.95	1.99

Note: The coastal provinces are in bold. Appointments refer to the share (in percentage) of years for the 1978–91 and 1992–2005 periods, respectively, in which a province witnessed new appointments of its provincial party secretary. Native sons refer to the share (in percentage) of years in each period in which a province was ruled by a provincial party secretary who was a native son. The data on the bureaucratic integration of provincial party secretaries refer to provincial average scores for each period. The coastal and inland average values reported at the bottom of the table and used in the mean comparison tests are the averages for all coastal and inland provinces in those periods, respectively. Since Hainan became a province in 1988, its data for the 1978–91 period cover only 1988–91. Chongqing's data for the 1992–2005 period cover 1997–2005, as Chongqing became a provincial unit in 1997.

***: $p < 0.01$ in two-group mean comparison tests for the coastal and inland provinces (two-tailed tests with unequal variances); **: $p < 0.05$; *: $p < 0.1$.

Source: Appendix to Chapter 4.

of central political control over the provincial governments might have weakened during these years. However, there was a reversal in the trend afterward. The share dropped to about 19 percent by 1999. In 2005, it was below 6.5 percent (two out of thirty-one provinces), as also shown in Figure 4.3. Meanwhile, the general reduction in the presence of native sons as provincial party secretaries in the later years is also mirrored in the provincial-level data for the two groups of provinces.

As we can see in the fourth and fifth columns of Table 4.2, the average share of years in which a province was ruled by a native son fell across the two periods for both the coastal and inland provinces. The average share for the coastal provinces was 34.8 percent during the 1978–91 period, but was down to about 22.6 percent during the 1992–2005 period. Similarly, the average share for the inland provinces dropped from 25 percent to about 15.7 percent. In fact, the inland provinces seemed less likely to be ruled by native sons than were their coastal counterparts (the simple two-group mean comparison test is significant at 0.05 for the 1978–91 period and at 0.1 for the 1992–2005 period). The center may have sought to exert tighter political control over the provincial governments in general by reducing the presence of native sons in the top provincial post over the years. However, there is little evidence that such exercise of central political control was targeted specifically toward the subnational governments of the coastal winner provinces in the global markets.[31]

Finally, following Huang (1996), I assign a score of 1, 2, 3, and 4 to provinces ruled by party secretaries who were localists, outsiders, centralists, and concurrent centralists during a certain year, respectively. A higher score indicates the exercise of tighter central political control. I first examine the annual national average of the bureaucratic integration score during the 1978–2005 period. The trend is broadly consistent with that for

---

[31] In fact, the center seemed to have mostly resorted to installing non-native sons as provincial party secretaries in the five provinces designated as autonomous regions for ethnic minorities. Four of these five provinces are in the inland, and none of them was ever ruled by a native-son party chief during this period. If we exclude these five provinces, the difference between the inland and the coast no longer attains statistical significance at the conventional levels in the two-group mean comparison test. In contrast, the results in Table 4.2 from the mean comparison tests for appointments of new provincial party secretaries (discussed earlier) and the bureaucratic integration of provincial party secretaries (see the following) will not change much if the minority regions are removed from the analysis. Nevertheless, to tackle the possibility that the center might find it harder to inject non-native-son party chiefs into provinces faring better in the global markets, I show systematic evidence in the Appendix to Chapter 5 that a greater degree of exposure to the global markets did not increase the chance of a province being ruled by a native son.

the native sons, as we can see in Figure 4.3. Central political control over the provincial governments was quite tight at the beginning of the period, especially in the late 1970s. The average bureaucratic integration score for provincial party secretaries was nearly 2.38 in 1978. This perhaps was due to the need to ensure political stability in the provinces in the early years after the end of the Cultural Revolution. The degree of central political control seemed to have gradually loosened up afterward before it began to tighten again in the latter half of the 1980s. Despite a temporary drop during the 1989–92 period for which the average score was only 1.89, an upward trend largely persisted thereafter. By 2003, the national average reached 2.48, even surpassing the previous high in 1978.

Exercise of overall tighter central political control since the early 1990s depicted in the national trend is also echoed in the rising average bureaucratic integration score of the provincial party secretaries for both the coastal and inland provinces across the two periods. Moreover, as we can see in the last two columns of Table 4.2, the average bureaucratic integration score was higher for the coastal provinces in both periods than for their inland counterparts, implying tighter central political control exercised over the provincial governments along the coast all along by this measure. The inland-coastal difference in simple two-group mean comparison tests is highly significant (at 0.01) for both periods.

Most important, the average score for the provincial party secretaries in the coastal provinces also witnessed a much sharper increase in the latter period. The coastal average rose from about 2.2 during 1978–91 to about 2.6 during 1992–2005. This implies that mostly outsiders ruled the coastal provinces in the earlier period, but on average these provinces were nearly ruled by centralists in the latter years. The inland average, in contrast, only increased slightly to about 1.99 in the latter years, from 1.95 earlier. In other words, for the most part, an outsider ruled the average inland province throughout the years under study. This suggests tighter central political control through appointing the more "bureaucratically integrated" provincial party secretaries to rule the provinces since the early 1990s, as reflected in the upward trend in Figure 4.3, was targeted mostly toward the provincial governments along the coast.

It is hardly surprising that party secretaries ruling some provincial units such as Beijing and Shanghai, the country's political capital and leading economic powerhouse respectively, always had a high bureaucratic integration score. Even during the earlier period of 1978–91, on average, the party secretaries in both Beijing and Shanghai were likely to be at least centralists. During the latter period of 1992–2005, their party chiefs were almost uniformly concurrent centralists (that is, party secretaries with sitting Politburo membership). More striking, of course, is the case of Guangdong, the standard-bearer of the country's post-1978 opening agenda. As was the case for most provinces, on average, an outsider ruled Guangdong during the 1978–91 period. During the latter period of 1992–2005, however, a concurrent centralist nearly always ruled Guangdong. Given its rise to become the country's most globalized province during this period, this is consistent with the notion that tighter central political control was targeted toward the provincial governments in the winner subnational regions in the global markets.

Thus, our aggregate data do not provide clear-cut cross-year trends regarding the incidence of new appointments for provincial party secretaries. However, the degree of political control exercised by the center seemed to have been on the rise in more recent years after an initial decline in earlier years if measured by the presence of native sons among provincial party chiefs and by the national average of the bureaucratic integration score of the provincial party secretaries. Moreover, the average data for the coastal and inland provinces provide prima facie evidence that throughout this post-Mao era the center exerted greater political control over the provincial governments along the coast by dispatching there the more "bureaucratically integrated" provincial party secretaries. By this measure, increasingly tighter central political control seemed to have been especially targeted toward the coastal provincial governments since the early 1990s. Regionally selective exercise of political control over the provincial governments, however, did not appear to have been sought through frequent replacements of their incumbent provincial party secretaries or via cutback in the presence of native sons as their provincial party chiefs.

4.5 CONCLUSION

One key factor helping the Chinese political center stave off the fissiparous tendencies unleashed by the opening to the global markets and hold the country together might be its resilient political strength. Party primacy and central political predominance under CCP single-party rule in China have imparted the political center the requisite institutional powers to exert political control over the provincial governments, not the least through its monopoly of the ruling-party nomenklatura authority over the top-echelon provincial cadres. Our preliminary evidence surveyed in this chapter shows no clear signs of the "withering" of the Chinese political center's overall ability to solicit policy compliance by the provincial governments through the exercise of political control since the commencement of reform and opening.

Indeed, in general, the center might have exercised a greater degree of political control over the provincial governments in more recent years. This has been manifested at the national aggregate level in the declining share of provinces ruled by native sons and the increasing average degree of bureaucratic integration of the provincial party secretaries, especially since the late 1980s and early 1990s. More important for our purposes, our first-cut evidence from provincial-level data reveals that throughout the post-1978 years – especially in the latter half of the period – the center seemed to have targeted provincial governments along the coast in particular for tighter political control by sending there reliable, pro-center agents predisposed to greater compliance with central policy preferences by their career trajectories.

This is hardly surprising. After all, compared with their inland counterparts, the coastal provinces seemed to have benefited more from exposure to the global markets, boasted more resources to spare, and grown more assertive in resisting central revenue demands amidst rising economic globalization and interprovincial disparity, as we have noted in Chapter 3. Tighter political control over their provincial governments could facilitate their compliance with the extractive demands from the center pursuing greater interregional fiscal transfers. Indicative as they are, findings from simple mean comparison analysis without accounting for the role of other possible factors than the geographic locations of the provinces can be crude and even potentially misleading. Is there systematic evidence that the Chinese political center actually exercised a greater degree of political control over the provincial governments in those regions thriving on foreign trade and exports during these years?

Although Huang (1996) has pioneered the rigorous, empirical research on the exercise of central political control in the reform era, his emphasis is on the consequences of such control at the provincial level for curbing local public investment urges and combating provincial inflationary pressures. Missing from this line of inquiry are efforts to explore the provincial-level determinants of such regionally differential exercise of political control by the Chinese national leadership via the ruling CCP. In other words, this body of scholarship does not shed much light on what provincial-level factors were more likely to provoke a greater dosage of political control from the center in the first place. For our purposes here, we know little about the role of the extent of provincial exposure to the global markets in affecting the degree of central political control over the provincial governments, a question I will take up next.

APPENDIX: CHINESE PROVINCIAL POLITICAL DATA

A4.1 Sources

For the names and their periods in office of the provincial party secretaries up to 1997, I have relied on He Husheng et al. (1993), Wang Jianying (1994), and Zhonggong Zhongyang Zuzhibu [Department of Organization of the CCP Central Committee] et al. (2000b). Information for the more recent years is available on the following official Web sites: http://www.xinhuanet.com, http://www.peopledaily.com.cn, and http://www.chinanews.com.cn.

Two of the most information-rich sources on China's provincial party secretaries are the volumes on members of the First through Sixteenth Central Committees of the Chinese Communist Party compiled by Shen Xueming and Zheng Jianying (2001), and Zhonggong Zhongyang Zuzhibu [Department of Organization of the CCP Central Committee] and Zhonggong Zhongyang Dangshi Yanjiushi [CCP Central Party History Research Office] (2004). They contain detailed biographical information on each individual, such as the year of birth, native province, education, and career trajectory. Some provincial party secretaries during the period were not Central Committee members, especially during but not limited to the early 1980s. For these officials, I have mostly relied on Liao Gailong et al. (1994) and Wang Zutang (1992). Very occasionally I have used Bartke (1997) for cross-checking whenever there are uncertainties or inconsistencies.

A4.2 Provincial Party Secretaries in the Dataset

Altogether, there were 186 distinct individuals serving as party secretaries in the Chinese provinces during the 1978–2005 period. For each province/year (for example, Beijing in 1988), the time-series cross-section dataset lists one unique provincial party secretary. As a rule, only officials who spent more than six months of the year in that province are listed for a given province/year. In calculating the number of months the person spent in the province in a year, December of the year is used as the end-point if the official's tenure did not end in that year; the actual month of his departure is used otherwise. The first month of that person's appointment in the province as the provincial party secretary is used as the starting point if the official started his top provincial job in that year; January is used as the starting month for the calculation otherwise. Thus, the cutoff point would be June of that year. For instance, Duan Junyi became party secretary of Beijing in January 1981 and left office in May 1984, when he was replaced by Li Ximing who served until December 1992. Thus, for Beijing/1981, Duan is listed as the party secretary. Because Duan's tenure in Beijing during 1984 was only five months when he left in May, his successor is listed for Beijing/1984. If an official started in June of a year, he or she is listed in that year as well. However, there are a few cases where additional rules are needed.

First, in certain cases, more than one change was made to the top provincial party office. For instance, Xie Xuegong was replaced by Lin Hujia as party secretary of Tianjin in June 1978. Lin served only until October of that year, when he left to become party secretary of Beijing and Chen Weida was appointed to succeed him in Tianjin. Under such circumstances, those who served the longest in the province for that year are listed. Since Xie Xuegong spent about six months of 1978 as Tianjin's party secretary, he is listed for Tianjin/1978, despite the fact that he left office in June of that year. Note that Xie's tenure in Tianjin during 1978 happened to be approximately six months (approaching our criterion in the previous paragraph), but this does not have to be the case. Even the longest-serving party secretary among several in a province during a certain year could have a tenure shorter than six months. The point is that I always list the person who served the longest among all the leaders who had spent some time as the provincial party secretary in a province in a year.

Party secretaries that are *not* listed under this rule are Lin Hujia (June 1978 to October 1978, Tianjin), Han Ningfu (August 1982 to January 1983, Hubei), Saifuddin (Seypidin Ezizi, October 1973 to January 1978, Xinjiang), Zhu Houze (March 1985 to July 1985, Guizhou), and Wang Renzhong (December 1978 to December 1978, Shaanxi). It is interesting to note that Wang Renzhong spent only two weeks as party secretary of Shaanxi in December of 1978. In addition, Wang Qishan (party secretary of Hainan from November 2002 to April 2003) is not listed in the dataset. His appointment in Hainan took place in November, too late to be included for 2002, but he left in April 2003, too early to be included in that year. A few officials who started as provincial party secretaries in the second half of 2005 are not included in the dataset either. They are Shi Zongyuan (starting in December 2005, Guizhou), Wang Yang (December

2005, Chongqing), Zhang Baoshun (July 2005, Shanxi), Zhang Chunxian (December 2005, Hunan), and Zhang Qingli (November 2005, Tibet).

Second, in a couple of cases gaps occurred between the time when one official left the post and the time when another appointment (acting or formal) was made to replace the outgoing official. Although Liu Fangren left the top party post in Guizhou in March 1985, for example, there was no successor until Hu Jintao formally assumed that post in October of that year. Here Hu is listed for Guizhou/1985 although his tenure in the province was shorter than six months in that year. Third, officials of Hainan province are listed from the date of its formal creation (September 1988 for the provincial party committee), even though a preparatory leadership was already in place in February of that year. Similarly, officials for Chongqing are listed since June 1997 when it became a centrally administered municipality. We thus have Hainan/1988 and Chongqing/1997 as two observations. Finally, there are rare cases when more than one individual occupied the same post at the same time. For instance, Zhao Haifeng, Ma Wanli, and Huang Jingbo were all party secretaries of Qinghai during the period from February 1983 to July 1985, without any clear indication as to whether any person was a first party secretary. In such cases, I list the first person.

A4.3 Issues of "Separately Listed Cities"

Between 1984 and 1990, fourteen cities – Chongqing, Wuhan, Shenyang, Dalian, Guangzhou, Harbin, Xi'an, Qingdao, Ningbo, Nanjing, Chengdu, Xiamen, Shenzhen, and Changchun – were granted the provincial-level status with respect to various economic policy issues (including the ability to conduct direct fiscal contracting with the center).[32] The status was phased out in 1994 for nine of the fourteen cities – except for Dalian, Qingdao, Ningbo, Xiamen, and Shenzhen. These nine cities were joined by Ji'nan and Hangzhou under the new category of deputy provincial cities, but Chongqing later attained its full provincial status in 1997 (Shi Yupeng and Zhou Li'an 2007). Therefore, China still has five "separately listed cities" and ten deputy provincial cities as of this writing in the summer of 2009.

---

[32] Literally, they are distinctly listed together with, rather than being submerged under, their host provinces in Chinese fiscal data sources. See, for instance, Zhongguo Caizheng Nianjian Bianji Weiyuanhui [Editorial Committee of the *Finance Yearbook of China*] (2006).

Even though all fourteen "separately listed cities" had direct fiscal ties with (as well as faced direct fiscal extraction by) the center before 1994, the provinces still held primary appointment responsibilities for the top leaders of these cities for most of this period under the one-level downward personnel management system. Since late 1998, however, the leading cadres of the five remaining "separately listed cities" and the ten deputy provincial cities have been placed under the direct management by the center (Chan 2004, 713, 726). Of course, only the five "separately listed cities," together with all the provinces, still maintain direct fiscal ties with the center.

Given the direct personnel powers held by the center over their leading officials and their direct fiscal relations with the center, it makes sense to treat these five "separately listed cities" as distinct provincial-level units during the post-1998 years.[33] In the main text of the book, however, I have refrained from doing so for two main reasons. First, partly due to their lower bureaucratic rank, the categories of bureaucratic integration according to Huang (1996) do not fully apply to the top cadres of these "separately listed cities." Because of the deputy provincial status of these cities, their top leaders are at most at the vice-provincial rank. That is, in the official hierarchy, the party chiefs of these cities always rank lower than do the provincial party secretaries ruling China's provinces. As such, these officials often have very different career trajectories, information used in the coding of the degree of bureaucratic integration of the provincial officials. For instance, as officials at the prefecture level, the top leaders of the "separately listed cities" are more likely to have had a prior career within the same province, rather than in other provinces. None of the incumbent party secretaries of the "separately listed cities" have ever become a concurrent centralist as a sitting Politburo member of the CCP Central Committee. Therefore, it is inappropriate to include these lower-ranking officials if our focus is on exercise of central political control with regard to the management of the provincial party secretaries, the top-ranking provincial-level cadres.

Second, including these cities as distinct provincial units for the relatively short period from 1999 to 2005 will complicate our statistical analysis in the later chapters by generating a more unbalanced dataset. For the five "separately listed cities" during the years of 1999 to 2005, only seven annual observations are available, whereas most other provinces have

---

[33] I thank Professor Pierre François Landry for exhorting me to tackle the possible issues related to these cities.

far more observations (except for Chongqing, which became a province in 1997, and Hainan, which became a province in 1988). Nevertheless, in later empirical analysis reported in the Appendix to Chapter 5, I will account for the role of these cities in the center's calculation of calibrating the amount of political control to exercise over the provincial governments. I will also conduct additional robustness tests that include the five "separately listed cities" as distinct provincial units since 1998, generating results that are substantively similar to the main statistical results reported in the text. This further justifies our focus on the provincial units in this book.

5

Global Market Integration and Central Political Control

5.1 INTRODUCTION

This chapter empirically investigates how the differential exposure to the global markets by the Chinese provinces affected the degree of political control the provincial governments incurred from the center by analyzing pooled provincial-level time-series cross-section data. As in Chapter 3, I measure the degree of economic openness of a province (that is, the degree to which a province benefits from a linkage to the global markets) with shares of exports and alternatively foreign trade in the provincial GDP. As in Chapter 4, I measure the extent of central political control exercised by the center over the provincial governments via Huang's (1996) notion of the "bureaucratic integration" of the provincial party secretaries, the top-ranking provincial officials.[1]

I find that provinces that engaged in more exports and foreign trade tended to be ruled by the more "bureaucratically integrated" provincial party secretaries predisposed to greater compliance with the policy preferences of the center during the 1978–2005 period. This lends strong empirical support to our hypothesis positing the exercise of more stringent

---

[1] Our broad-gauged analysis in Chapter 4 suggests the center did not seem to have sought tighter political control over the coastal provincial governments through frequent replacement of provincial party chiefs or reduced presence of native-son provincial party secretaries. Statistical analysis of the provincial-level data to be reported in the Appendix to Chapter 5 further indicates that provincial exposure to the global markets did not affect the incidence of new appointments or the presence of native sons among provincial party secretaries during this period.

political control over the subnational governments in those richer but more assertive winner provinces by the Chinese national leadership that rules the country via a most centralized political party. The empirical results from this chapter will make three major contributions, one to the broader study of the domestic politics of economic globalization and two to the existing research on China's central-provincial relations in the post-1978 era.

First, these findings are in consonance with an argument privileging the role of – the incentives of and institutional resources available to – the national political leadership in response to the centrifugal tendencies unleashed by rising economic globalization, as elaborated in Chapter 2. They challenge the prevailing economic research on globalization and domestic intergovernmental conflicts that solely focuses on rising intransigence from those subnational units thriving in global commerce and that predicts inexorable national-level political decline and collapse (for example, Alesina and Spolaore 1997; Bolton and Roland 1997; Bolton et al. 1996). Provincial-level evidence from China of the exercise of regionally targeted central political control echoes cross-national findings (Camões 2003; van Houten 2003) that cast doubts over an inevitable nexus between global market integration and national political disintegration.

Second, the results highlight the crucial role played by the institutions within the single ruling CCP in helping the national leaders rein in economically resourceful but fiscally unruly provinces in the post-Mao era. They are thus in line with a number of studies suggesting that central political strength has remained resilient despite economic reform and opening, and the center's overall grip of national political power has remained tenacious in China throughout this period (Huang 1995b; Kim 2002; Landry 2008; Naughton and Yang 2004b; Sheng 2005a; Solinger 1996). It takes issue with concerns about growing provincial bargaining power and autonomy in the fiscal and other economic policy realms at the expense of the center (for instance, Jia Hao and Lin Zhimin 1994; Walder 1995b; Wang 1995) or prognostications of an imminent outright collapse of the Chinese state (Chang 2001; Chang 1992; Friedman 1993; Goldstone 1995; Waldron 1990).

Third, joining a growing body of recent scholarship (Gallagher 2005; Huang 2003; Pearson 1991; Wang 2001; Zheng 2004a; Zweig 2002), the findings from this chapter will shed new light on the vital importance of a link to the global markets in China's post-1978 political economy. Departing from existing research on the role of economic globalization in shaping the political ties between the Chinese central and provincial governments (for example, Goodman and Segal 1994; Shirk 1994; Zheng 1994), I highlight *how* Beijing actually responded to the fissiparous pressures of economic openness by taking advantage of the institutional resources imparted by the sole governing political party. By unpacking the very determinants of such control, moreover, I will also help further advance the research on the regionally selective exercise of central political control in China during the reform era pioneered by Huang (1996) who has largely focused on its macroeconomic consequences.

In the remaining sections of this chapter, I first briefly discuss the data and lay out the hypothesis to be tested. I next conduct systematic analysis of annual provincial-level data to assess the relationship between the extent of provincial exposure to the global markets and the degree of central political control over the provincial governments. Exercise of tighter central political control over the provincial governments via the appointment of the more "bureaucratically integrated" provincial party secretaries, however, may imply better provincial informal "connections" at the center. Would this then translate into a greater provincial ability to obtain from the central government preferential policies in the foreign economic sector for the jurisdictions they oversaw, which in turn would help expand provincial exports and foreign trade? Following our earlier empirical tests, therefore, I also tackle these concerns of possible endogeneity.

5.2 TESTING THE EFFECT OF ECONOMIC GLOBALIZATION

5.2.1 Data and Hypothesis

Our time-series cross-section dataset consists of annual data for each province during the 1978–2005 period. The unit of analysis is province/year. Our survey of the broad data patterns earlier in Chapter 4 indicates that the center seemed to have resorted to exercising tighter political control over the coastal provincial governments by posting there more compliant party chiefs by virtue of their career backgrounds. I thus focus on this measure of central political control as the dependent variable for our empirical analysis in this chapter – the bureaucratic integration score for the provincial party secretaries for each province/year. I simply call our dependent variable *Political Control*. The coding methods discussed in the Appendix to Chapter 4 ensure that there is one unique top party official for each province in any given year. As discussed at length in Chapter 4, the notion of bureaucratic integration was first developed by Huang (1996) to gauge the varying propensity of provincial officials to comply with central policy preferences due to their career trajectories.

Provincial officials holding a concurrent position at the center (via membership in the Politburo), whom Huang calls "concurrent centralists," are the most likely to stay in tune with central policy preferences. Better monitored by their senior colleagues in the Politburo, these officials also have more "encompassing" interests in the success of national policies because in essence they are central and provincial officials simultaneously. The "centralists" are those with significant prior work experiences at the national level (in the line ministries of the central government or the national organs of the CCP). They are sympathetic to central policy directives due to their earlier career socialization at the center. Next are the "outsiders" who spent their previous careers in other provinces before moving to the provinces where they are currently stationed. Their province-based careers might make them more susceptible to the sway of local interests than the concurrent centralists or the centralists. Finally, "localists" are officials who worked their way up in the same province that they lead now. They are the least likely to comply with central policy preferences in cases of central-provincial conflicts due to their most entrenched local ties.

Such varying incentives to comply with the policy directives of the national leaders due to different career trajectories could have been further reinforced by, as well as manifested in, the different career rewards for these officials later on. As our preliminary analysis in Chapter 4 has indicated, immediately after completion of their provincial stints provincial party secretaries who were concurrent centralists seemed most likely to be promoted to higher-level substantive or ceremonial posts in the national capital, followed in that order by the centralists and the outsiders. Unsurprisingly, the localists were the least likely to be lavished with such career advancement opportunities by the Chinese political center in this period.

I assign values of 4, 3, 2, and 1 to provinces/years ruled by party secretaries who are concurrent centralists, centralists, outsiders, and localists, respectively. As noted earlier, the careers of leading provincial cadres lie in the hands of the Chinese political center. All else being equal, therefore, a higher value for our dependent variable denotes the exercise of a greater degree of central political control over a provincial government. This takes place when the center assigns a more "bureaucratically integrated" provincial party secretary predisposed to greater compliance with central policy preferences due to career experiences to rule a certain province in a given year.

I mainly use the percentage share of provincial exports in provincial GDP – denoted as *Export* – to measure provincial exposure to and potential gains from participation in the world markets because this allows us to have slightly more observations. For robustness checking, I also use the percentage share of total provincial foreign trade (exports plus imports) in provincial GDP – *Trade*. Although overall China has made rapid strides in its embrace of economic openness, there has been wide variation among the provinces in the degree of integration with the global markets, as we have examined in Chapter 3. Echoing cross-national findings, many existing econometric studies have shown that Chinese provinces that engage in more trade and exports tend to grow faster and to be wealthier. In other words, more economically open provinces are more likely to benefit from a window to the outside.

For the main analysis in this chapter, I will not control for the provincial ability to attract FDI because systematic provincial-level FDI data for the most part only became available in the mid- to late 1980s. Their inclusion would result in a significant loss in the number of observations for empirical analysis. Moreover, because of the important role of FDI in promoting China's foreign trade and exports during this period, it might be difficult to disentangle the effects of foreign trade and exports from those of FDI. I thus focus on measures of exports and total foreign trade that should sufficiently capture much of the same underlying degree of provincial exposure to the global markets of interest here.[2]

Consistent with the general argument laid out in Chapter 2, our hypothesis suggests that the Chinese political center has incentives to exert tighter political control over the provincial governments that oversee the winner provinces in the global markets – those subnational regions faring better in the post-Mao era of economic reform and opening. A major impetus behind the center's seeking a tighter political grip over these provincial governments could be to ease central resource extraction from the winner provinces for funding interprovincial redistribution to help maintain balanced regional development and to keep the national leadership in power.

---

[2] In additional robustness tests not reported here, *FDI*, measured by the percentage share of actually utilized FDI in provincial GDP, fails to attain statistical significance at the conventional levels regardless of whether or not *Export* is included. Results for *Export*, however, are broadly similar in the presence or absence of *FDI*. I control for the effect of FDI for the sample period of 1978–2002 for our dependent variable elsewhere (Sheng 2007b), also with largely similar results.

With rising economic openness, regional disparity within China deteriorated as the gap in economic performance and wealth further widened between the thriving coastal provinces and the inland provinces that were doing less well in the global markets, as already reviewed in Chapter 3. Successful efforts by the central government to redress the uneven regional economic development through interprovincial fiscal transfers hinge on submission to Beijing of adequate resources from the winner provinces. Consistent with the predictions of fiscal conflicts in the age of rising economic globalization, however, the preferences of those provincial governments in regions thriving in the global markets are especially likely to diverge from those of the center. Above all, they are more likely to resist demands for greater fiscal contributions to the interregional fiscal redistributive scheme pursued by the central government and to seek greater autonomy in disposing of their own fiscal resources.

Partly reflecting the abhorrence of the local economic actors in the winner provinces toward the heftier tax burdens entailed, recalcitrance on the part of these provincial governments toward central extractive demands could also be due to the fiscal imperative they confront themselves. As also noted in Chapter 3, all Chinese local governments have been hard-pressed to maximize revenues in their own hands in the age of decentralized expenditure responsibilities and increased local self-financing. The need for more revenues could be especially acute for the provincial governments in those regions more exposed to the volatile international markets, perhaps because of the more daunting task of internal redistribution and balancing within their own jurisdictions. After all, the economic schism among the different localities within these winner provinces might have also deteriorated under rising economic openness.

Such fiscal constraints can pit the provincial governments in the winner provinces against the political center if more revenue contributions to Beijing necessarily dictate a concomitant reduction in the fiscal resources at their own disposal. Indeed, the provincial governments in the winner regions often resorted to a host of ploys to hide revenues from the center during this period. In defiance of the preferences of the center, leaders of some of the winner provinces even openly opposed the 1994 fiscal centralization initiative by the central government, as the well-known cases of Ye Xuanping of Guangdong and Shen Daren of Jiangsu have amply illustrated. Tacit resistance toward central extractive demands through tax evasion and public clamors for greater fiscal autonomy by the winner provinces, however, could only be appeased at the expense of the power and authority of the national leaders at the center.

Without adequate revenue remittances from these provinces, meanwhile, the center would not be able to perform the requisite interprovincial transfers to placate the provinces faring less well and crying for more assistance. Many of these latter provinces in China were already simmering with ethnic unrest. Absent infusion of central aid, unabated discontent of these loser provinces (if only relative to the winners) would equally threaten the country's political stability. Thus, it is conceivable that the centrifugal tendencies unleashed by China's embrace of the global markets, if left unchecked, could eventually challenge the very raison d'être and undermine the political authority of the Chinese central government.

A more robust redistributive agenda pursued by the center but financed via greater extraction from the winner provinces, in contrast, could enhance central government legitimacy. By helping to reduce the regional income gap and mollify the country's disaffected inland provinces, interregional redistribution could allay a key factor fanning the fiscal intransigence of the winner regions in the first place. Thus, the Chinese national leaders have incentives to extract more resources from the winner provinces to help underwrite interregional redistribution in this era.

As surveyed in Chapter 3, the Chinese political center indeed continued to carry out substantial fiscal transfers favoring the inland provinces throughout this period. If anything, the extent of fiscal redistribution across the Chinese provinces could have expanded in the more recent years. Persistent central redistributive efforts must have been funded by continuing fiscal extractions by the center from the unruly winner provinces. This could have been facilitated by the personnel tools afforded the Chinese national leaders by the ruling CCP regarding the management of the top provincial leadership, as discussed in Chapter 4. In theory, such institutional resources imparted by the CCP enable the Chinese political center to exert substantial political control over *all* subnational governments, including those overseeing the winner provinces in the global markets. Given the vital importance of these winner provinces for the center's redistributive and political goals in this era, therefore, I hypothesize:

H1. *Other things being held constant, the Chinese political center in the post-1978 period has sought to exercise a greater degree of political control over the subnational governments in those provinces that have benefited more from a linkage to the global markets.*

Tighter political control could be exercised by installing at the helm of these more economically resourceful but fiscally intransigent winner regions party chiefs who are predisposed to greater policy compliance with the national leadership by virtue of their career trajectories. More sympathetic to the policy agenda of their national superiors, these officials are more likely to work diligently to ensure compliance with the latter's extractive demands from the local economic actors in their own jurisdictions. Appointing pliable, pro-center provincial party secretaries effectively helps the center cut its agency costs in delegating the task of running the winner provinces and extracting their resources. More concretely, we expect the Chinese political center to assign its more trustworthy agents, the more "bureaucratically integrated" provincial party secretaries (centralists and concurrent centralists), to rule those provinces that are more exposed to the global markets during these years.[3]

5.2.2 Model Specifications and Estimation Issues

It is certainly unlikely that the Chinese political center would be solely motivated by the extent of provincial economic openness in exercising political control over the provincial governments. In addition to our main independent variable on the degree of provincial exposure to the global markets (*Export* and, alternatively, *Trade*), I include a number of variables measuring the socioeconomic and other political traits of the provinces. First, it is straightforward to argue that, *ceteris paribus*, wealthier, faster-growing, and larger provinces could be worthy of a tighter political grip from the center in their own right, regardless of whether they are highly exposed to the global markets. I thus account for the possible

---

[3] One might wonder whether the same hypothesized logic linking the extent of provincial exposure to the global markets and the degree of central political control over a provincial government during the post-1978 period could apply to the pre-1978 era. This is unlikely to be the case. First, as noted earlier in Chapter 4, during the last decade of Mao's rule (the chaos of the Cultural Revolution), the CCP was in a shambles. As the institutional tool of personnel management of the CCP that is privileged in my study fell into disarray in those years, it must have been difficult for the center to exercise any effective political control over the provincial governments via the ruling party. Second, China before 1978 embraced self-imposed autarky under which there was little foreign trade (Lardy 1992) for any province, coastal or inland. Thus, even if the CCP was functioning well before the Cultural Revolution (that is, during 1949–66) to exercise some form of regionally selective control over the provincial governments, the rationale should have been different from a logic revolving around the extent of provincial participation in the global markets. This suggests that tighter central political control over the provincial governments overseeing the more globalized economies should have only begun in the post-1978 era. Due to lack of comparable systematic data on the provincial level for other economic variables, however, it is extremely difficult to assess empirically the exact logic at work for the years of 1949–66.

effect of the level of economic development – *Per Capita GDP*, measured by the natural log of 1977 constant RMB values. Provincial economic dynamism is captured by *Growth*, the real growth rate (in percentage) of per capita GDP (again at 1977 constant values). Following Su and Yang (2000, 224), I measure the provincial size as the size of the population – *Population* – the percentage share of the provincial population in the national total.[4]

As noted, starting from the early 1980s, about fourteen cities in several provinces were elevated to the special status of cities "separately listed under the plan" (*jihua danlie chengshi*) until the category was phased out for most of them in the early to mid-1990s. Municipal governments in these cities, which are often major industrial centers within their respective host provinces, were granted economic powers normally reserved for provincial governments, such as the ability to conduct direct fiscal dealings with the center. These governments would directly remit revenues to and receive subsidies from the center, *just like*, rather than *through*, their host provincial governments. The municipal governments involved often favored such arrangements because they enhanced their own economic policymaking authority.[5]

From the perspective of the national leadership, the separate listing of these mainly "cash cow" cities in the national plan allowed the center to tap into their fiscal resources directly by skipping the provincial-level hurdle altogether. This reduced need to deal with the provincial governments also implied that the center could afford to exercise less stringent

---

[4] Because some segments of the population such as the military are not included in the population figures for any single province, I use the national population data from Guojia Tongji Ju [National Bureau of Statistics] (1999a, 2002, 2005), which are larger than the sum of the provincial totals in the provincial statistical yearbooks. Alternatively, I have tried to measure the provincial size with the natural log of real aggregate provincial GDP. The variable itself is not significant, regardless of whether *Population* is included while the results for all other variables remain largely unchanged. Because the two variables both capture the same underlying size of the provinces, I report the results including only population size in the estimation.

[5] For an interesting account of the feud between Hubei province and its capital city – Wuhan – and the politics of making the latter a separately listed city, see Schroeder (1992). Meanwhile, none of these "separately listed cities" seems to have fully severed their fiscal links with the provincial-level governments in their host provinces after they established direct fiscal ties with the central government. For one thing, throughout the post-1994 era, each year these cities still remit budgetary revenues to and/or receive budgetary transfers from the provincial governments in their host provinces. Nevertheless, the bulk of the fiscal flows for these cities seem to be taking place with the central government (Zhongguo Caizheng Nianjian Bianji Weiyuanhui [Editorial Committee of the *Finance Yearbook of China*] 1996, 1997–2005).

political control over the provincial leadership in those jurisdictions host-ing such "separately listed cities," all else being equal. I thus create a dummy variable – *Central City Host*, taking on a value of 1 if a province hosted any such cities in a certain year and 0 otherwise.[6] We expect its coefficient to be negative because the presence of such cities should lessen the need to exercise tight central political control directly over the gov-ernments of their host provinces.

In his seminal work, Bates (1981) argues that government policies in the developing world have been biased in favor of the urban sectors, which are more concentrated geographically (hence, more prone to solv-ing their collective action problems in launching rebellions), more threat-ening to political stability, and thus more likely to be pacified by the state. Others, however, point to worsening political unrest in rural China in the reform era due to the excessive peasant burdens spawning wide-spread protests (Bernstein and Lü 2003). For our purposes, either more or less urbanized (that is, more rural) provinces might pose a more cred-ible threat to rule by the Chinese national leaders. It would be interest-ing to examine empirically whether tighter central political control was exercised over the provincial governments in those more or less urban-ized provinces to guard against potential instability. Therefore, I include *Urban Employment*, measured by the percentage share of urban employ-ment in the total provincial employment.

Building on Huang's (1996) argument that the exercise of central polit-ical control has been effective in checking local public investment urges, Huang and Sheng (2009) show that a greater degree of central political control exercised over the provincial governments was indeed associated

---

[6] The original fourteen cities (with the years when they were listed separately and the provinces where they are located) are Chongqing (1984–95, Sichuan province), Wuhan (1985–95, Hubei), Shenyang (1985–95, Liaoning), Dalian (1985-, Liaoning), Guangzhou (1985–95, Guangdong), Harbin (1985–95, Heilongjiang), Xi'an (1985–95, Shaanxi), Qingdao (1987-, Shandong), Ningbo (1988-, Zhejiang), Nanjing (1990–95, Jiangsu), Chengdu (1990–95, Sichuan), Xiamen (1989-, Fujian), Shenzhen (1989-, Guangdong), and Changchun (1990–95, Jilin). Although officially the status was to be phased out for nine of the cities by the end of 1994 (Shi Yupeng and Zhou Li'an 2007, 19), it appears that direct fiscal relations between the center and these cities, a key definition of the special status, were still maintained as of 1995 (Zhongguo Caizheng Nianjian Bianji Weiyuanhui [Editorial Committee of the *Finance Yearbook of China*] 1996). Therefore, I use 1995 as the last year, rather than 1994 for these nine cities, which became deputy provincial cities, joined by Ji'nan and Hangzhou, as discussed in the Appendix to Chapter 4. Using 1994 as the last year for the nine cities does not affect the analysis reported later. Several provinces hosted more than one separately listed city in some years. Using a variable taking on a value of 0 with no such cities, 1 with one such city, and 2 with two such cities generates broadly similar results to those reported later.

with lower provincial inflation during the reform era. However, they do not directly explore whether tighter central political control could have been exercised over those provincial governments witnessing higher inflation in their jurisdictions in the first place, a possibility I investigate here. I thus add *Inflation*, measured by the annual percentage change in provincial consumer price indices, to our robustness analysis.[7] The main analysis by Huang and Sheng focuses on the 1978–97 period because inflation became less of a concern to the national leaders in the aftermath of the Asian financial crisis. Here for purposes of consistency and comparison with the other model specifications, I report the results from analysis that includes the entire period of 1978–2005, but the results are broadly similar if only data from the 1978–97 period are included.

Finally, I add two dummy variables that are nonvarying across the years. *CAM* is a dummy variable taking on a value of 1 for provinces that are centrally administered municipalities – Beijing, Shanghai, Tianjin, and Chongqing (since 1997). This special administrative status might denote their additional but unobservable political and economic importance for the Chinese national leadership not already captured by the other variables. *Minority* is a dummy variable that equals 1 for provinces designated as "autonomous regions for ethnic minorities" – Inner Mongolia, Tibet, Xinjiang, Guangxi, and Ningxia. Due to their greater susceptibility to ethnic unrest,[8] including this variable will help us assess whether the center has been intent on exercising tighter control over the subnational governments in these regions. Because the value of these two dummy variables does not change over time, a model with provincial fixed effects (see the following) does not allow us to examine the effects of these variables (Beck and Katz 2001). Therefore, I only include these two variables for robustness testing in models without the provincial fixed effects.

All these additional variables, like *Export* and *Trade*, are lagged by one year to remedy mutual causality in our analysis. Our independent and dependent variables thus effectively cover the periods of 1978–2004 and 1979–2005, respectively. Besides these independent variables, I also add a province-specific intercept designed to capture those unobservable effects "fixed," that is, invariant to each provincial-level unit. This is equivalent

---

[7] Moreover, they use inflation data from both the provincial retail price indices and the provincial consumer price indices. I report the results using the more commonly used measure based on consumer prices here, but using inflation data based on the provincial retail price indices will generate similar results.

[8] See, for example, Bovingdon (2002) regarding the case of Xinjiang, and Karmel (1995) regarding the situation in Tibet.

to adding a dummy variable for each individual province (Green et al. 2001). Similarly, an annual dummy variable to account for year-specific effects not accounted for in the model is also included. However, there could be another important function served by the presence of the year dummy variables in our model. More specifically, we have to control for temporal autocorrelation due to the time-series dimension of our data. That is, the bureaucratic integration score of the top official and the related degree of central political control over a provincial government in a province for a year could be related to that of the earlier (or next) year.

I am not aware of any methodological consensus on how best to remedy problems arising from potential serial correlation in ordered logit or probit models with more than two outcomes (see the following). Beck et al. (1998) recommend the use of year dummy variables in models with binary outcomes as a remedy for potential temporal autocorrelation, advice I decide to adopt for our purposes here even though our dependent variable has four outcomes.[9] In the robustness analysis reported later, I also follow Green et al. (2001) to tackle possible serial correlation by adding a lagged dependent variable in the model while dropping the year dummy variables. As we will readily see, the results remain largely unchanged for our main independent variable measuring the extent of provincial exposure to the global markets.

Although we are interested in how the extent of provincial participation in economic globalization affects the degree of central political control exercised over the provincial governments, I regard the dependent variable as a latent variable to be gauged by our observable data. In this book, I use the bureaucratic integration score of the provincial party secretaries as its observable indicator. Although the latent variable can be continuous, the measure of bureaucratic integration is discrete, taking on the four integer values of 1 to 4, with 1 denoting the lowest degree of central control. Even though I have theorized about the direction of control, unfortunately, we do not know whether a value of 4 denotes exactly four times as much control as a value of 1. That is, the distance between the different values of our bureaucratic integration variable may not be uniform. When such variables are used as dependent variables, ordinary least squares estimation can be misleading; an ordered logit or probit model seems more appropriate (Greene 2000,

---

[9] As I report later, I also recode the dependent variable into a dummy variable and estimate it with a simple logit model, again yielding broadly similar results.

Chapter 19). Therefore, I only report results from estimating an ordered logit model in this section.[10]

5.2.3 Findings

The results from the ordered logit estimation are presented in Table 5.1. Model 1 is the baseline estimation. I drop all other variables except the province and year dummy variables in Model 2 to address possible concerns over multicollinearity among some of the variables included in the same model. After all, many of the provincial economic variables such as wealth levels or economic growth may be highly correlated with provincial exports and trade, or with one another. I mainly focus on the analysis using the export-based measure of provincial exposure to and benefits from the global markets, but the alternative trade-based measure yields broadly similar findings, as in Model 3. Model 4 excludes observations from Tibet, Hainan, and Chongqing, the three provinces that often do not appear in much of the political economy research on China employing provincial-level data. Dropping observations from one of the three provinces at a time will generate similar results. Finally, Model 5 replaces the year dummy variables with a lagged dependent variable to control for serial correlation.

Overall, our results are consistent with the hypothesis that the center seeks to exercise a greater degree of political control over the provincial governments in those regions that are more exposed to the global markets by installing in their leadership post pro-center agents with career trajectories predisposing them to greater compliance with central policy preferences. Provincial exports are *positively* associated with the degree of bureaucratic integration of the provincial party secretaries. The coefficient for *Export* is highly significant (at 0.01) across all models. The magnitude of the coefficient for *Export* is somewhat diminished in Model 5 when a lagged dependent variable is added. However, this is not surprising because the presence of a lagged dependent variable tends to suppress the effects of the other variables in the model (Achen 2000). Most important for our purposes, our *Export* variable remains positive and highly significant.

---

[10] Using an ordered probit model with the same specification as our baseline ordered logit model presented later generates nearly identical results. Estimating an ordinary least squares regression yields broadly similar results for our *Export* variable in terms of the direction and level of statistical significance of its effect.

TABLE 5.1. *The Effect of Economic Globalization on Central Political Control Over the Provincial Governments*

Models	1	2	3	4	5
Export	0.08***	0.07***		0.08***	0.04***
	(0.01)	(0.01)		(0.01)	(0.01)
Trade			0.04***		
			(0.01)		
Central City	−1.15***		−0.98***	−1.00***	−0.65**
Host	(0.35)		(0.34)	(0.34)	(0.33)
Per Capita GDP	−0.32		−0.37	−1.05	0.11
	(0.61)		(0.61)	(0.67)	(0.15)
Growth	−0.03		−0.03	−0.03	0.01
	(0.02)		(0.02)	(0.02)	(0.01)
Population	−0.40		−0.39	−0.35	−0.36
	(0.36)		(0.37)	(0.35)	(0.36)
Urban	0.08***		0.08***	0.10***	0.04
Employment	(0.03)		(0.03)	(0.03)	(0.03)
Political					3.29***
Control$_{i,t-1}$					(0.26)
Cut 1	−6.49	−0.88	−3.14	−6.59	2.84
	(4.38)	(0.78)	(5.79)	(5.04)	(3.21)
Cut 2	−3.82	1.70	−0.43	−3.98	7.11
	(4.36)	(0.79)	(5.79)	(5.03)	(3.24)
Cut 3	−1.56	3.92	1.82	−1.89	10.83
	(4.31)	(0.81)	(5.78)	(5.00)	(3.28)
Province dummy	Yes	Yes	Yes	Yes	Yes
Year dummy	Yes	Yes	Yes	Yes	No
Log pseudo-likelihood	−781.19	−794.78	−768.40	−733.61	−507.42
Provinces included	31	31	31	28	31
Observations	797	797	791	745	797
Wald χ^2	398.10	425.81	392.19	343.40	309.28
Probability > χ^2	0.00	0.00	0.00	0.00	0.00
Pseudo R^2	0.22	0.21	0.22	0.22	0.49

Note: The dependent variable, *Political Control*, is the annual bureaucratic integration score of the provincial party secretaries for each province, and is estimated with ordered logit regressions. It covers the 1979–2005 period. *Political Control*$_{i,t-1}$ is the dependent variable lagged by one year. All other independent variables are lagged by one year. Model 4 does not include observations from Tibet, Hainan, or Chongqing. Results for the province and year dummy variables are omitted to economize on space. Robust standard errors are in parentheses.

***: $p < 0.01$; **: $p < 0.05$; *: $p < 0.1$ (two–tailed tests).

TABLE 5.2. *The Effect of Economic Globalization on Central Political Control: Robustness Tests*

Models	6	7	8	9	10
Export	0.08***	0.08***	0.05***	0.05***	0.05***
	(0.02)	(0.02)	(0.01)	(0.01)	(0.01)
Central City Host	−1.32***	−1.03***	−1.50***	−0.94***	−1.37***
	(0.36)	(0.40)	(0.25)	(0.26)	(0.41)
Per Capita GDP	−0.92	−0.94	0.73***	−0.09	1.40*
	(0.73)	(0.86)	(0.24)	(0.28)	(0.79)
Growth	−0.03	−0.01	−0.02	−0.02	−0.03
	(0.02)	(0.02)	(0.02)	(0.02)	(0.02)
Population	−0.17	0.34	0.05	0.12***	−0.51
	(0.59)	(0.66)	(0.04)	(0.04)	(0.36)
Urban Employment	0.11***	0.17**	0.01	0.00	0.01
	(0.03)	(0.07)	(0.01)	(0.01)	(0.04)
Inflation	0.01				
	(0.04)				
CAM				2.40***	
				(0.38)	
Minority				0.54***	
				(0.17)	
Cut 1	−8.89	0.41	3.17	−1.25	
	(6.84)	(7.19)	(1.25)	(1.48)	
Cut 2	−6.19	2.97	5.29	0.92	
	(6.80)	(7.19)	(1.26)	(1.48)	
Cut 3	−4.01	5.36	7.08	2.86	
	(6.75)	(7.16)	(1.27)	(1.47)	
Constant					−7.71
					(5.57)
Province dummy	Yes	Yes	No	No	Yes
Year dummy	Yes	Yes	Yes	Yes	Yes
Log pseudo-likelihood	−716.34	−574.11	−917.27	−895.05	−329.08
Provinces included	31	31	31	31	26
Observations	738	586	797	797	682
Wald χ^2	379.74	487.17	120.81	156.32	173.01
Probability > χ^2	0.00	0.00	0.00	0.00	0.00
Pseudo R^2	0.23	0.21	0.08	0.11	0.24

Note: The dependent variable, *Political Control*, is the annual bureaucratic integration score of the provincial party secretaries for each province, and is estimated with ordered logit regressions. The exception is Model 10, where the dependent variable is a dummy variable equaling 1 if the original bureaucratic integration score is 3 or 4 and 0 otherwise, and is estimated with a logit model. All independent variables are lagged by one year. Model 7 covers data during the 1979–98 period. In Model 10, observations from Inner Mongolia, Zhejiang, Jiangxi, Hunan, and Chongqing are automatically dropped from the analysis due to model perfect predictions. Results for the province and year dummy variables are omitted to economize on space. Robust standard errors are in parentheses.
***: $p < 0.01$; **: $p < 0.05$; *: $p < 0.1$ (two-tailed tests).

The results of additional robustness tests are presented in Table 5.2. Model 6 accounts for the role of provincial inflation in affecting the degree of political control exercised by the center over the provincial governments. Since late 1998, the leading cadres in the five remaining "separately listed cities" have been directly managed by the center (Chan 2004, 713, 726). Model 7 thus examines a subsample covering only the 1979–98 period for the dependent variable, presumably with more homogenous data prior to this structural change. In other words, the results from Model 7 should help us better determine whether it is justifiable to analyze data from the entire period together. Model 8 drops the province fixed effects; Model 9 is estimated without the provincial fixed effects but with the addition of *CAM* and *Minority*, dummy variables that indicate the special status of some provinces and are nonvarying over time. In Model 10, I recode the dependent variable into a dummy variable equaling 1 if the original bureaucratic integration score is 3 or 4 (for provinces ruled by a concurrent centralist or centralist) and 0 otherwise. I then re-estimate the data with a simple logit model in order to test the robustness of the findings to the alternative coding of the dependent variable.

As we can see clearly, the results for *Export* have remained largely unchanged in all these models. It is important to note that its estimated coefficient in Model 7 covering only data for the 1979–98 subsample is also strikingly similar to the one in our baseline Model 1, both in terms of magnitude and statistical significance. This suggests that the decision to pool the data from the entire period of 1979–2005 in the analysis does not seem to be affected by the changes introduced in late 1998 for the five "separately listed cities." However, since we cannot directly observe the latent variable of political control measured through the bureaucratic integration score of the top provincial officials – our dependent variable, we cannot interpret an ordered logit model by reading off the estimated coefficients.

One intuitive way to interpret the results of ordered logit analysis is to simulate the "first difference" effects of the independent variables. Following King et al. (2000) and Tomz et al. (2003), I simulate these effects based upon our baseline Model 1 and present them in Table 5.3. Holding all other variables at their mean values, increasing the value of *Export* by one standard deviation (about 12.69 percent in provincial share of exports in GDP) from its mean (around 10.25 percent) can, on average, reduce the probability of a province being led by a localist party secretary by about 0.11, and by an outsider by about 0.12. In sharp contrast, the probability of a province being ruled by a centralist or concurrent centralist (the two more tightly controlled and more pro-center groups) in a certain year rises by about 0.17 and 0.05, respectively.

TABLE 5.3. *Simulated "First Difference" Effects*

	Localist	Outsider	Centralist	Concurrent Centralist
Export	−0.11	−0.12	0.17	0.05
	(0.01)	(0.03)	(0.03)	(0.01)
	[−0.13, −0.08]	[−0.18, −0.06]	[0.11, 0.23]	[0.03, 0.08]
Central City Host	0.21	−0.04	−0.14	−0.03
	(0.07)	(0.04)	(0.04)	(0.01)
	[0.08, 0.35]	[−0.13, 0.01]	[−0.21, −0.07]	[−0.04, −0.01]
Per Capita GDP	0.05	−0.02	−0.03	−0.00
	(0.08)	(0.03)	(0.06)	(0.01)
	[−0.08, 0.22]	[−0.08, 0.01]	[−0.13, 0.11]	[−0.02, 0.03]
Growth	0.03	0.00	−0.02	0.00
	(0.02)	(0.00)	(0.02)	(0.00)
	[−0.01, 0.06]	[−0.01, 0.01]	[−0.05, 0.01]	[−0.01, 0.00]
Population	0.18	−0.09	−0.09	−0.01
	(0.17)	(0.10)	(0.08)	(0.02)
	[−0.09, 0.55]	[−0.35, 0.01]	[−0.19, 0.13]	[−0.03, 0.04]
Urban Employment	−0.12	−0.18	0.21	0.09
	(0.03)	(0.09)	(0.07)	(0.06)
	[−0.17, −0.05]	[−0.36, −0.03]	[0.07, 0.32]	[0.01, 0.23]

Note: The results are based on Model 1 in Table 5.1, according to *CLARIFY* simulations (1,000 times) recommended in King et al. (2000) and Tomz et al. (2003) by holding all the variables in the model at their mean and moving the variable of interest by 1 standard deviation from its mean. The exception is the dummy variable *Central City Host*, whose results are obtained by moving the variable from 0 to 1. The standard errors are in parentheses, and the 95 percent confidence intervals are in brackets.

Yet another way of interpreting the results from ordered logit models is to plot the predicted probabilities for the four outcomes along different values of our main independent variable while holding constant all other variables in the model. This is shown in Figure 5.1. When the export/ GDP share of a province is 5 percent in a certain year, the predicted probability of that province being ruled by a localist party secretary is, on average, about 0.25, ruled by an outsider 0.58, ruled by a centralist 0.15, and ruled by a concurrent centralist only 0.02.[11] When the export/GDP

---

[11] It is interesting to point out that the higher probability of having an outsider party secretary than of having a localist at the helm even at this low level of economic openness might reflect the fact that in general, provincial party secretaries are less likely to be localists. This suggests that, the center might have always tried to exert some measure of control over all the provincial governments by ensuring that few provinces would be ruled by localist party secretaries.

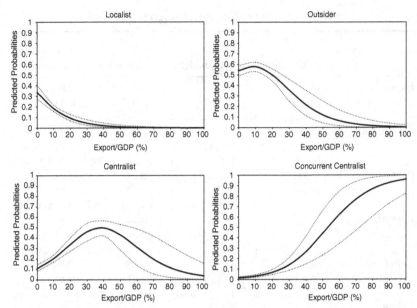

FIGURE 5.1. Predicted probabilities of the degree of central political control by provincial export/GDP share.

Note: Dark solid lines refer to the mean predicted probabilities for different types of provincial party secretaries along different values of *Export* (the percentage share of provincial exports in GDP). Light dotted lines are the upper and lower 95 percent confidence intervals. They are calculated and plotted according to *CLARIFY* simulations (1,000 times) recommended in King et al. (2000) and Tomz et al. (2003) by holding all other variables (including the year and provincial dummies) at their mean values except for our variable of interest here – *Export*.

share rises to 60 percent, however, the average predicted probability of a province being ruled by a localist party secretary drops to merely 0.01, and by an outsider to about 0.06. In contrast, the mean predicted probability of it having a centralist party secretary climbs to 0.31, and of it having a concurrent centralist surges to as much as 0.62.

One example is Guangdong. As shown in Tables 3.3 and 4.2, the average export/GDP share for Guangdong was about 16.9 percent for the 1978–90 period, while its average secretary bureaucratic integration score was slightly less than 1.9 during the 1978–91 period. This implies that Guangdong was, on average, nearly always ruled by an outsider party secretary then. During the 1991–2004 period, Guangdong's average export/GDP share soared to about 74 percent; its average secretary bureaucratic integration score also grew to almost 3.8 for the 1992–2005 period. In fact, ever since 1993, Guangdong's provincial party secretary has been a concurrent centralist. At the other end is Guizhou province, one of the most economically insular provinces in China during the period. Its average export/GDP share was barely 1.3 and 4.2 percent during the periods of 1978–90 and 1991–2004, respectively, and its average secretary bureaucratic integration score was only about 2.5 and 2.1 during the periods of 1978–91 and 1992–2005, respectively. Unsurprisingly, for the most part since 1993 an outsider party secretary has ruled Guizhou.

As expected, the coefficient of our *Central City Host* variable is negative and statistically significant across all the models. This is consistent with the notion that separately listing the cities in the national budget and establishing direct central fiscal ties with (and enabling direct central fiscal extraction from) these "cash cow" cities might mitigate the need to exercise tight political control over the government leadership in the host provinces. In fact, according to the simulated "first difference" effects reported earlier in Table 5.3 for our baseline Model 1, holding all other variables at their mean values, hosting a separately listed city increases the probability of a province being led by a localist party secretary (the least controlled) by on average about 0.21 in a given year. In sharp contrast, the probability of a province/year being ruled by any other category of provincial party secretary – an outsider, centralist, or concurrent centralist – declines by about 0.04, 0.14, and 0.03, respectively.[12]

Meanwhile, our *Urban Employment* variable is positively associated with our dependent variable. The results are mostly significant, except in Model 5 including a lagged dependent variable, in Models 8–9 that exclude province fixed effects, and in Model 10 with the alternative coding of the dependent variable. This provides some empirical support to the idea that the center is more interested in keeping a short leash over the provincial governments of the more urbanized (that is, less rural) provinces. Thus, governments in developing countries may adopt policies to pacify the urban population for fear of political instability (Bates 1981). Our evidence from China in the post-1978 period shows that the central government might have tried to exercise tighter political control over the provincial governments in the more urbanized provinces. This could reflect a two-pronged strategy of simultaneous appeasement and

---

[12] In additional analysis reported in the Appendix to Chapter 5, I list Dalian, Qingdao, Ningbo, Xiamen, and Shenzhen as separate provincial-level units for the post-1998 period in the dataset and conduct the tests with or without including observations from the five "separately listed cities." The results are broadly similar for our *Export* variable in both magnitude and statistical significance for the coefficient.

control toward the more politically menacing urban areas by the Chinese political center despite recent unrest in the countryside (Bernstein and Lü 2003). However, some caution is in order here because this variable fails to be significant in some specifications.

Inflation is not significantly related to the dependent variable. The center did not appear to have exercised regionally differential political control based upon the preexisting levels of provincial inflation, even though tighter political control exercised over the provincial governments could lead to lower provincial inflation in this period (Huang and Sheng 2009). Finally, the subnational government overseeing a centrally administered municipality or an autonomous region for ethnic minorities, on average, tended to incur tighter central political control, given the positive and significant effects for the two dummy variables of *CAM* and *Minority* in Model 9 without provincial fixed effects. This suggests that the center seemed to have kept under its firmer grip the major municipalities or those provinces prone to ethnic restiveness.

However, the results for the remaining variables are more uncertain. *Per Capita GDP* is highly significant (at 0.01) only in Model 8 excluding province fixed effects, *CAM* and *Minority*, and slightly significant (at 0.1) when the dependent variable is recoded into a dummy variable in Model 10. Similarly, *Population* is only significant (at 0.01) in Model 9 leaving out the province fixed effects but including *CAM* and *Minority*. Meanwhile, *Growth*, measuring provincial economic dynamism, does not seem to be a significant predictor of central political control over the provincial governments measured in terms of the bureaucratic integration of the provincial party secretaries appointed.[13] Most important, even after we take into account the possible effect on the dependent variable of all these other factors, the effect of our *Export* variable remains consistently positive and significant.

To summarize, the empirical results in this section suggest that, all else being equal, the center tended to assign to the more export-oriented provinces party chiefs – the top-ranking provincial officials – who were holding a concurrent central office or had significant prior career experiences working at the center. These officials were considered more likely to comply with the policy preferences of the Chinese national leadership due to their career backgrounds. In other words, by sending in these

---

[13] This general lack of statistical significance for *Growth* also mitigates the possibility of mutual causality when we analyze the effect of the regionally differential exercise of central political control on provincial economic growth during this period in Chapter 6.

more loyal officials, the political center in China sought to place the provincial governments in Chinese provinces with greater exposure to the global markets under more stringent political control, as measured by Huang's (1996) bureaucratic integration score of the provincial party secretaries.

5.3 TACKLING POSSIBLE ENDOGENEITY

5.3.1 Reverse Causality

The most serious critique of the statistical findings presented earlier in this chapter is that the implied logic might be reversed. In order to ease revenue extraction for interprovincial redistribution under the centrifugal pressures of the global markets, I have posited that the national political leaders in China sought to exercise tighter political control over the sub-national governments overseeing those provinces that thrived in exports and foreign trade by assigning there more pliable top cadres. The degree of economic openness is treated as exogenous, largely a product of provincial natural resource endowments, as discussed at length in Chapter 3. Privileging the importance of possible "personal connections," however, an alternative logic could conceivably argue that the more "bureaucratically integrated" officials are better able to obtain the plum jobs of governing the "more comfortable" provinces in the first place. These could include the cosmopolitan provinces along the coast that are more closely linked with the global markets, for example.

Better connections with the highest leadership in the nation's capital can certainly be facilitated by previous central work experiences or concurrent office holding at the national level such as a seat in the Politburo. At the least, both offer unrivaled opportunities for personal socialization and even ingratiation. After all, "factionalism" has always been a staple in the study of Chinese elite politics for this period, as noted earlier (for example, Dittmer and Wu 1995; Huang 2000; Pye 1992; Shih 2008). In short, this alternative hypothesis of "personal connections" might generate results that are observationally equivalent to those implied by the logic of the regionally selective exercise of central political control pursued in this book.

Nevertheless, suggestions that these presumably "better-connected" officials are favored by China's national leaders and thus are posted in the more prosperous, globalized provinces do not appear to be warranted by empirical evidence. One obvious difficulty with this alternative logic is that it does not provide a good explanation for why any well-connected (highly "bureaucratically integrated") official would necessarily want to be assigned to an ethnic minority region with high political instability, such as Tibet or Xinjiang. After all, our empirical evidence from Model 9 has clearly shown that these ethnic minority regions tended to be overseen by the more "bureaucratically integrated" provincial party secretaries. This, however, is consistent with my argument suggesting the exercise of tighter central political control over the provincial governments in regions more prone to ethnic unrest.

Another problem is that in most cases – indeed over 80 percent – of the provinces/years ruled by the concurrent centralists in our dataset, those provincial party secretaries were promoted to the Politburo while they had already been working in the more globalized provinces. Only fewer than 20 percent of them were transferred to these provinces later as sitting Politburo members (see also Sheng 2009a). In other words, the vast majority of the concurrent centralists did not have to take advantage of the "personal connections" made possible by Politburo membership to obtain jobs in those "coveted" provinces. They had already been there in the first place. These officials were later brought into the Politburo because of the incentives of the Chinese national leaders to ensure their greater compliance with central revenue extraction from the winner provinces that they ruled on behalf of the center. In other words, the center made these officials Politburo members out of its interest in exerting tighter political control over the provincial governments the officials led.

A related, yet still distinct, line of skepticism also revolves around the notion of stronger factional ties with the national leadership for the more "bureaucratically integrated" provincial party secretaries. However, it suggests that the differential provincial ability to conduct foreign trade and exports might be a function of the different preferential policies obtained from the central government. Under this view, the degree of provincial exposure to the global markets was not determined by the relatively immovable provincial resource endowments such as geographic locations, historical legacies, or preexisting skill levels, as I have argued in Chapter 3. Instead, it might be endogenous to having party secretaries with better connections at the center via prior work experiences in the national capital or concurrent membership in the Politburo. After all, it would be far easier for these officials to bring back policy pork from the center that in turn could have helped make the provincial economies over which they presided more successful in the global markets.[14]

Interviews conducted with the relevant Chinese central government officials by Zweig (2002, 80–81) do suggest that local governments often fiercely lobbied the central government for the establishment of economic development zones in their respective jurisdictions in order to attract foreign capital and promote exports. Provincial governments led by party secretaries with a higher bureaucratic integration score – those who once worked side by side with the officials in the central government in charge of approving the establishment of the development zones or who regularly attended meetings with the highest national leadership in the Politburo – would perhaps be more effective in such lobbying efforts. Indeed, such reasoning has led Lieberthal and Oksenberg (1988, 351) to note the paradox that "closer scrutiny" by the central government – for instance, through appointment of the more pro-center provincial officials – might actually lend the "wealthier, revenue-producing areas" in China a "greater opportunity to influence policies of concern to them." To the extent that the provinces could benefit from greater exposure to the global markets, presumably these better-connected provincial party chiefs would also push for more favorable policies from the central government that later enabled the provinces to open further to the outside.

Recall also from Chapter 3 that regionally slanted preferential policies in the foreign economic sector were indeed pursued by the center in the early years of the opening to the world markets. To be sure, there is no clear evidence that policies in all areas were uniformly biased in favor of the coastal provinces. For example, during 1984 foreign exchange retention policies clearly favored the five ethnic minority regions, most of which are landlocked (Zhang 2002). Still, policies regarding the establishment of the various types of national-level development zones, with the Special Economic Zones (SEZs) granting the greatest local policy autonomy and economic benefits, were in fact mostly lavished on the coastal provinces, especially in the early years. Even after the preferential policies began to spread to other provinces in the early 1990s, data collected by Démurger et al. (2002b) suggest that the coastal provinces still benefited to a greater extent from these policies despite the narrowing gap during the latter period (see also Table 3.2 in Chapter 3).

---

[14] In a similar vein, Shih (2008, Chapter 5) argues that provincial leaders boasting closer factional ties to the dominant Chinese national leaders could bring in more favorable bank loan policies from the central government.

The coastal provinces were more exposed to the global markets in terms of the role of exports and foreign trade in the provincial economies during the entire period under study. They enjoyed faster economic growth, were wealthier in terms of their per capita GDP level, and in general were more likely to gain from economic globalization. The better business environment and infrastructure with lower "transaction costs" in these development zones must have contributed to the better ability of their host provinces to compete in the international markets, hence allowing them to grow faster and richer. In Chapter 3, I have argued that the natural resource endowments of the coastal provinces were the main reason behind their becoming the main beneficiaries of the preferential policies from the central government early on. Nevertheless, for our purposes, I still have not systematically tackled the question of whether the more "bureaucratically integrated" provincial party secretaries actually managed to bring to the provinces they oversaw more policy pork from the central government.

The prima facie evidence, however, seems to contradict the notion of policy pork being doled out to the provinces led by the more "bureaucratically integrated" party secretaries. The difference in the average bureaucratic integration score for the provincial party secretaries since 1992 diverged between the coastal and inland provinces, with the value being higher for the coastal provinces (Table 4.2 in Chapter 4). At about that time, however, the gap between the two groups of provinces in terms of the extent of the regionally tilted preferential policies received from the center began to narrow (Table 3.2 in Chapter 3). Intuitively, this at least suggests that our measure of the degree of central political control might not be positively associated with the extent of central preferential policies in the foreign economic sector for the provinces. The remainder of this section provides systematic evidence in support of this intuition.

5.3.2 Determinants of Provincial Preferential Policies

Here I use the preferential policy index – simply denoted as *Policy* – from the dataset on the regional distribution of preferential policies constructed by Démurger et al. (2002b) as the dependent variable. As discussed in Chapter 3, for each Chinese province during the 1978–98 period (except Chongqing, which became a provincial unit in 1997), these economists assign an annual score ranging from 0 to 3, based on the types of economic development zones located in the provincial jurisdiction that were authorized by the central government. A score of 0 indicates the absence of development zones of any kind, while a value of 3 suggests the presence of an SEZ (including the Pudong New Area). In essence, a higher score implies the establishment of development zones that imparted greater policy autonomy in the foreign economic sector to the hosting local governments and more tangible benefits to the provinces where the zones were located in terms of their greater ability to attract foreign capital, boost foreign trade and exports, promote economic development, etc.

Démurger and her colleagues are mainly interested in the effect of such preferential policies on provincial economic growth, but they do not examine the provincial-level determinants of these policies. For our purposes, we want to find out whether provincial governments led by the more "bureaucratically integrated" provincial party secretaries tended to be rewarded with more generous policy pork in the foreign economic sector for the provincial jurisdictions they oversaw, as measured by the preferential policy index. As noted earlier, a major expansion in the geographic coverage of these preferential policies took place in 1992. In order to determine whether there was any structural change between the pre-1992 period and subsequent years, I first conduct cross-sectional analysis with averaged provincial-level data for the two periods. I then run pooled time-series cross-section analysis that employs data from the entire period of 1978–98. Consistent with the overall thesis of this book, the following empirical results indicate that our measure of the degree of central political control over the provincial governments – the bureaucratic integration score of the provincial party secretaries – is not positively related to the extent of preferential policies from the central government for the provinces.

5.3.2.1 Cross-sectional Analysis

I first report the results from our cross-sectional analysis. *Policy*, our dependent variable, is the average score of the preferential policy index for each province during the periods of 1979–91 and 1992–98, respectively. Although the index covers the period of 1978–98, I only use the years of 1979–98 due to the need to lag by one year the independent variables that start from 1978, as in our previous analysis. Thus, I run separate tests for these two periods. *Political Control* is our main independent variable. I use the average values of the bureaucratic integration score of the provincial party secretary during the 1978–90 and 1991–97 periods for each province.

A number of provincial-level economic and political variables are also included. I have argued that the provincial natural resource endowments were the primary determinants of why some provinces were selected as the initial recipients of central preferential policies. In terms of opening to the world markets, the most important and logical factor may be whether a province is located along the coast (Chapter 3). Thus, I include in the model a dummy variable, *Coast*, taking on a value of 1 for the coastal provinces and 0 otherwise, as defined in the previous chapters. In addition, I include *Export*, the percentage share of exports in provincial GDP, or *Trade*, the share of total provincial foreign trade in provincial GDP, to examine whether provinces with better preexisting performance in terms of exports or foreign trade were also more likely to be targeted with preferential policies regarding the establishment of economic development zones.[15]

Meanwhile, Shirk's influential "political logic" argument suggests that during the post-1978 era, Chinese national leaders embroiled in succession contests at the center might have courted those provinces that enjoyed a larger presence on the CCP Central Committee with preferential policies (Shirk 1993, 1996). Thus, I include a variable, *Full CC*, measuring the annual percentage share of incumbent officials in the total full Central Committee membership for each province.[16] This is the membership category actually endowed with the requisite voting powers at the plenary sessions of the Central Committee (Jing Shan 1991, 170) and most relevant to the "Selectorate" logic of Shirk. Again, as with the other variables, I use the average values of *Full CC* of 1978–90 and 1991–97, respectively, for the two period samples.

Zhang (2002) has suggested that those provinces that are autonomous regions for ethnic minorities tended to receive preferential foreign economic policies regarding foreign exchange retention. To control for the possibility that these ethnic regions were also favored with policies to establish the development zones, I add a dummy variable, *Minority*, which takes on a value of 1 for these five official autonomous regions for ethnic minorities and 0 for all others. Finally, I control for the effect of being a border province on the regional distribution of preferential policies granted by the central government with a dummy variable, *Border*, which takes on a value of 1 for any province that shares a land border with a foreign country.[17]

---

[15] Provincial exports or foreign trade might also have been affected by the preferential policies from the central government, but dropping *Export* or *Trade* does not affect the results for *Coast*, our main variable of concern here.

[16] For details of the coding and sources of the *Full CC* variable used here, see Sheng (2005a).

[17] Border provinces in China include Inner Mongolia, Liaoning, Jilin, Heilongjiang, Guangxi, Yunnan, Tibet, Gansu, and Xinjiang. Of these, Liaoning and Guangxi are also coastal provinces.

TABLE 5.4. *The Determinants of Preferential Policies: Cross-sectional Analysis*

Models	1979–91		1992–98	
	11	12	13	14
Political Control	−0.24	−0.26	−0.04	−0.10
	(0.23)	(0.21)	(0.12)	(0.11)
Coast	1.12***	0.88***	0.59***	0.61***
	(0.36)	(0.30)	(0.18)	(0.17)
Export	0.04		0.03***	
	(0.03)		(0.005)	
Trade		0.05**		0.02***
		(0.02)		(0.003)
Full CC	−0.30	−0.28	−0.28	−0.27
	(0.36)	(0.22)	(0.30)	(0.29)
Minority	0.02	0.03	−0.01	−0.01
	(0.21)	(0.20)	(0.25)	(0.25)
Border	−0.28	−0.26	0.31	0.28
	(0.21)	(0.21)	(0.24)	(0.22)
Constant	0.80	0.75*	1.45***	1.54***
	(0.57)	(0.41)	(0.35)	(0.36)
Observations	30	30	30	30
F	6.15	8.95	9.93	9.72
Probability > F	0.00	0.00	0.00	0.00
Adjusted R^2	0.59	0.68	0.56	0.60

Note: The dependent variable, *Policy*, is the average preferential policy index of the 1979–91 period and 1992–98 period for each province for Models 11–12 and 13–14, respectively, and is estimated with ordinary least squares regressions. *Political Control, Export, Trade,* and *Full CC* are averages of the 1978–90 period and 1991–97 period, respectively. Hainan became a provincial unit in 1988. The dependent variable for Hainan is thus the average value of the 1989–91 period in Models 11–12. Excluding Hainan from our analysis does not affect the results. Because Chongqing only attained its provincial status in 1997, its observations are not included in the analysis. Robust standard errors are in parentheses.
***: $p < 0.01$; **: $p < 0.05$; *: $p < 0.1$ (two-tailed tests).

Presumably, border provinces enjoy natural advantages in terms of land-based foreign commerce – advantages that might not be fully captured by our *Coast* variable alone, and thus could also receive special consideration from the central government (Zheng 1994).

The results are reported in Table 5.4. Models 11–12 are estimated with data from the 1979–91 period for our *Policy* variable; Models 13–14 employ data for the 1992–98 period. Above all, *Political Control*, the bureaucratic integration score of the provincial party secretaries, is *not* positively correlated with our dependent variable measuring the extent of preferential policies for the provinces. In fact, the coefficient for *Political Control* is negative across all the models, but it is not statistically significant at any conventional level. These results contradict the notion that some provinces should be better able to lobby for policy pork from the central government through their party chiefs who were better connected in the national capital by virtue of prior central work experiences or concurrent Politburo membership.

These findings should not be surprising if the bureaucratic integration of the provincial party secretaries is construed in terms of the degree of political control exercised over the provincial governments by the Chinese political center (Huang 1996), as I pursue in this volume, rather than in terms of the personal connections of the leading provincial cadres under an alternative logic. In the meantime, the *Full CC* variable measuring provincial representation on the CCP Central Committee is not statistically significant at the conventional levels. Interestingly, its coefficient is also negative in all models. These findings lend little support to the implications of Shirk's argument that those provinces boasting higher shares of full CC membership and greater "Selectorate" power should be better able to bring in policy pork from the top national leaders in constant, intense succession struggles for the supreme power of the land (Shirk 1993, 1996).

In contrast, consistent with our argument privileging the role of provincial natural resource endowments, the coefficient for the *Coast* dummy variable is positive and highly significant across all four models. This suggests that the coastal provinces were indeed more likely to be favored with preferential policies in the foreign economic sector, given their natural comparative advantage in foreign trade, as noted in Chapter 3. Not surprisingly, the coefficient has somewhat diminished in both magnitude and statistical significance levels in the latter sample covering the 1992–98 period (Models 13–14). This largely reflects the expansion of regional preferential policies since 1992 to the inland provinces, thus dampening the importance of provincial natural resource endowments, as noted previously. Nevertheless, even in this latter period, being located along the coast apparently had an advantage. It was still a positive and significant determinant of the regional distribution of foreign economic preferential policies.

Meanwhile, the positive and significant effects of *Export* (Model 13) and *Trade* (Models 12 and 14) are also consistent with the results for our *Coast* dummy variable. Generous policies in the foreign economic sector from the central government might have also been granted to provinces with substantial preexisting export and foreign trade capacity, mostly but perhaps not always, located along the coast. Still, some caution is in order here because the effect of *Export* is not significant in Model 11 for the 1978–91 subsample. Finally, being an autonomous region for ethnic minorities or a border province did not appear to have affected the extent of preferential policies regarding the establishment of development zones received by a province in either period in our analysis here, even though these provinces might have received more generous foreign exchange retention rates in the 1980s (Zhang 2002).

Our cross-sectional analysis suggests that provincial geographic locations and to some extent preexisting export and foreign trade performance seemed to be the most important factors in explaining the regional distribution of preferential policies to establish the various types of economic development zones in China. The political ties between the center and the provinces measured either by the bureaucratic integration score of the provincial party secretaries or by provincial representation on the Central Committee of the ruling CCP did not appear to be significant predictors. The value of cross-sectional findings for the two periods, however, may be limited due to the unavoidable loss of information through the averaging of the data over the years. Next, I conduct time-series cross-section analysis that allows us to examine both diachronic and spatial variation in the dependent variable with a larger number of observations.

5.3.2.2 *Time-Series Cross-section Analysis*

Policy, the preferential policy index score for each province/year during the 1979–98 period, is again our dependent variable. It takes on discrete values of 0–3, as described earlier. Thus, we use an ordered logit model, as in our previous estimation of the bureaucratic integration of the provincial party secretaries. Year-specific dummy variables are added to control for year-specific effects and to remedy serial correlation (Beck et al. 1998). Alternatively, I replace the year dummy variables with a lagged dependent variable to address possible temporal autocorrelation. Although it would be ideal to add a province dummy variable for each province (Green et al. 2001), the model would no longer converge during estimation when we control for provincial-level fixed effects. They are thus not included in our analysis here.

Once again, I use *Political Control* as our main independent variable, the bureaucratic integration score of the provincial party secretary for a province in a given year. It is lagged by one year to mitigate mutual causality. Similarly, I also control for *Export* and, alternatively, *Trade*, as well as *Full CC*, the percentage share of incumbent provincial officials in the full membership of the CCP Central Committee. As in our cross-sectional analysis, dummy variables such as *Coast*, *Minority*, and *Border* are also included. These variables are all lagged by one year. The results are presented in Table 5.5. Models 15–16 include *Export*; Models 17–18 use the alternative variable *Trade*. The year dummy variables are included in Models 15 and 17; they are replaced with a lagged dependent variable in Models 16 and 18.

Above all, as in our cross-sectional analysis, our *Political Control* variable is not a positive predictor of the extent of preferential policies for the provinces during these years. In fact, in Models 15 and 17, its coefficient is *negative* and significant (at 0.1 and 0.05, respectively). However, *Political Control* is no longer statistically significant at the conventional levels in Models 16 and 18 when a lagged dependent variable is included. Again, these results suggest that the prior work experiences or concurrent Politburo membership for the provincial party chiefs were not very useful assets when it came to helping bring in preferential policies in the foreign economic sector to the provinces overseen by these officials. Likewise, shares of incumbent provincial officials in the full membership of the CCP Central Committee were not significant predictors of the regional distribution of the preferential policies for the establishment of economic development zones.

In contrast, the positive and highly significant (0.01 or 0.05) coefficient for our *Coast* dummy variable across all four models again implies that the geographic locations and natural resource endowments of the provinces were far more important. To be sure, the magnitude and level of statistical significance of the coefficient declines somewhat when the year dummy variables are supplanted with a lagged dependent variable, but this is again largely expected given the well-known role of lagged dependent variables in suppressing the possible effects of other independent variables (Achen 2000). Nevertheless, the coefficient of the *Coast* dummy variable remains positive and significant (at 0.05 for Model 16 and 0.01 in Model 18). Furthermore, both *Export* and *Trade* are statistically significant. This largely echoes the cross-sectional findings. The center might have targeted those provinces that were already highly capable of exporting to or trading in the global markets with more generous preferential policies. Finally, as in the cross-sectional analysis, *Minority* and *Border* were not significant determinants, implying that foreign economic preferential policies related to the economic development zones were not specifically targeted toward these regions.

TABLE 5.5. *The Determinants of Preferential Policies: Time-series Cross-section Analysis*

Models	15	16	17	18
Political Control	−0.19*	0.04	−0.24**	0.01
	(0.11)	(0.16)	(0.11)	(0.16)
Coast	3.71***	0.74**	3.59***	0.88***
	(0.33)	(0.35)	(0.36)	(0.32)
Export	0.08***	0.06***		
	(0.02)	(0.02)		
Trade			0.07***	0.04***
			(0.02)	(0.01)
Full CC	−0.07	−0.28	−0.06	−0.20
	(0.21)	(0.19)	(0.21)	(0.18)
Minority	−0.01	0.05	−0.03	−0.08
	(0.22)	(0.34)	(0.22)	(0.35)
Border	−0.04	−0.20	−0.10	−0.20
	(0.21)	(0.30)	(0.20)	(0.30)
Policy$_{i,t-1}$		4.88***		4.83***
		(0.48)		(0.48)
Cut 1	6.00	2.68	−0.81	2.60
	(1.31)	(0.46)	(0.39)	(0.45)
Cut 2	7.77	6.56	0.99	6.44
	(1.38)	(0.77)	(0.39)	(0.75)
Cut 3	11.62	13.95	5.09	13.89
	(1.64)	(1.30)	(0.67)	(1.30)
Province dummy	No	No	No	No
Year dummy	Yes	No	Yes	No
Log pseudolikelihood	−384.04	−200.89	−373.32	−200.49
Provinces included	30	30	30	30
Observations	590	590	584	584
Wald χ^2	272.38	129.56	251.55	131.11
Probability > χ^2	0.00	0.00	0.00	0.00
Pseudo R^2	0.46	0.72	0.48	0.72

Note: The dependent variable, *Policy*, is the annual preferential policy index for each province, and is estimated with ordered logit regressions. It covers the 1979–98 period. Because Chongqing only attained its provincial status in 1997, its observations are not included in the analysis. *Policy$_{i,t-1}$* is the dependent variable lagged by one year. All other independent variables are lagged by one year. Results for the year dummy variables in Models 15 and 17 are omitted to economize on space. Robust standard errors are in parentheses.
***: $p < 0.01$; **: $p < 0.05$; *: $p < 0.1$ (two-tailed tests).

In sum, these time-series cross-section findings are consistent with the results of the earlier cross-sectional analysis. Concerns of possible endogeneity regarding the main empirical results of this chapter do not appear to be empirically warranted. There is little evidence that a greater degree of central political control over the provincial governments actually denotes a greater ability of these officials to lobby for central preferential policies that in turn could help the provincial jurisdictions they oversaw become more exposed to the global markets. Instead, the findings tend to support the notion that provincial natural resource endowment profiles ultimately played the major role in helping determine why some provinces received a greater extent of central preferential policies in the foreign economic sector than other provinces. Their more abundant economic resources as they began to thrive in the international markets, of course, also prompted the center to exert tighter political control over their provincial governments later on.

5.4 CONCLUSION

Employing systematic provincial-level data, our empirical analysis in this chapter indicates that the Chinese political center sought to exert tighter political control over the provincial governments in the winner provinces in the era of economic reform and opening to the world markets. A greater degree of *ex ante* political control was exercised by the center via appointing provincial party secretaries with center-friendly career trajectories. More specifically, the more "bureaucratically integrated" provincial party secretaries holding concurrent central posts or boasting significant prior central career experiences were more likely to be dispatched to rule the provinces more integrated with the global markets. Furthermore, our examination of the determinants of the regional distribution of preferential policies on the economic development zones should also assuage possible concerns about mutual causality between our measures of the degree of central political control and the extent of provincial economic openness.

Despite popular predictions otherwise, therefore, there is little evidence that the fiscally assertive winner provinces had indeed been gaining an inordinate amount of political influence at the expense of the center in the Chinese polity. Had they had their way, the winner provinces might have preferred to block the Chinese national leaders from installing pro-center agents at their provincial helms. The systematic evidence from this chapter clearly suggests that the opposite seems to be the case. This is also supported by anecdotes. For example, "strong local resistance" and resentment in Guangdong apparently did not stop the center from sending in Li Changchun, a Politburo member (concurrent centralist), to be its provincial party secretary in early 1998 (Li 2001, 65). Indeed, since 1993, only concurrent centralists have ruled the province as its party chief. Not surprisingly, despite Guangdong's widely reported "fiscal revolt" in the early 1990s, it has been rare to see the province again grab the headlines for openly defying the center.

This chapter shows how the Chinese political center resorted to the exercise of regionally selective political control via the institutions of the sole governing CCP to redress possible central-provincial conflicts engendered in the process of opening up to the global markets. I stress the role of a single ruling political party with its national leaders effectively wielding personnel powers at the subnational level as the institutional linchpin enabling the center to continue to exert a tight political grip over the provincial governments in general and those overseeing the winner provinces in the global markets in particular. Future research might look at whether national-level politicians in similar institutional settings imparting great central political powers sought to exercise similar, territorially targeted political control in the age of economic globalization. I will further discuss these issues in Chapter 7.

By now, we have examined the role of economic globalization in explaining the degree of central political control exercised over the Chinese provincial governments in the era of reform and opening. The question that logically follows is whether as a result such regionally differential exercise of central political control over the provincial governments during these years worked. I turn to this question next.

APPENDIX: APPOINTMENTS, NATIVE SONS, AND "SEPARATELY LISTED CITIES"

A5.1 New Appointments and Native Sons

In Table A5.1, I first report the results of estimating the effect of provincial exports on the incidence of new appointments and the presence of native sons among the provincial party secretaries for each province/year during 1979–2005. The dependent variables are two dummy variables. For Models 19–20, it equals 1 if a new appointment of a provincial party secretary occurred for a province in a given year and 0 otherwise. For Models 21–24, it equals 1 if the provincial party secretary for a province/year was a native son and 0 otherwise. As noted in Chapter 4, the appointment of new people to lead the provinces implies exercise of tighter central political control and keeping a native son at the provincial helm suggests the opposite, other things being equal. I use a logit

TABLE A5.1. *The Effect of Economic Globalization on the Incidence of New Appointments and Presence of Native Sons Among the Provincial Party Secretaries*

Models	New Appointments			Native Sons		
	19	20	21	22	23	24
Export	−0.01	−0.02	−0.01	−0.01	0.01	0.01
	(0.02)	(0.02)	(0.02)	(0.02)	(0.01)	(0.02)
Central City Host	−0.25	−0.37	1.24**	1.23**	0.36	0.42
	(0.41)	(0.37)	(0.56)	(0.62)	(0.29)	(0.53)
Per Capita GDP	0.54	0.07	0.34	−1.29***	0.97**	−0.78**
	(0.74)	(0.19)	(1.18)	(0.40)	(0.39)	(0.33)
Growth	0.02	0.03**	0.01	−0.01	−0.004	−0.001
	(0.02)	(0.01)	(0.03)	(0.03)	(0.02)	(0.02)
Population	−0.10	−0.12	−0.20	0.20	0.30***	0.25***
	(0.36)	(0.37)	(0.27)	(0.41)	(0.05)	(0.08)
Urban Employment	−0.01	−0.01	−0.11**	0.03	−0.03***	0.01
	(0.03)	(0.03)	(0.05)	(0.08)	(0.01)	(0.02)
CAM					−2.14**	−0.29
					(0.87)	(1.27)
Appointment$_{i,t-1}$		−2.04***				
		(0.36)				
Native$_{i,t-1}$				4.04***	−7.63***	5.29***
				(0.38)	(2.14)	(1.35)
Constant	−5.28	−0.60	−1.47	4.54	0.39	0.39
	(6.57)	(3.68)	(10.69)	(4.52)		(1.99)

Province dummy	Yes	Yes	Yes	Yes	No	No
Year dummy	Yes	No	Yes	No	Yes	No
Log pseudolikelihood	−373.84	−373.24	−169.17	−112.05	−340.72	−140.60
Provinces included	31	31	14	14	31	31
Observations	767	797	378	378	797	797
Wald χ^2	62.46	59.21	129.64	146.38	167.59	258.00
Probability $> \chi^2$	0.42	0.01	0.00	0.00	0.00	0.00
Pseudo R^2	0.07	0.09	0.35	0.57	0.22	0.68

Note: The dependent variable for Models 19–20 is *Appointment*, a dummy variable equaling 1 if a province witnessed a new appointment of its provincial party secretary in a year and 0 otherwise. *Appointment*$_{i,t-1}$ is the dependent variable lagged by one year. The dependent variable for Models 21–24 is *Native*, a dummy variable equaling 1 if a province was ruled by a native-son provincial party secretary. *Native*$_{i,t-1}$ is the dependent variable lagged by one year. All other independent variables are lagged by one year. All models are estimated with logit regressions. In Model 19, thirty observations for year 1996 are dropped because of model perfect predictions (no new appointments in 1996). In Models 21–22, observations from seventeen provinces are automatically dropped from the analysis due to model perfect predictions (none was ever ruled by a native son). Results for the province and year dummy variables are omitted to economize on space. Robust standard errors are in parentheses.

***: $p < 0.01$; **: $p < 0.05$; *: $p < 0.1$ (two-tailed tests).

model for these estimations. The variables included are the same as in the estimations for the bureaucratic integration of the officials in the text of this chapter. I tackle possible serial correlation with year dummy variables (Models 19, 21, and 23) and, alternatively, a lagged dependent variable (Models 20, 22, and 24).

Observations from a little over one-half (17 out of 31) of the provinces were dropped from Models 21–22 that include province-specific dummy variables, due to the lack of variation in the dependent variable (none of these provinces was ever ruled by a native son during the sample period). They include Beijing, Guangxi, Hainan, Shanghai, Gansu, Guizhou, Heilongjiang, Henan, Hubei, Jilin, Ningxia, Inner Mongolia, Zhejiang, Qinghai, Tibet, Xinjiang, and Chongqing. In order to see whether the results will change if we include these observations, therefore, in Models 23–24, I drop the provincial dummy variables, but add *CAM*, a dummy variable equaling 1 for the four centrally administered municipalities – Beijing, Shanghai, Tianjin, and Chongqing (since 1997), as in Model 9 of Table 5.2 earlier. However, I do not add the dummy variable *Minority* to the estimation here because none of the five provinces designated as "autonomous regions for ethnic minorities" was ever ruled by a native son during this period.[18]

As we can see, *Export* is *not* significantly related to the dependent variable in any of the models. This suggests that the degree of provincial exposure to the global markets did not appear to matter much in the center's decision to replace an incumbent provincial party secretary or allow a native son to run a province. The results for the other variables, however, are more uncertain and often dependent on the model specifications, implying the need for further research here. For example, hosting a separately listed city that enjoyed direct fiscal ties with the center and was thus subject to direct central fiscal extraction seems to increase the probability that a province would be led by a native son, as seen in the positive and significant (at 0.05) coefficient for *Central City Host* in Models 21–22. Carving out a "cash cow" city for direct fiscal extraction certainly reduced the need for tight political control so that the center could afford to send in a native son. Yet the variable was no longer statistically significant in Models 23–24, leaving out the provincial dummy variables in order to include more observations, even though its coefficient remains positive.

---

[18] Inclusion of the *Minority* variable automatically results in dropping all the observations from these five provinces due to "perfect predictions," but does not meaningfully affect the results reported here.

TABLE A5.2. *The Effect of Economic Globalization on Central Political Control: Accounting for the "Separately Listed Cities"*

Models	25	26	27	28
Export	0.08***	0.03**	0.08***	0.03**
	(0.02)	(0.01)	(0.02)	(0.01)
Per Capita GDP	−0.60	0.02	−0.63	0.01
	(0.62)	(0.25)	(0.63)	(0.27)
Growth	−0.03	0.01	−0.03	0.01
	(0.02)	(0.01)	(0.02)	(0.01)
Population	−0.55	−0.39	−0.58*	−0.41
	(0.34)	(0.32)	(0.35)	(0.33)
Nonagricultural Population	0.05	0.03	0.05	0.03
	(0.04)	(0.03)	(0.05)	(0.04)
Political Control$_{i,t-1}$		3.23***		3.32***
		(0.25)		(0.26)
Cut 1	9.11	11.57	−10.20	1.98
	(6.43)	(2.38)	(4.43)	(3.14)
Cut 2	11.65	15.66	−7.58	6.23
	(6.43)	(2.45)	(4.40)	(3.17)
Cut 3	13.88	19.36	−5.40	9.91
	(6.42)	(2.51)	(4.35)	(3.21)
Province dummy	Yes	Yes	Yes	Yes
Year dummy	Yes	No	Yes	No
Log pseudolikelihood	−809.40	−530.31	−786.06	−505.62
Provincial units included	34	34	31	31
Observations	817	814	793	793
Wald χ^2	428.87	319.55	429.55	308.17
Probability > χ^2	0.00	0.00	0.00	0.00
Pseudo R^2	0.21	0.48	0.21	0.49

Note: The dependent variable, *Political Control*, is the annual bureaucratic integration score of the provincial party secretaries for the thirty-one provinces (covering the 1979–2005 period) and the five "separately listed cities" (covering the 1998–2005 period). It is estimated with ordered logit regressions. *Political Control*$_{i,t-1}$ is the dependent variable lagged by one year. All other independent variables are lagged by one year. Due to lack of data on urban employment for the "separately listed cities," I use *Nonagricultural Population*, which is the percentage share of the nonagricultural population in the total population for all the observations. In Models 25–26, observations from Qingdao and Xiamen are dropped from the analysis because of lack of variation in the dependent variable. Results for the province and year dummy variables are omitted to economize on space. Robust standard errors are in parentheses.

***: $p < 0.01$; **: $p < 0.05$; *: $p < 0.1$ (two-tailed tests).

A5.2 The Role of "Separately Listed Cities"

In Table A5.2, I report the results of additional robustness analysis in order to address the concerns raised by the issue of "separately listed cities" with direct fiscal relations with and under the direct purview of the center's nomenklatura control since 1998, as discussed in Chapter 4. In other words, since 1998, these cities effectively could be regarded as enjoying a provincial-level status for purposes of political control by the center. Here I list Dalian, Qingdao, Ningbo, Xiamen, and Shenzhen as *separate* provincial-level units for the post-1998 period (including 1998) in the dataset. Following strictly the same criteria discussed in Chapter 4 for the provincial party secretaries, I also code the degree of bureaucratic integration for the party secretaries of these cities since 1998.[19]

Analysis in Models 25–26 pools all available data in this period from all thirty-one provinces and five "separately listed cities." However, data from Qingdao and Xiamen are eventually dropped because of lack of variation in the dependent variable – all party secretaries serving in these two cities during this period were localists with only in-province work experiences. Models 27–28 exclude all observations from the "separately listed cities," even though data for the five host provinces involved do not contain data from these cities. Models 26 and 28 replace the year dummy variables with a lagged dependent variable. As we can see, the results for *Export*, our major political independent variable of interest, are broadly similar to those reported earlier in the text for the main estimations of the chapter.

[19] Except for the export data, which are taken from China Ministry of Foreign Trade and Economic Cooperation (1987–2003) and China Ministry of Commerce (2004–2005), the economic data for the five "separately listed cities" are from Guojia Tongji Ju [National Bureau of Statistics] (1998–2005). Data for the municipal party secretaries of these cities are mostly from the Web sites of the *People's Daily*, Xinhua News, and occasionally http://www.chinajunzheng.com/bbs/htm_data/89/0704/58814.html, accessed on June 5, 2007.

6

Consequences for Fiscal Extraction
and Economic Growth

6.1 INTRODUCTION

Amidst the country's rapid opening to the global markets and rising fiscal conflicts between the central and provincial governments, the Chinese political center, via the ruling CCP, did seek to exercise a greater degree of political control over the provincial governments in those regions more exposed to foreign trade and exports during the 1978–2005 period. Provincial party secretaries with career trajectories predisposing them to greater compliance with the policy preferences of the national leadership tended to be sent to rule the more globalized provinces. I argue that such territorially targeted political control was aimed at tapping more fiscal resources from the winner provinces to compensate those provinces that were faring less well in the global markets. How effective was such regionally selective exercise of central political control?

If tighter political control was exercised over the subnational governments overseeing the localities that were more closely integrated with the international markets in order to facilitate central resource extraction, we expect the more tightly controlled provincial governments headed by the pro-center agents to fulfill such revenue demands from above more diligently. Strenuous resource extraction on behalf of the center, however, can vitiate the protection of property rights and distort the incentives of the economic actors populating the jurisdictions ruled by those provincial governments. In short, the exercise of a greater degree of central political control for purposes of resource extraction may ultimately retard economic growth in the targeted provinces.

In this chapter, I proceed to assess empirically the effect of the regionally differential exercise of central political control on central revenue extraction from the provinces and on provincial economic growth in post-Mao China. I first show striking time-series trends during the 1979–2004 period, as reflected in the data at the national aggregate level, that indicate higher budgetary revenue shares for the central government in years with overall tighter central political control exercised over the provincial governments. Consistent with these national trends, furthermore, annual cross-sectional evidence covering the years since the 1994 fiscal reform suggests that Chinese provinces ruled by the more tightly controlled provincial governments were subject to greater budgetary revenue extraction by the central government. Finally, there is robust panel evidence that greater political control tended to have a dampening effect on provincial economic growth throughout the post-1978 years.

In the age of growing economic globalization, such territorially targeted exercise of central political control for resource extraction and redistribution may have arrested some of the worst momentum in the rising regional economic gap if growth in the otherwise more dynamic Chinese provinces was hampered.[1] Still, for those negatively affected regions, stunted economic growth could be a hefty price to pay. My emphasis on the role of the regionally differential exercise of political control in central resource extraction and provincial economic growth is thus consistent with a leading perspective on economic development. This school stresses the crucial importance of "credible commitment" from the central government to protecting the property rights of local economic actors (for example, North and Weingast 1989). Here, however, I apply its underlying insight to the subnational level in examining how the varying degrees of central political control over the different Chinese provincial governments could affect de facto local property rights protection and incentives for economic expansion in the different provinces.

Meanwhile, existing research has highlighted the role of the regionally differential exercise of central political control in affecting the tendency of the provincial governments to surmount the "collective action"

---

[1] While provincial governments in regions more exposed to the global markets were under tighter central political control, this does not mean that economies in the more globalized provinces also tended to grow more slowly in general. The empirical results in this chapter suggest that when other things are held constant, exercise of tighter central political control was associated with slower provincial economic growth. The implication is that those more globalized provinces could have grown even faster absent the more stringent political control over their provincial governments for greater fiscal extraction.

problem in contributing to macroeconomic stability during the post-1978 era. For instance, tighter political control via planting pro-center provincial party secretaries seemed to have enabled the Chinese political center to secure greater compliance from the targeted provincial governments in its constant fight against inflation. Outcomes closer to the preferences of the national leaders – lower public investment growth and inflation – were indeed more likely to obtain in those jurisdictions presided over by the more tightly controlled provincial governments in this period (Huang 1996; Huang and Sheng 2009). The empirical analysis presented in this chapter, however, indicates that on balance, the economic impact of such control over the provincial governments by the Chinese national leaders can be mixed.

In the rest of this chapter, I first examine how the degree of central political control over the provincial governments affected formal fiscal extraction from the provinces by the center during this period. I then discuss the possible effect of such control on provincial economic growth. In particular, I take issue with the "market-preserving federalism" school on China's reform-era economic growth. Its advocates tend to dwell, quite inappropriately, on the national level in discussing the role of political decentralization in post-Mao China. They also overemphasize the importance of the "credible commitment" from the central government to local property rights protection via *fiscal* contracts with the provinces. While stressing central political primacy at the national level, I highlight how the *political* relations between the center and the different provincial governments can affect provincial-level economic growth, a conjecture I then test.

6.2 CENTRAL POLITICAL CONTROL AND FISCAL EXTRACTION

6.2.1 Role of Provincial Governments in Central Fiscal Extraction

There are two main forms of fiscal extraction from the provinces by the Chinese central government. One is more formal and implemented through the budgetary channel. The other can be less formal or observable; in fact, it can be more unpredictable and arbitrary, for instance, through ad hoc "forced borrowings" by the central government, as noted earlier in Chapter 3. Ideally, to assess how tighter political control can facilitate revenue extraction from the provinces, we need to examine both the formal and informal aspects of fiscal flows between the central and provincial governments. Even though anecdotes abound, unfortunately, publicly available information on the latter does not exist on a systematic basis. As a second-best strategy, here I focus on the more formal budgetary revenue flows with publicly accessible data.

Throughout this period, local governments in China did not enjoy independent authority to define their own tax base or to set the tax rates in their own jurisdictions (Wong 1997). Yet they could still play an important role in fiscal revenue extraction from the localities by the central government. Above all, the provincial governments could be directly involved with the center's revenue collection efforts in the provinces, especially before the introduction of the tax sharing system and the establishment of the center's own tax collection agencies nationwide in 1994. While collecting local revenues for themselves, they had to collect on behalf of the central government revenues strictly defined as "central," such as those from public enterprises owned by the central government but located in the provinces (Wong et al. 1995).

Since the fiscal reform of 1994, the direct extractive role of the provincial governments for Beijing has diminished, but they continue to influence the collection of central taxes in their jurisdictions, if more indirectly. For instance, even though the local branches of the national-level State Taxation Administration are no longer politically beholden to the local governments at the same level, their staff still depend on the latter for a variety of amenities related to working and living in the localities. This has allowed the local governments to intervene in their own favor in cases of central-local conflict. For instance, they can step in to help determine the disputed nature of certain business activities to be taxed and the proper tax categories (local, central, or shared taxes) to apply. They can also help taxpayers with insufficient funds for paying both central and local taxes decide on their payment priorities (Yang Bing and Jiao Wei 2001).[2] Since 2002, moreover, the provincial governments have continued to collect the personal and local enterprise income taxes from their jurisdictions, taxes that are later shared with the central government (Guojia Shuiwu Zongju [State Tax Administration] 2002). This can certainly enhance the role in the central government's revenue collection from the provinces played by the provincial governments that actually collect these taxes.

---

[2] Not surprisingly, problems of tax evasion and tax arrears in the provinces during the early post-1994 period were often more serious for taxes accruing to the center than those going to local coffers, as "the local tax bureaus enjoyed tax collection priorities over the branches of the national tax bureau" in the localities (Wang 1997, 813–814).

In addition, the provincial governments might be able to leave their mark on the terms of formal fiscal obligations toward the center in the first place. For instance, during the pre-1994 period of fiscal contracting, the provincial governments often sought to bargain with the national leaders over the marginal retention rates for budgetary revenues in their fiscal contracts with the central government (Fewsmith 1997, 517; Yang 1994, 86). Even the onset of the fiscal reform in 1994 aimed at institutionalizing central-provincial fiscal ties did not eliminate such attempts at influence from below. From time to time, the provincial governments continue to haggle with the central government over the amount of provincial remittances to the center or the size of central fiscal subsidies to the provinces (Chang Yimin 1999; Zhao Yining 2003).

To be sure, lower-level governments within the provinces were responsible for collecting a sizable share of the tax revenues themselves, some of which would go to the center (Oi 1999). However, the provincial governments could influence their tax collection efforts through more or less intensified monitoring and auditing of these lower-level governments (Whiting 2001). In short, the central government's ease in extracting fiscal revenues from the provinces could vary with the extent of fiscal compliance by the provincial governments. Central fiscal extractive efforts would benefit from greater cooperation by the provincial governments in their tax collection efforts on behalf of Beijing (directly or indirectly), in their negotiation of the terms of fiscal contracts and the size of fiscal transfers with the central government, and in their monitoring of tax collection by local governments below the provincial level.

6.2.2 Trends at the National Level

I first examine the broad relationship, as reflected in aggregate diachronic trends, between the average degree of central political control exerted over all the provincial governments and the extent of central budgetary revenue extraction from the provinces, measured as the country's degree of formal fiscal centralization. The goal here is simply to get a rough sense of how the degree of central political control could be related to provincial compliance with central fiscal extractive demands over the years in post-1978 China.

Again, the degree of central political control exercised over the provincial governments is measured by the bureaucratic integration score of the provincial party secretaries leading the provincial governments (Huang 1996). Recall that in order of diminishing central control and declining tendency of the provincial governments led by these officials to comply with central policy preferences, there are four categories of provincial party secretaries. Concurrent centralists (with the provinces/years ruled by this type of officials) are coded with a score of 4, centralists with 3, outsiders with 2, and localists with 1. Because I assume the direction of causality runs from central political control to fiscal extraction from the provinces, I lag *Political Control* by one year to mitigate mutual causality. Thus, I use data on *Political Control*, measured by the annual average bureaucratic integration score of the provincial party secretaries for all the provinces for the period of 1978–2003.

Following other scholars (Wang 1995; Wang Shaoguang and Hu Angang 1993), I assume that the degree of fiscal centralization is higher – implying greater fiscal extraction by the central government from the provinces – when there are more revenue resources in the hands of the central government. I mainly focus on *Fiscal Centralization I*, the share of budgetary revenues collected by the Chinese central government that does not include budgetary remittances from below in its calculation, as noted earlier in Chapter 3. This measure constituted one of the "two ratios" (together with the share of total government budgetary revenues in national GDP) that were explicitly emphasized by the Chinese central government as indicators of its fiscal strength. Their increases were also one of the ostensibly sought goals of the 1994 fiscal reform (Zhang 1999, 116, 131–132). Thus, it is a reasonable proxy of the degree of fiscal centralization for our purposes here. Furthermore, it covers the entire 1979–2004 period.[3] If a tighter political grip by the central government over the provincial governments could facilitate fiscal extraction from the provinces, the average bureaucratic integration score of the provincial party secretaries should be closely and positively associated with the central budgetary revenue shares. The over time trends of the two series are presented in Figure 6.1.

As we can see, since the early 1980s, the lagged values of the average bureaucratic integration scores of the provincial party secretaries have moved closely with the shares of budgetary revenues collected by the central government. Indeed, the positive correlation is very strong. The simple correlation coefficient is as high as 0.77 (p = 0.000) between the

---

[3] Because of its shorter coverage (1990–2004), as noted in Chapter 3, I only present *Fiscal Centralization II*, the share of budgetary revenues available to the central government that includes revenue remittances from the provinces, as a robustness check. The two fiscal series are highly correlated with each other, at over 0.93 (p = 0.000).

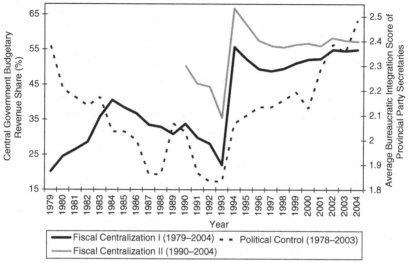

FIGURE 6.1. Central political control and fiscal centralization, 1978–2004. *Note: Political Control* is the annual average bureaucratic integration score of the provincial party secretaries for all provinces during the 1978–2003 period. *Fiscal Centralization I* is the annual share of total government budgetary revenues (excluding remittances from the provinces) collected by the central government during the 1979–2004 period. *Fiscal Centralization II* is the share of revenues available to the central government (including remittances from the provinces) during the 1990–2004 period.

Source: See Appendix to Chapter 4 for data sources of *Political Control. Fiscal Centralization* data are from Zhongguo Caizheng Nianjian Bianji Weiyuanhui [Editorial Committee of the *Finance Yearbook of China*] (2006, 396–398).

lagged values for *Political Control* (1981–2003) and the values for *Fiscal Centralization I* (1982–2004). As discussed earlier in Chapter 4, this was right after the center carried out the first wave of personnel reform during the post-1978 era to institutionalize cadre management at the local levels in 1980.[4] Overall, these time-series trends indicate that a higher share of total government budgetary revenues seemed to have flown to the central

---

[4] The correlation is even higher at about 0.84 (p = 0.000) if we only include the 1984–2003 period for *Political Control* after the 1983 reform reinstituting the one-level downward personnel management system whereby only the major provincial-level officials fall under the purview of the central nomenklatura. The exception was during 1978–80 for *Political Control*. The high average bureaucratic integration score and low central revenue share in the immediate aftermath of the Cultural Revolution probably reflected both the need for tighter political control through the installation of pro-center officials in the provinces and central fiscal weakness during these years.

government during those years when the Chinese political center was on average exercising a greater degree of central political control over the provincial governments.[5]

The positive correlation of these national trends is encouraging, but some other unobservable variables might have driven both the changes in the overall degree of political control over the provincial governments and the changes in the degree of fiscal centralization in China over the years. For instance, one might wonder whether any new policy preferences of Chinese national leaders can explain both the overall tighter central political grip over the provincial governments and the more centralized revenue collection since the early 1990s.[6] In other words, did some form of preference change prompt the center to pursue centralization on both the political and fiscal fronts? Such skepticism is reasonable, but the notion of possible change in the policy preferences of the center is entirely consistent with the underlying theme of this book.

The Chinese political center, in response to the centrifugal pressures of economic openness, resorted to the institutional power imparted by the single ruling CCP to exert tighter political control over the subnational governments of the winner provinces. The goal of such regionally targeted political control, I argue, is to ease resource extraction from these provinces, which will help fund interregional redistribution and prolong national rule by the center. If party chiefs more sympathetic to the center were less likely to champion provincial resistance to Beijing's extractive efforts, exertion of tighter political control by appointing the more loyal agents to oversee the provincial governments would facilitate provincial compliance with the center's revenue demands. Indeed, provincial governments led by the more "bureaucratically integrated" party secretaries (such as the government of Shanghai) seemed more receptive to the fiscal centralization initiative during the 1994 fiscal reform that was widely perceived to be against the interests of the rich provinces along the coast (Zhao Yining 2003).

As noted in Chapter 4, the upward trend in the average bureaucratic integration score since the early 1990s in Figure 6.1 mostly reflects the increasingly tighter central political control over the coastal provincial governments. Such regionally selective exercise of political control must

---

[5] Despite its shorter series, the correlation of *Fiscal Centralization II* (1990–2004) with *Political Control* (1989–2003) is also quite strong (at about 0.65, p = 0.000).

[6] I am indebted to Professor Dali L. Yang for reminding me of this possible line of critique.

have helped the center overcome opposition from the coastal provinces and ensure the relatively smooth implementation of the 1994 reform centralizing China's fiscal structure. The need for both tighter central political control and greater fiscal centralization might have stemmed from the center's growing concern about the territorial challenges arising from China's embrace of the global markets (hence, its "new policy preferences"). The national temporal trends of the average bureaucratic integration score of the provincial party secretaries and the central budgetary revenue share during these years thus suggest that the degree of central political control over the provincial governments may be positively associated with the extent of central fiscal extraction from below, especially from the coastal provinces thriving in the global markets.

6.2.3 Provincial-level Evidence

Nevertheless, the time-series trends at the national aggregate level above are suggestive at best. By themselves, they do not directly show whether at the provincial level the exercise of more stringent political control by the center actually made any difference in helping the center extract fiscal resources. After all, our story of territorially selective political control posits that subnational governments presiding over the winner provinces that have benefited more from opening to the global markets are subject to a greater degree of political control by the Chinese political center. Were those more tightly controlled provincial governments more compliant with the extractive demands from the central government? At the provincial level, did those provinces that were ruled by the pro-center party secretaries in fact submit more revenue to the Chinese central government?

Because provincial party secretaries more sympathetic to the policy preferences of the national leaders should be more likely to comply with the central government demands for revenue extraction, I hypothesize:

H1. Other things being equal, Chinese provinces presided over by more tightly controlled provincial governments tend to submit more budgetary revenues to the central government.

Before the fiscal reform of 1994, provincial-level data on even formal fiscal flows are sketchy. Using data from Lin and Liu (2000), elsewhere I have provided some evidence that provinces ruled by the more "bureaucratically integrated" party secretaries on average received less favorable marginal budgetary revenue retention rates in their fiscal contracts with the central government during the 1985–93 period (Sheng 2007b). This implies greater budgetary revenue submissions to the center by these provinces. Although the central government could violate the contractual terms during later implementation, central political control seemed to have mattered even during the stage of fiscal contract negotiation with the provincial governments.

For the post-1994 period, relatively consistent provincial-level data on formal central-provincial fiscal flows are now publicly available. Some more direct, albeit still imperfect, evidence on the possible role of central political control in facilitating central fiscal extraction can thus be gleaned from the provincial-level data on net inward budgetary transfers from the central government. Compared with their inland counterparts, the coastal regions in China tended to be ruled by the more tightly controlled provincial governments, as I have noted in Chapter 4. They also tended to receive, on a per capita basis, fewer net central fiscal subsidies from (effectively remitting more revenues to) the center during these years, as shown in Chapter 3. In the following, I examine how the regionally differential exercise of central political control over the provincial governments affected annual provincial budgetary revenue remittances to the center.

The dependent variable, *Revenue Remittance*, is the net provincial per capita budgetary revenue remittances (constant 1977 RMB) to the central government for each year during the 1995–2004 period. It is obtained by subtracting per capita central budgetary subsidies from per capita provincial budgetary remittances to the center.[7] All else being equal, a higher value of the dependent variable denotes greater provincial revenue remittances to (and hence greater fiscal extraction by) the Chinese central government. The subsidy data do not contain data on tax rebates for the provincial governments because the levels and fixed growth formulas for calculating these rebates were determined at the outset of the fiscal reform in 1994.

As noted, tax rebates were used by the central government to compensate the provinces for anticipated revenue losses during the 1994 fiscal reform. By nature, they were *not* redistributive, but rather mostly a function of the preexisting provincial fiscal strength as of 1993 (An Xiumei and Yang Yuanwei 2008; Wang 1997; Yep 2008, 239–240). Not

[7] This is equivalent to multiplying by minus one the figures on the net per capita central fiscal subsidies for the provinces reported in Table 3.6 in Chapter 3.

surprisingly, provincial governments that had been more fiscally resourceful tended to receive more rebates (Wang 2004). Therefore, data on tax
rebates for the provinces are less relevant to our understanding of the
extent of central fiscal extraction for interregional fiscal redistribution.
More important for our purposes, almost by definition, it is unlikely
that these base levels of and fixed growth formulas for calculating the
tax rebates could be affected by later changes in the type of provincial
party secretaries and in the related degree of political control exercised by
the center over the provincial governments. They were part of the fiscal
reform package of 1994. In other words, these data will not be very useful for helping us assess the effect of the degree of central political control
in the later years.

In addition to our main independent variable *Political Control*, I
include *Export* – provincial exports as a percentage share of provincial
GDP – due to the possibility that the more globalized provinces might
also be subject to greater fiscal extraction by the central government.
I also add a dummy variable, *Minority*, that equals 1 for the five ethnic minority regions – Guangxi, Inner Mongolia, Ningxia, Tibet, and
Xinjiang. Consistent with the findings from scholarship on the politics of
regional fiscal transfers in post-Soviet Russia (Treisman 1999), research
on central-provincial fiscal transfers in China for the year of 1998 suggests that subnational regions susceptible to ethnic unrest also tended
to be fiscally appeased by the center (Wang 2004). Indeed, targeting
the ethnic minority regions with central fiscal subsidies was an integral
part of the Western Development Program launched in the late 1990s to
help the country's less-developed inland regions (An Xiumei and Yang
Yuanwei 2008; Naughton 2004). Following Treisman (1999), I run separate regressions with provincial data for each year because panel unit-
root tests suggest that provincial data on fiscal flows, with our relatively
short series, are not stationary and not suitable for pooled time-series
cross-section analysis.

I report the results from the annual cross-sectional regressions in
Table 6.1. As we can see, our *Political Control* variable is positively
correlated with the dependent variable for every single year during the
1995–2004 period for which data are available.[8] Despite the relatively

---

[8] In the Appendix to Chapter 6, I report the results of analysis that treats the "separately
listed cities" as distinct provincial-level units for the 1999–2004 period because of their
direct fiscal ties with the central government and the fact that their top leadership has
been directly managed by the center since late 1998. The results for these years are similar to those presented here in Table 6.1.

TABLE 6.1. *The Effect of Central Political Control on Central Budgetary Revenue Extraction from the Provinces, 1995–2004*

Panel A

Year Coverage	1995	1996	1997	1998	1999
Models	1	2	3	4	5
Political Control	18.97*	21.04**	20.72**	16.82*	5.83
	(10.95)	(9.80)	(9.82)	(9.20)	(8.01)
Export	0.06	0.50	0.48	0.64	1.50
	(0.64)	(0.80)	(0.75)	(0.71)	(0.94)
Minority	−94.70*	−94.20*	−97.13*	−111.99*	−137.19
	(54.53)	(46.37)	(50.29)	(58.84)	(82.58)
Constant	−39.6*	−51.1**	−52.0**	−57.4***	−63.2**
	(20.16)	(20.36)	(20.35)	(19.70)	(23.05)
Observations	30	30	30	31	31
F	1.95	2.82	2.65	2.33	1.73
Probability > F	0.15	0.06	0.07	0.097	0.19
Adjusted R^2	0.27	0.37	0.36	0.34	0.29

Panel B

Year Coverage	2000	2001	2002	2003	2004
Models	6	7	8	9	10
Political Control	8.91	18.59	27.98*	28.85*	48.66**
	(8.84)	(12.04)	(15.30)	(14.54)	(21.29)
Export	1.52*	2.26**	2.59*	2.62*	1.44
	(0.83)	(1.10)	(1.37)	(1.35)	(0.95)
Minority	−162.55*	−248.05*	−320.52*	−290.00	−322.32*
	(89.91)	(138.26)	(185.95)	(188.73)	(174.17)
Constant	−83.3***	−151.8***	−185.8***	−201.6***	−283.8***
	(22.97)	(39.43)	(49.42)	(48.21)	(58.44)
Observations	31	31	31	31	31
F	2.42	2.93	2.45	2.68	3.53
Probability > F	0.09	0.05	0.09	0.07	0.03
Adjusted R^2	0.31	0.33	0.33	0.31	0.36

Note: The dependent variable, *Revenue Remittance*, is the net provincial per capita budgetary revenue remittance (constant 1977 RMB) to the central government in each year, and is estimated with ordinary least squares regressions. Data for each year during the 1995–2004 period are estimated separately. All independent variables are lagged by one year. Robust standard errors are in parentheses.

***: $p < 0.01$; **: $p < 0.05$; *: $p < 0.1$ (two-tailed tests).

small sample size, its coefficient is statistically significant at the conventional levels for most of these years, except for 1999 through 2001. Taken together, this indicates that other things being equal, subnational regions in China overseen by the more tightly controlled provincial governments – those led by the more "bureaucratically integrated" party secretaries – remitted more budgetary revenue to the central government during most of these years than other provinces. The magnitude of the coefficient grew gradually from 5.8 in 1999 to 48.7 in 2004, after an initial decline from around 21 in 1996. This implies that the positive effect of *Political Control* may have become more pronounced in more recent years.

Meanwhile, the positive coefficient of *Export* across all models supports the notion that the more globalized Chinese provinces tended to remit more revenue to the center (and the less globalized provinces would receive more subsidies from Beijing). The coefficient, however, is only significant for the 2000–03 period. This is perhaps due to the presence in the same models of our *Political Control* variable that could already have absorbed/attenuated some of the effect of provincial exports (King 1991, 1050). After all, *Export* was a significant predictor of the degree of central political control over the provincial governments in the first place, as our analysis in Chapter 5 shows. Nevertheless, the increasing magnitude of the coefficient in models for the more recent years suggests that the role of provincial exposure to the global markets in interregional fiscal redistribution in China has grown more salient.

Finally, the coefficient for the *Minority* dummy variable is negative and statistically significant at the conventional levels for the most part, except for 1999 and 2003. It suggests that these provinces might have been subject to less strenuous formal fiscal extractions by the central government during these years. In fact, ethnic minority regions in China tended to be fiscally pacified with greater inward budgetary revenue transfers from the central government. The increasing magnitude of the coefficient of *Minority* since the late 1990s may also reflect the growing reliance on fiscal appeasement of the ethnic minority regions via subsidies by the Chinese central government under the Western Development Program.

Our first-cut evidence thus indicates that the exercise of tighter central political control over the provincial governments seemed to have facilitated formal fiscal extractions by the Chinese central government from the provinces during the post-1978 era. Applying a greater degree of central political control might have aimed at ensuring greater fiscal compliance from the targeted provincial governments. Other things being equal, pro-center cadres leading the more tightly controlled provincial governments might have been more willing to comply with the extractive demands of the national political leaders. Perhaps these provincial party secretaries were more effective in ensuring the delivery to the central government of fiscal resources collected in their jurisdictions. They might have been more amenable during negotiations with the center on the terms of the fiscal contracts during the period of fiscal contracting, or more willing to send remittances to Beijing (less adamant in demanding central fiscal subsidies) afterward. They might also have striven harder to keep a close eye on the tax collection efforts by the lower-level governments on behalf of the center.

Indeed, interpretation of our statistical evidence along these lines is consistent with the findings from existing case-study research. In a fascinating study of three coastal provinces in the Yangtze delta during the early 1990s, Whiting (2001, 213–217) shows how the government of Shanghai worked harder than the government of Jiangsu province to fulfill the revenue targets set by the center through, among other things, more intensified monitoring of the tax efforts of the lower-level governments. For Whiting, the Shanghai government acted more like a conscientious agent of the center due to the city's heavier fiscal burdens imposed by Beijing. Yet this does not explain why the Shanghai government was required or willing to contribute more to central coffers than its Jiangsu counterpart in the first place. In contrast, our analysis here would suggest that tighter central political control exercised over the Shanghai government through the stationing there of loyal party chiefs can better explain both its more onerous fiscal obligations to the center and its more diligent efforts to fulfill them. During 1978–91, for example, the average bureaucratic integration score for the party secretaries of Shanghai was over 3.1, while that of Jiangsu was only 2.5 (as shown in Table 4.2 in Chapter 4). During 1978–90, Shanghai also had the most globalized subnational economy in China (as seen in Table 3.3 in Chapter 3), hence the tighter central political control over its government.[9]

---

[9] In Table 3.3, Hainan's trade/GDP for 1978–90 was the highest because its data only cover 1988–90 for which Shanghai's trade/GDP was 43.66 percent, much higher than that of Hainan in the same period. As also discussed in Chapters 3 and 4, Shanghai continued to be the largest net contributor to the Chinese central government, while the government of Shanghai remained under a most tenacious political grip by the national leadership in the post-1994 period.

6.3 CENTRAL POLITICAL CONTROL AND PROVINCIAL ECONOMIC GROWTH

6.3.1 Credible Commitment and Market-Preserving Federalism

The exercise of more stringent political control by the center through placing trustworthy agents in the top post of the provincial governments might not only facilitate provincial compliance with central resource extraction. It can also attenuate the credibility of the central government's commitment to protecting the property rights of the local economic actors who are more vulnureable to the political pressures from above through the more sedulous efforts of their provincial leaders to comply with the central government's extractive demands. Faced with heftier taxes and left with fewer resources at their own disposal, therefore, economic actors in jurisdictions ruled by the more tightly controlled provincial governments might have fewer incentives to pursue economic expansion, other things being equal.

This emphasis on the vital importance of "credible commitment" from the central government to the sanctity of local property rights for regional economic development is consistent with a longstanding thesis in research on the political economy of development (North and Weingast 1989). A central tenet of this school is that governments capable of binding their own hands should be less likely to become "grabbing" or predatory toward local economic actors (Olson 1993, 1996). In the context of post-1978 China, this line of scholarship stresses the role of economic incentives emancipated by the credible commitment from the central government to protecting local property rights via decentralized fiscal arrangements.

Wary of the potential menace of predation posed by an overly powerful central government, this school argues that sustainable economic development requires meaningful political constraints imposed on the national leaders. Federalist institutions that formally divide authority among multiple tiers of government might promise one source of such constraints. In particular, credible commitment to protecting local property rights from the central government is politically "durable" under one particular brand of federalism, known as "market-preserving federalism" (MPF) (Montinola et al. 1995; Qian and Weingast 1997; Weingast 1995). For the theory's adherents, China's post-1978 stellar economic record seems to have provided ample proof of the country's embrace of growth-friendly MPF.

One putative mechanism for signaling the credible commitment of the central government to protecting local property rights in reform-era China was fiscal contracting between the central and provincial governments until it was phased out in 1994. Among other things, fiscal contracts specifying above-quota marginal revenue retention rates for the provincial governments made them de facto "residual-claimants" allowed to keep more locally generated economic resources. Above all, this transformed the provincial governments into pseudocorporate firms obsessed with maximizing economic gains by pursuing sounder economic policies and cultivating faster economic growth in their own jurisdictions. Indeed, such fiscal incentives might have driven much of China's post-1978 economic growth by fostering the rise of the quasi-nonstate economic sector often owned and operated by the local governments themselves (Jin et al. 2005; Lau et al. 2000; Lin and Liu 2000; Naughton 1995; Walder 1995a).

Underpinning this body of research, therefore, is the assumption that the central government in China was capable of "credibly committing" itself to the contractual terms of revenue division with the provincial governments, which would single-mindedly promote economic development under minimal central political meddling. Largely missing, however, has been any serious discussion of the role of *political* factors that are so fundamental to the original MPF formulation. In fact, a fundamental requirement of MPF is that any fiscal arrangements between the central and local governments be "politically durable." Some form of institutional guarantee would ensure that lower-level governments manage their economic and fiscal affairs with little political interference from the central government. Even though they acknowledge the lack of truly institutionalized political powers for the localities as a major limitation, the MPF scholars still highlight the possibility of such "political durability" in China (Montinola et al. 1995, 52–53):

... Viewed from the perspective of the political relationships among the different levels of government, China's political decentralization shares much in common with Western federalisms. The modern Chinese system includes a division of authority between the central and local governments. The latter have primary control over economic matters within their jurisdiction. Critically, there is an important degree of political durability built into the system ... meaning that the decentralization of [economic and fiscal] power is not merely at the discretion of the central political authorities.

I do not dispute the crucial role of a truly credible commitment by the national political leaders to the protection of local economic actors' property rights in unleashing the local incentives to pursue economic expansion. Applying MPF to post-Mao China, however, may be misleading due to its focus on the national level by characterizing China's national political system in this period as "politically decentralized," or because of its overemphasis on the *fiscal* rather than *political* dimension, even in studies that do seek to account for provincial-level variation.

Above all, China's national political system is *not* a conventional political federation featuring a hierarchy of governments with truly autonomous policymaking in their respective domains (say, regarding fiscal affairs) and little meddling by the central government into distinctly local matters (Riker 1964, 11). If political decentralization is measured in terms of governing political party decentralization, as in Chapter 2, China simply has a most centralized political system because its political center is endowed with the capability to exert political control over all the provincial governments via the sole governing CCP. That is, the center enjoys political primacy through its monopoly personnel powers within the ruling CCP to appoint and remove the top provincial cadres. Given the center's political preponderance under CCP single-party rule throughout this period, as I have already discussed at length in Chapter 4, any central government commitment, regardless of whether it was through fiscal contracting or otherwise, should not be very credible in China. In fact, what seems to be lacking under China's political system where the center still predominates politically over the provincial governments is exactly the kind of "political durability" envisioned by the MPF scholars.

With respect to fiscal contracting with the provincial governments, the Chinese central government had not been reluctant to take advantage of its political might to engage in opportunistic behavior. This could undermine the credibility of any commitment to the sanctity of local property rights that is so elemental in the stories of MPF. As already surveyed in Chapter 3, the central government's political supremacy could have eased involuntary "borrowings" from the provinces, often in explicit contravention of the nominal terms of the fiscal contracts. Likewise, few fiscal contracts survived their original, full five-year terms. Ultimately, central political predominance via its personnel powers over the provincial governments can always be the last resort whenever there are conflicts over fiscal matters with the provinces. This was certainly the case when the provincial party secretary of Jiangsu was fired for protesting with the central government on the eve of the 1994 fiscal reform to centralize revenue collection. In sum, the terms of the fiscal contracts with the provincial governments by themselves were hardly binding upon China's national political leaders.[10]

More important, evidence from Chapter 5 indicates that the exercise of a greater degree of political control via appointment of pro-center provincial party chiefs seemed to have been deliberately targeted by Beijing toward the subnational governments in those provinces that were more exposed to the world markets. I have argued that such regionally selective exercise of central political control could aim at tapping the more abundant resources of the winner provinces in the age of globalization in order to help fund interregional redistribution, to remedy regional disparity, and to prolong national rule by the Chinese political center.

Indeed, our evidence presented earlier in this chapter suggests that the exercise of tighter central political control over the provincial governments seemed to be associated with a greater extent of central fiscal extraction from the provinces. This implies a higher probability of fiscal compliance by those provincial governments under tighter central control. The incentives of economic actors are more likely to be distorted in the localities run by these provincial governments, localities where the center's ability to engage in fiscal extraction is less constrained and its commitment to protecting local property rights less credible. The exercise of varying degrees of central political control over the different provincial governments denotes varying degrees of de facto local property rights protection from possible central infringement and predation.

In other words, at the provincial level, the degree of "credibility" and "political durability" in the central government's commitment to protecting local property rights and the resultant incentives of local economic actors to pursue economic growth could *vary* with the degree of central political control exerted over their provincial governments. Largely absent in the existing discussions of MPF,[11] the role of such *provincial-level* variation in

---

[10] Recognizing these inherent difficulties, Chung (2000, 6) observes that the greatest challenge for the political center in actually inducing local incentives and efficiency promised by economic decentralization "is to convince the localities that ... the centre's commitment is genuine and trustworthy," often a no small feat to accomplish in China's center-dominated political system under CCP single-party rule.

[11] Even studies that do recognize possible provincial-level variation in the degree of local property rights protection by the central government tend to attribute such variation to the differences in the nominal terms of the fiscal contracts with the central government for the different provinces (for example, Jin et al. 2005; Lin and Liu 2000). Conventional critiques of MPF in the context of reform-era China (for instance, Cai and Treisman 2006; Mertha 2005; Tsai 2004; Tsui and Wang 2004; Yang 2006) have also taken issue with its fiscal focus and the inapplicability of its logic at the national level. However,

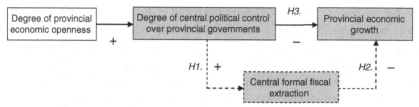

FIGURE 6.2. Central political control, fiscal extraction, and provincial economic growth: Hypothesized causal pathways.
Note: The highlighted boxes specify the hypotheses directly tested in this chapter. The dashed lines map out one possible mechanism linking central political control and provincial economic growth via central formal fiscal extraction; "+" and "–" are the signs of the predicted effect.

the *political* ties linking the central and provincial governments in accounting for provincial economic growth in post-1978 China is our focus here.

6.3.2 Hypotheses

In short, economic actors in localities ruled by the more tightly controlled governments and subject to greater fiscal extraction by the central government should have fewer incentives to expand the economy because the promises of "residual claims" by the central government are less politically sustainable. This, in turn, might hurt economic growth in these provinces. At the provincial level, variation in the degree of central political control over the provincial governments and in the extent of central fiscal extraction should be negatively related to variation in provincial economic growth, as I schematize in Figure 6.2.

As noted, central fiscal extraction from the provinces can take both formal and informal forms. The dampening effect of central political control on provincial economic growth can first be mediated through budgetary revenue extractions by the central government. The more tightly controlled provincial governments tended to submit more budgetary revenues to the central government. They often received less favorable terms for budgetary revenue retention in the fiscal contracting schemes before 1994 (Sheng 2007b), or sent larger budgetary remittances during the post-1994 period. To be sure, due to its greater certainty and predictability, rule-based formal fiscal extraction by the central government

none of the critiques has suggested how the underlying reasoning can be applied at the subnational level with a focus on the regionally selective exercise of central political control, as I have tried to do here.

might be less predatory and less detrimental to local economic growth. It may be easier to build such extraction into the expectations of local economic actors. Nevertheless, even the more predictable, formal extraction reduces locally available resources and can dampen the incentives of the local economic actors within the provinces. Thus, it should still be negatively associated with provincial economic growth.

In an in-depth case study, for example, White (1989) argues that the heftier tax burdens for Shanghai, compared with those for the other provinces, were at least partly responsible for the city's languid economic growth in the 1980s. Among other things, higher effective tax rates for Shanghai may have stunted the development of the nonstate sector, turned away foreign investment, inhibited enterprise capacity for innovation, and deprived the local government of the resources to invest in infrastructure upgrading crucial for future economic growth. In a similar vein, Whiting (2001) finds from her field work in the early 1990s that greater fiscal extraction by the center led to relatively lower pay for the workers, technicians, and managers in Shanghai, when compared with those in the neighboring Jiangsu and Zhejiang provinces. This might have helped contribute to an exodus of talented skill from Shanghai, hurting its economic dynamism. Therefore, I first focus on the more formal aspect by hypothesizing:

H2. Greater formal fiscal extraction from the provinces by the central government tends to be associated with slower economic growth at the provincial level, other things being equal.

Meanwhile, the pernicious effect of central political control on local economic growth can also be filtered through the more informal, arbitrary extraction from the provinces. In particular, provinces led by pro-center party secretaries can succumb to central fiscal predation through the more unpredictable and less visible fiscal ploys of the central government as well as through the more formal budgetary channel. Leading provincial cadres who are more compliant with the center's policy preferences might be more quiescent in face of unwarranted ruses of resource extraction by the center. For instance, they might be less resistant toward central requests for ad hoc "loans" or involuntary sharing of central fiscal burdens through additional revenue contributions beyond their formal fiscal obligations.

Because informal fiscal extraction by the center is more difficult for local economic actors to anticipate, such greater uncertainty can make its effect on the economic incentives particularly deleterious in those targeted provinces. Unfortunately, information on such unofficial fiscal flows is mostly anecdotal, making it much harder for researchers to account for them directly in actual empirical analysis. Nevertheless, the harm on the provincial economy from possible informal fiscal extraction unobservable to the eyes of researchers cannot be adequately captured by the detrimental effect of the center's formal fiscal extraction alone. Instead, the degree of central political control exercised over a provincial government should better help us gauge the ability of the Chinese central government to extract resources outside the formal fiscal channels.

If the exercise of tighter central political control can facilitate central resource extraction that is more arbitrary and invisible, as well as the more formal and rule-based budgetary revenue extraction, it is also more likely to vitiate the protection of de facto property rights and hurt the incentives of local economic actors, and thus hamper provincial economic growth. In other words, if the center's overall credibility in its commitment to protecting local property rights is questionable due to its ultimate political supremacy in a most centralized political system, such credibility should be especially dubious for regions ruled by the more tightly controlled provincial governments. These are provinces led by provincial party chiefs more sympathetic to and compliant with the center's extractive demands, informal or formal. Economic actors in these provinces should enjoy more attenuated de facto property rights protection and hence have weaker incentives to pursue economic growth. We expect the effect of the degree of central political control exercised over a provincial government on provincial economic growth to be negative. Therefore, I hypothesize:

H3. Tighter central political control over the provincial governments tends to be associated with slower economic growth at the provincial level, other things being equal.

In contrast to my focus on possible horizontal variation at the provincial level, a nuanced "organizational" variant of the political economy argument privileging the role of property rights protection in economic development has highlighted *vertical* variation in reform-era China. For instance, Walder (1995a, 270–272) argues that as economic actors in their own right, local governments at the lowest level (that is, at the township level) actually enjoy the least attenuated property rights protection because they operate locally owned public firms farthest away from Beijing and are thus under the least "central regulation." Indeed, the township and village enterprises (TVEs) in rural China were arguably the most vibrant drivers of the country's economic growth, at least until the early 1990s.

For our purposes, however, this line of argument does not address the potentially baneful effect on local economic incentives of the political predominance in the Chinese political hierarchy of the next-higher-level local government vis-à-vis the local officials-cum-entrepreneurs owning, operating, or overseeing the TVEs. In other words, even for local economic actors at the grassroots level, politically empowered fiscal extraction and even predation from *above* – their next-upper-level government – is still possible and indeed often practiced, as Whiting (2001) has found from her field research in Shanghai, Jiangsu, and Zhejiang, although it can also *vary horizontally* for the different localities at each level.

I have shown in Chapter 5 that different provincial governments in China tended to be placed under varying degrees of political control by the center – their immediate upper-level political superiors. Here in this chapter I examine the consequences of possible *horizontal* variation in provincial property rights protection for economic growth among the different Chinese provinces ruled by different types of provincial party chiefs and subject to varying degrees of central fiscal extraction. Drawing on a leading political economy thesis that emphasizes the role of government credible commitment and property rights protection in economic development (North and Weingast 1989), I apply its fundamental insight to the *subnational* level to study the effect of central political control on provincial economic growth in post-Mao China.

6.4 TESTING THE EFFECT OF POLITICAL CONTROL ON ECONOMIC GROWTH

6.4.1 Model Specifications and Estimation Issues

With a subnational research design drawing on provincial-level data from China, I use the annual real growth rate (in percentage) of provincial per capita GDP (constant 1977 RMB) as our measure of provincial economic growth.[12] Our dependent variable, *Growth*, is the real per capita

---

[12] Using aggregate, rather than per capita, GDP growth as the dependent variable as in Zhang and Zou (1998) yields broadly similar results (Sheng 2005b). Here I use per capita growth rates in order to be consistent with most existing empirical studies of economic growth.

GDP growth rate for each province/year during the 1979–2004 period. *Political Control*, the bureaucratic integration score of the provincial party secretary for each province/year during the 1978–2003 period, is our political independent variable. Lagged by one year to remedy mutual causality in the analysis, it is included to test the effect of the degree of central political control over the provincial governments on provincial economic growth, as specified in *H3*.

To test the effect surmised in *H2*, I use different measures of central budgetary revenue extraction from the provinces for the different periods. The existing literature on economic growth in reform-era China has highlighted the use of central-provincial fiscal contracts before 1994 as a credible commitment device by the central government. All else being equal, provinces receiving higher above-quota retention rates for budgetary revenue in the fiscal contracts were subject to a lesser extent of formal fiscal extraction by the central government. Contractual rates for provincial revenue retention thus serve as an indirect though still imperfect proxy for the degree of central formal fiscal extraction from the provinces during this period. I only employ this variable to estimate a subsample for the years of 1979–93, the period to which the practice of fiscal contracting is most relevant.

Specifically, *Revenue Retention* is measured by the marginal rate of budgetary revenue retention for the provinces in the fiscal contracts with the central government, as in Lin and Liu (2000). Alternatively, I draw on data from Jin et al. (2005), which cover the years of 1980–92.[13] Its coefficient should take on a positive sign, as higher revenue retention rates could encourage local economic expansion. Nevertheless, contractual terms do not equate the actual amount of provincial revenue remittances to the central government; in fact, they can be arbitrarily violated from time to time. We thus also expect more uncertainty in the results for this variable.

Earlier in this chapter, our analysis based on budgetary resource flows between the central and provincial governments since 1995 shows how a greater degree of central political control is associated with greater provincial revenue remittances to the central government. Thus, for the 1995–2004 period, I include *Revenue Remittance*, the net provincial per

[13] In contrast, Lin and Liu (2000) study a longer period (1970–93) by assuming the rate for all provinces before 1985 to be zero. Neither study employing *Revenue Retention* includes observations from Tibet. Observations from Hainan are also absent from Lin and Liu (2000). I thank Dr. Hehui Jin and Professors Justin Yifu Lin, Zhiqiang Liu, and Yingyi Qian for sharing their data on provincial marginal revenue retention rates.

capita budgetary revenue remittance to the central government, as defined previously. Note again that our measure only incorporates the formal budgetary transfers between the central and provincial governments. It does not necessarily include the more arbitrary but largely invisible portions of revenue extraction, such as involuntary contributions from the provinces. Still, all else being equal, larger provincial budgetary remittances imply a greater extent of formal fiscal extraction by the center that leaves fewer resources for the provinces. We expect the effect of this variable on our dependent variable to be negative.

I also include a number of economic variables that often appear in empirical studies on economic growth, utilizing post-1978 Chinese provincial-level data. Unless otherwise noted, I do not lag these economic variables because their effect on economic growth is assumed contemporaneous, as in the existing research. *Employment Growth* is the annual growth rate (in percentage) of provincial employment. It accounts for the role of the increase of labor inputs in provincial economic growth (Lin and Liu 2000; Zhang and Zou 1998). Similarly, *Investment Growth*, the annual percentage growth in real provincial per capita total fixed asset investment (constant 1977 RMB), controls for the role of the growth of capital inputs (Lin and Liu 2000). We expect the effect of both variables to be positive.

Per Capita GDP$_{i,t-1}$, the natural log of real provincial per capita GDP (in constant 1977 RMB, lagged by one year), accounts for the preexisting level of economic development of a province. If the "economic convergence" thesis is right (Barro 1991), growth should be slower in the more economically developed places, all else being equal. This would yield a negative expected sign for its coefficient. I also add *Export*, the percentage share of provincial exports in provincial GDP. Greater exposure to the global markets is linked to faster economic growth in a number of studies on China and East Asia, as well as in much cross-national research (for instance, Amsden 1989; Chen and Feng 2000; Dacosta and Carroll 2001; Feder 1983; Frankel and Romer 1999; Park and Prime 1997). We expect a *positive* sign for its coefficient.[14]

For analysis of some subsamples for which consistent data are available, I also control for the effect of *NONSOE GIOV*, the percentage share of provincial gross industrial output value (GIOV) contributed by nonstate-owned enterprises. Many scholars (for example, Lau et al.

---

[14] There are no changes in our main results if we use the share of provincial exports plus imports in provincial GDP.

2000; Lin and Liu 2000; Naughton 1995; Walder 1995a) suggest that the nonstate sector has played a vital role in China's post-1978 economic success. New statistical standards for GIOV data, however, were introduced in 1997 (Henan province seemed to have adopted the new standards in 1994). Thus, I only include this variable for analysis covering the pre-1997 data. Finally, I add province-specific and year-specific intercepts to capture the unobservable effects "fixed" to each provincial-level unit and to each year. This is equivalent to adding to the statistical model a dummy variable for each individual province and for every single year (Green et al. 2001).

Our pooled time-series cross-section data consist of annual observations from thirty-one provincial units for about twenty-six years (1979–2004) for our dependent variable. The data are slightly unbalanced; Hainan and Chongqing attained their provincial status in 1988 and 1997, respectively. Because the fiscal reform of 1994 ended the system of fiscal contracting, I estimate the pre-1994 and post-1994 subsamples separately before analyzing the data for the entire period together. I use ordinary least squares regressions with panel-corrected standard errors, the standard estimation technique for such data in political science (Beck and Katz 1995, 1996). Proper use of this technique, however, requires that there be no autocorrelation in the residuals (Beck 2001, 279). Simple tests show that including one level of lag for our dependent variable is sufficient to cleanse serial correlation in the errors for the full sample covering 1979–2004 and for the subsample covering 1995–2004. Addition of a lagged dependent variable, however, is not necessary for the pre-1994 subsample.

6.4.2 Results

Table 6.2 presents the main empirical findings. Models 11–14 analyze the data from the pre-1994 subsample. Models 11 and 13 include the measures on provincial budgetary revenue retention rates in the fiscal contracts with data from Lin and Liu (2000) and Jin et al. (2005), respectively. I drop *Revenue Retention* from Models 12 and 14 to check the robustness of the findings for *Political Control*. Models 15–16 estimate the data from the 1995–2004 subsample for which relatively consistent data on provincial net per capita revenue remittances to the central government are available. Model 15 includes *Revenue Remittance*; Model 16 analyzes the same data without controlling for the role of provincial revenue remittances. Finally, Model 17 covers the full sample of 1979–2004.

TABLE 6.2. *The Effect of Central Political Control on Provincial Economic Growth*

Year Coverage	1979–93		1986–92		1995–2004		1979–2004
Models	I1	I2	I3	I4	I5	I6	I7
Political Control$_{i,t-1}$	-0.81**	-0.88***	-0.89**	-0.91***	-0.53**	-0.51**	-0.61***
	(0.32)	(0.32)	(0.35)	(0.35)	(0.24)	(0.24)	(0.21)
Employment Growth	-0.004	0.004	0.01	0.00	0.00	-0.02	-0.03
	(0.12)	(0.12)	(0.11)	(0.11)	(0.07)	(0.07)	(0.07)
Export	0.19**	0.20***	0.23**	0.23**	0.15***	0.11**	0.12***
	(0.07)	(0.07)	(0.09)	(0.09)	(0.05)	(0.05)	(0.02)
Per Capita GDP$_{i,t-1}$	-11.46***	-11.16***	-14.18***	-13.44***	-23.64***	-21.54***	-8.62***
	(2.23)	(2.25)	(2.82)	(2.71)	(3.68)	(3.96)	(1.34)
NONSOE GIOV	0.15***	0.14***	0.12**	0.11**			
	(0.04)	(0.05)	(0.06)	(0.05)			
Investment Growth	0.04**	0.04**	0.05***	0.05***	0.09***	0.10***	0.07***
	(0.02)	(0.02)	(0.02)	(0.02)	(0.02)	(0.02)	(0.01)
Revenue Retention	0.04**		-0.02				
	(0.02)		(0.02)				
Revenue Remittance					-0.007**		
					(0.003)		

Growth$_{i,t-1}$					0.21***	0.24***	0.18***
					(0.06)	(0.06)	(0.04)
Constant	73.60***	74.32***	94.97***	89.19***	181.02***	166.12***	65.32***
	(14.08)	(14.28)	(18.20)	(17.22)	(27.10)	(29.11)	(9.10)
Provinces included	28	28	29	29	31	31	31
Observations	401	401	355	355	307	307	758
Province dummy	Yes	Yes	Yes	Yes	Yes	Yes	Yes
Year dummy	Yes	Yes	Yes	Yes	Yes	Yes	Yes
F	13.28	13.37	12.53	12.80	11.00	10.74	16.78
Probability>F	0.00	0.00	0.00	0.00	0.00	0.00	0.00
Adjusted R^2	0.60	0.59	0.60	0.61	0.60	0.59	0.56

Note: The dependent variable, *Growth*, is the annual real provincial per capita GDP growth rate (in percentage), and is estimated with ordinary least squares regressions. *Growth$_{i,t-1}$* is the dependent variable lagged by one year. Although *Political Control$_{i,t-1}$* and *Per Capita GDP$_{i,t-1}$* are lagged by one year, none of the other independent variables are lagged. In Model 11, data on *Revenue Retention* are from Lin and Liu (2000); data used in Model 13 are from Jin et al. (2005). Results for the province and year dummy variables are omitted to economize on space. Panel-corrected standard errors are in parentheses.

***: $p < 0.01$; **: $p < 0.05$, *: $p < 0.1$ (two–tailed tests).

Above all, there is some evidence for H_2 that posits the negative effect on provincial economic growth of the extraction of budgetary revenues by the central government. More important, we have found strong empirical support for H_3 that links tighter central political control over the provincial governments with slower economic growth in the provinces.

The coefficient for *Revenue Retention* is positive and highly significant (at 0.05) in Model 11, largely confirming the original findings of Lin and Liu (2000). This implies that higher marginal revenue retention rates for the provinces in the fiscal contracts and hence less formal fiscal extraction by the central government could be conducive to provincial economic growth during the pre-1994 period. Conversely, lower provincial revenue retention and greater central formal extraction from the provinces may be associated with lower provincial economic growth. Covering neither Hainan nor Tibet, the data on provincial marginal budgetary revenue retention rates from Lin and Liu (2000) effectively begin in 1985 by assuming the rate for all provinces in the earlier years to be zero. The alternative measure from Jin et al. (2005) begins in 1980 and includes observations from Hainan. However, it ends in 1992, one year earlier than the data in Lin and Liu (2000), and one year before fiscal contracting was phased out. If the latter data series are used, as in Model 13, the coefficient for this variable is no longer statistically significant at the conventional levels. Such uncertainty might reflect our reliance on the marginal revenue retention rates specified in the fiscal contracts with the central government rather than the actual revenue retained by the provinces as our proxy of the center's formal fiscal extraction from the provinces. After all, terms in the fiscal contracts were seldom set in stone and might not accurately reflect the true extent of formal fiscal extraction by the center.

Revenue Remittance, the net provincial per capita budgetary remittance to the center during the post-1994 era, is negatively correlated with provincial economic growth in Model 15. The effect is highly significant (at 0.05). A negative correlation between provincial revenue remittances and provincial economic growth is consistent with a conjecture (H_2) highlighting the growth-hampering effect of formal fiscal extractions by Beijing. Thus, there seems to be some empirical evidence indicating that a greater extent of formal fiscal extractions by the center, more likely from those provinces led by the more tightly controlled provincial governments under the watch of pro-center party chiefs, might have hurt provincial economic growth.

Meanwhile, a greater degree of central political control over the provincial governments would also have allowed the Chinese central government to engage in the more arbitrary and informal fiscal extraction that is not captured by our measure of provincial revenue retention or remittance, but could be especially detrimental to provincial economic growth. Indeed, our findings strongly support *H3* predicting stunted per capita GDP growth in provinces that were led by provincial governments under tighter central political control. This was perhaps due to their greater susceptibility to the less visible forms of central fiscal opportunism as well as the more formal budgetary extraction, and hence the more distorted local economic incentives. As we can see in Table 6.2, the degree of central political control over the provincial governments is consistently and negatively associated with provincial economic growth. The coefficient for *Political Control* is highly significant (either at 0.01 or 0.05) in the 1979–93 (Models 11–14) and 1995–2004 (Models 15–16) subsamples, regardless of whether we control for formal budgetary extraction, and in the full sample (Model 17).

According to Model 17 covering the entire period of 1979–2004, the coefficient for *Political Control* is about -0.61. If this is used as the baseline, it translates into a reduction of around 1.83 percent in real provincial per capita GDP growth if we move from a province under a least tightly controlled government led by a localist provincial party secretary to a province under a most tightly controlled provincial government headed by a concurrent centralist. This is consistent with the notion that officials more sympathetic to the center's policy outlook are more likely to comply with central demands for revenue extraction, arbitrary or rule-based. However, eased fiscal extraction by the center via exercise of tighter political control over the provincial governments can undermine the credibility of the central government's commitment to safeguarding the property rights of local economic actors and can hurt local incentives for economic expansion.

Echoing the findings of much existing research, *Export*, the percentage share of provincial exports in GDP, exerts a positive and significant (at 0.01 or 0.05) effect upon provincial economic growth, as shown in all models in Table 6.2. The effect of *Per Capita GDP$_{i,t-1}$* measuring the preexisting level of provincial economic development, is negative and highly significant (at 0.01) in all models. This provides strong evidence of possible economic "convergence" among China's provinces, as growth of the more economically developed provinces tended to be slower than that of the other provinces during this period, other things being equal. Again confirming the findings of Lin and Liu (2000), growth in provincial capital inputs, measured by real per capita fixed asset investment – *Investment*

Growth – is a positive and significant predictor of provincial economic growth across all models. Similarly, for our pre-1994 subsamples, the contribution by the nonstate sector to provincial gross industrial output, measured by our *NONSOE GIOV* variable, is a positive and highly significant (at 0.05 or 0.01) determinant of provincial economic growth. This is consistent with research that highlights the salutary contributions of the nonstate sector to China's growth record in the reform period. A little surprisingly, however, *Employment Growth*, measuring annual growth in the provincial labor force, fails to attain statistical significance at the conventional levels in our models.

6.4.3 Summary and Discussion

I have so far presented empirical evidence linking the exercise of tighter central political control over the provincial governments with slower provincial economic growth in China during the post-1978 period. While facilitating formal revenue extraction from the provinces, a greater degree of central political control over the provincial governments by appointing the more compliant provincial party chiefs can also help the central government engage in the more informal and arbitrary revenue extraction. A greater extent of fiscal extraction by the center (formal and informal) can attenuate protection of the property rights of the local economic actors, twist their incentives, and hinder economic expansion in those Chinese provinces presided over by the more tightly controlled provincial governments.

One concern at this point is whether the direction of causality surmised in this chapter can be reversed.[15] Is it possible that the center tended to keep a more tenacious political grip over those provincial governments that presided over slower-growing local economies? For example, did the center try to send in the more trustworthy officials to improve the economic performance in provinces with a lackluster record, perhaps due to cadre incompetence? Our empirical evidence, however, does not appear to support the notion that the center would opt to exercise tighter political control to promote provincial growth. Indeed, empirical analysis presented in Chapter 5 regarding the determinants of the degree of central political control exercised over the provincial governments indicates that the rate of provincial economic growth was not a significant predictor

[15] I thank the late Professor Michael Wallerstein for suggesting the need to address possible reverse causality here.

of the bureaucratic integration score of the provincial party secretaries appointed during the post-1978 era. In short, a province's past growth record by itself did not seem to be an important consideration in the center's decisions regarding the type of provincial party secretaries to send to the provinces in this period.

Another plausible objection is that instead of the story of central credible commitment and local property rights protection pursued in this chapter, tighter central political control might hurt provincial economic growth via an entirely different mechanism. By virtue of being "better" agents of the center, some provincial party secretaries may be more likely to share the center's policy aversion to excessive public investment growth that can endanger national macroeconomic stability, despite the temptation to overheat the local economy confronting all provincial governments (Huang 1996). After all, provincial governments under tighter central political control – that is, those headed by the more "bureaucratically integrated" provincial party secretaries – did preside over lower inflation in their jurisdictions during much of the post-1978 era (Huang and Sheng 2009).

In other words, it could be a "collective action" story whereby tighter political control over the provincial governments discourages free riding in the provision of a national-level public good – lower inflation – eventually suppressing provincial economic growth. To explore whether and how inflation can affect economic growth in the provinces, I redo the analysis reported in Table 6.2 by accounting for the possible role of *Inflation*, the annual percentage change in the provincial consumer price indices in provincial economic growth. I also use both the lagged (by one year) and unlagged values of provincial inflation to see whether lagging makes any difference. Following the original analysis, I estimate the 1979–93 and 1995–2004 subsamples and the full sample for 1979–2004 separately.

As we can see from Table 6.3, provincial inflation is significantly but *negatively* associated with provincial economic growth in the models where *Inflation* is *not* lagged for the two subsamples (Models 18 and 20) or for the full sample (Model 22). This supports the notion that inflation might increase the transaction costs of economic activities and thus reduce economic growth (Zhang and Zou 1998, 230). When the variable is lagged by one year, however, the negative coefficient of the variable is only significant in the 1979–93 subsample (Model 19). If economic growth in those localities ruled by the more tightly controlled provincial governments were slower due to the sympathy of provincial leaders with the aversion of the national leaders to high inflation, we should have

TABLE 6.3. *The Effect of Inflation on Provincial Economic Growth*

Year Coverage	1979–93		1995–2004		1979–2004	
Models	18	19	20	21	22	23
Political Control$_{i,t-1}$	−1.02***	−0.81**	−0.64***	−0.53**	−0.63***	−0.50**
	(0.33)	(0.34)	(0.24)	(0.24)	(0.20)	(0.21)
Employment Growth	−0.05	−0.04	−0.05	−0.02	−0.04	−0.02
	(0.12)	(0.12)	(0.06)	(0.07)	(0.07)	(0.07)
Export	0.16**	0.19**	0.10**	0.11**	0.11***	0.13***
	(0.08)	(0.09)	(0.05)	(0.05)	(0.02)	(0.02)
Inflation	−0.38***		−0.35***		−0.34***	
	(0.10)		(0.13)		(0.08)	
Inflation$_{i,t-1}$		−0.21**		0.05		−0.04
		(0.11)		(0.12)		(0.08)
NONSOE GIOV	0.15***	0.12**				
	(0.05)	(0.05)				
Per Capita GDP$_{i,t-1}$	−10.53***	−11.55***	−20.44***	−21.33***	−9.08***	−9.65***
	(2.33)	(2.41)	(3.93)	(4.01)	(1.28)	(1.27)
Investment Growth	0.07**	0.06***	0.11***	0.10***	0.09***	0.08***
	(0.02)	(0.02)	(0.02)	(0.02)	(0.01)	(0.01)

Growth$_{i,t-1}$			0.21***	0.24***	0.18***	0.18***
			(0.06)	(0.06)	(0.04)	(0.04)
Constant	73.58***	78.96***	159.91***	164.55***	71.01***	72.44***
	(15.16)	(15.68)	(28.96)	(29.54)	(8.74)	(8.77)
Provinces included	30	30	31	31	31	31
Observations	385	378	304	304	719	712
Province dummy	Yes	Yes	Yes	Yes	Yes	Yes
Year dummy	Yes	Yes	Yes	Yes	Yes	Yes
Adjusted R^2	0.61	0.60	0.60	0.58	0.60	0.58
F	12.94	12.21	10.91	10.28	18.39	17.14
Probability>F	0.00	0.00	0.00	0.00	0.00	0.00

Note: The dependent variable, *Growth*, is the annual real provincial per capita GDP growth rate (in percentage), and is estimated with ordinary least squares regressions. *Growth$_{i,t-1}$* is the dependent variable lagged by one year. *Inflation* is measured by the annual percentage change in the provincial consumer price indices. Although *Inflation$_{i,t-1}$*, *Political Control$_{i,t-1}$*, and *Per Capita GDP$_{i,t-1}$* are lagged by one year, all other independent variables are not lagged. Results for the province and year dummy variables are omitted to economize on space. Panel–corrected standard errors are in parentheses.

***: $p < 0.01$; **: $p < 0.05$, *: $p < 0.1$ (two–tailed tests).

observed exactly the opposite in our analysis. *Inflation* would have taken on a positive sign, with higher provincial inflation being linked with faster provincial economic growth and lower inflation with slower growth. For our purposes, these findings provide little support for the notion that provincial inflation was a positive and significant predictor of provincial economic growth.[16]

Our empirical evidence thus does not corroborate the observable implications of a possible "collective action" story that predicts lower provincial economic growth in the presence of lower inflation. Most important for our purposes, inclusion in the estimation of a variable on provincial inflation – regardless of whether or not it is lagged by one year – does not seem to affect the negative and significant effect of our *Political Control* variable. Its results are indeed broadly similar to those reported in Table 6.2. Still, an inflation variable does not normally appear in most recent studies on economic growth in China (for instance, Lin and Liu 2000; Park and Prime 1997) or estimations of economic growth in the cross-national literature (Barro 1991, 1996; Przeworski et al. 2000). This is probably due to the lack of clear theoretical rationales or possible endogeneity of the variable, as acknowledged even by scholars who do add such a variable in their estimations employing Chinese provincial-level data (Zhang and Zou 1998, 230). Thus, I do not include the variable in the main analysis reported earlier in this chapter.

Of course, if an alternative "collective action" logic can better explain the empirical findings from this chapter of tighter central political control associated with lower provincial economic growth, it would imply that provincial governments under tighter central political control were more sympathetic to the policy preferences of the Chinese political center for lower economic growth during this era. While the Chinese national leaders, like their counterparts elsewhere, are generally concerned about macroeconomic instability and inflation, there is little evidence that they actually prefer lower economic growth. Indeed, our discussions from Chapter 3 suggest that they launched economic reform and embraced the global markets in the post-1978 years in order to pursue greater efficiency gains and faster economic growth for the country.

---

[16] I only report the results from the specifications that exclude *Revenue Retention* or *Revenue Remittance* for the sake of space. Including variables on the revenue retention rates in the fiscal contracts and on the net provincial per capita revenue remittance does not meaningfully affect the results for *Political Control*; the effect of *Inflation* tends to be either negative (if not lagged or even if lagged for the 1979–93 period) or not significant, as in Table 6.3.

6.5 CONCLUSION

Confronting the mounting need for interregional fiscal redistribution as China opened to the world markets, the political center, via the ruling CCP, resorted to exerting tighter political control over the subnational governments in the winner provinces in order to extract resources, mitigate regional economic disparity, and maintain its national rule. Indeed, Chinese provinces ruled by the more tightly controlled provincial governments – headed by provincial party secretaries more compliant with central policy preferences by virtue of their career trajectories – tended to obtain lower marginal budgetary revenue retention rates in their fiscal contracts with the central government (Sheng 2007b). They also remitted more budgetary revenues to the center after the fiscal reform of 1994. Presumably, these provinces might have been equally susceptible to greater informal fiscal extraction by the central government that was more arbitrary and unpredictable, but less observable.

As long as national-level leaders via the sole-ruling CCP still directly manage the political careers of the top provincial cadres, it is difficult to imagine that the political center will be institutionally bound to not engaging in fiscal opportunism vis-à-vis the provinces. A greater degree of central political control exercised over the provincial governments not only facilitates formal and informal resource extraction by the central government. It can also increase the likelihood of central fiscal predation, dampen the incentives of local economic actors, and retard local economic growth in those very provinces targeted for greater control and extraction. Our analysis of the provincial-level data in this chapter confirms such a negative link between the degree of central political control exercised over a provincial government and the rate of local economic growth presided over by the provincial government during the 1979–2004 period.

A longstanding thesis in the literature on the political economy of development highlights the positive role of the "credible commitment" of the central government to the protection of local property rights in unleashing the incentives for economic expansion among local economic actors. In the context of studying economic growth in post-Mao China, the MPF scholars implicitly assume that a form of "credible commitment" by the center was automatically built into the fiscal contracts with the provincial governments. Sweeping notions of a central credible commitment to local property rights protection through fiscal contracting, however, are inappropriate for explaining China's impressive economic record during this period due to the political supremacy of the center.

To carry out interregional redistribution and redress rising regional disparity under economic openness, the Chinese central government might have been tempted to ignore the nominal terms of the fiscal contracts in order to extract revenue from the winner provinces with more resources to spare. The credibility of its commitment to protecting local property rights via fiscal contracting could thus be eroded by the center's resilient political predominance within a most centralized political system – a single-party state. Instead, we can apply the logic of credible commitment and local property rights protection more fruitfully to understanding how regionally selective central political control over the different provincial governments might affect economic growth in the different provinces. Thus, I try to bring politics back into our discussion of the role of the "credible commitment" from the central government in local economic development and to situate the argument on a more appropriate (provincial) level of analysis.

Evidence of tighter central political control facilitating central fiscal extraction and hindering provincial economic growth, however, does not necessarily imply that the sole consequence of such control wielded by the Chinese political center was excessive resource extraction from and even possible fiscal predation upon the targeted provinces that hampered provincial economic growth. While undermining local property rights protection and distorting incentives, the exercise of more stringent political control over certain provincial governments to extract resources and help finance interprovincial fiscal transfers by the central government might have mitigated the uneven regional economic development among the provinces. Thus, if tighter political control was exercised over the subnational governments in the winner provinces in the global markets (Chapter 5), stunted growth in these otherwise economically more dynamic provinces suggests the possible equalizing effect of central revenue extraction and redistribution eased by the regionally targeted political control through a single governing political party.

Finally, the potentially incentive-distorting effect of tighter central political control over the provincial governments should also be considered together with its more benevolent role in curbing excessive public investment growth and containing inflationary pressures in the provinces (Huang 1996; Huang and Sheng 2009). After all, exercise of a

greater degree of central political control over the provincial governments can help remedy the subnational-level "collective action" curse
by contributing to such national-level public goods as macroeconomic
stability. Arguably, a stable national macroeconomic environment might
be just as vital for ensuring sustained economic development as secure
local property rights protection. The net economic consequences of the
regionally differential exercise of central political control under single-
party rule thus could be complex. I will further discuss these implications in the next chapter.

APPENDIX: ACCOUNTING FOR "SEPARATELY LISTED CITIES"

As noted, since late 1998, the top government and party leadership of
the "separately listed cities" have been directly appointed by the center.
Because these cities also enjoy direct fiscal ties with the Chinese central
government, it might make sense that these cities are included in the analysis as separate provincial-level units for the post-1998 years (including
1998). In this Appendix, I present the results for our robustness analysis
that lists these cities as additional, distinct provincial-level units in the
dataset.

In Table A6.1, I present the empirical results from cross-sectional analysis of the effect of central political control on net provincial per capita
budgetary remittances to the central government. The data from these
"separately listed cities" became relevant for our purposes in 1998. Our
data for analysis effectively cover the 1999–2004 period due to the need
to lag the independent variables by one year to mitigate mutual causality. The specifications follow those of Table 6.1, except that here I also
add a dummy variable, *Central City*, that equals 1 if a provincial-level
unit was actually a separately listed city (for Dalian, Ningbo, Qingdao,
Shenzhen, and Xiamen) and 0 otherwise. The expectation is that these
cities should be subject to greater central fiscal extraction because they
are essentially "cash cow" enclaves carved out of existing provincial
boundaries for exactly such purposes. The positive and mostly significant coefficients for *Central City* seem to bear out this hunch. More
important for our purposes, the results for *Political Control* are broadly
similar to those presented in Table 6.1. Its coefficient has taken on a
positive sign in all models. Despite the small sample sizes, it is also statistically significant (at 0.05 or 0.1) for models using data from 2001,
2002, and 2004.

TABLE A6.1. *The Effect of Central Political Control on Central Revenue Extraction: Accounting for the "Separately Listed Cities"*

Year Coverage	1999	2000	2001	2002	2003	2004
Models	24	25	26	27	28	29
Political Control	9.89	12.88	23.76*	39.20**	28.89	54.83**
	(9.55)	(9.78)	(13.33)	(19.05)	(18.14)	(22.16)
Central City	69.36***	69.74***	77.69*	111.89**	78.28	204.25**
	(20.78)	(21.03)	(38.43)	(50.77)	(66.99)	(76.14)
Export	0.72**	0.87**	1.07**	0.97	0.77	0.08
	(0.31)	(0.33)	(0.52)	(0.70)	(0.89)	(0.84)
Minority	−141.79	−166.81*	−256.40*	−332.89*	−308.67	−338.14*
	(84.00)	(90.04)	(138.15)	(186.15)	(191.06)	(174.83)
Constant	−61.82***	−83.37***	−146.00***	−189.59***	−172.60***	−272.47***
	(21.30)	(22.41)	(37.68)	(51.40)	(49.29)	(59.45)
Observations	36	36	36	36	36	36
F	11.90	12.67	6.82	5.04	2.47	4.21
Probability > F	0.00	0.00	0.00	0.00	0.07	0.01
Adjusted R^2	0.39	0.41	0.37	0.35	0.29	0.39

Note: The dependent variable, *Revenue Remittance*, is the net provincial per capita budgetary revenue remittance (constant 1977 RMB) to the central government in each year during 1999–2004, and is estimated with ordinary least squares regressions. The five "separately listed cities" during these years are included as additional, separate observations in the analysis, together with the thirty-one existing provincial units whose data now do not contain data for these cities. All independent variables are lagged by one year. Robust standard errors are in parentheses.

***: $p < 0.01$; **: $p < 0.05$; *: $p < 0.1$ (two-tailed tests).

TABLE A6.2. *The Effect of Central Political Control on Provincial Economic Growth: Accounting for the "Separately Listed Cities"*

Year Coverage	1995–2004		1979–2004
Models	30	31	32
Political Control$_{i,t-1}$	−0.60**	−0.59**	−0.64***
	(0.26)	(0.26)	(0.20)
Employment Growth	−0.12*	−0.14**	−0.11
	(0.07)	(0.06)	(0.07)
Export	0.12***	0.10**	0.12***
	(0.04)	(0.04)	(0.02)
Per Capita GDP$_{i,t-1}$	−21.65***	−19.72***	−8.50***
	(3.57)	(3.78)	(1.36)
Investment Growth	0.05***	0.05***	0.06***
	(0.01)	(0.01)	(0.01)
Revenue Remittance	−0.007**		
	(0.003)		
Growth$_{i,t-1}$	0.24***	0.28***	0.18***
	(0.06)	(0.06)	(0.04)
Constant	169.81***	155.79***	65.20***
	(26.68)	(28.18)	(9.32)
Provinces included	36	36	36
Observations	336	336	787
Province dummy	Yes	Yes	Yes
Year dummy	Yes	Yes	Yes
F	9.24	9.08	16.03
Probability>F	0.00	0.00	0.00
Adjusted R^2	0.56	0.55	0.56

Note: The dependent variable, *Growth*, is the annual real provincial per capita GDP growth rate, and is estimated with ordinary least squares regressions. *Growth*$_{i,t-1}$ is the dependent variable lagged by one year. *Political Control*$_{i,t-1}$ and *Per Capita GD*$_{i,t-1}$ are lagged by one year. None of the other independent variables are lagged. The five "separately listed cities" during 1998–2004 are included as additional, separate observations in the analysis, together with the thirty-one existing provincial units whose data now do not contain data for these cities. Data on *Employment Growth* are missing for Qingdao for 1999. Results for the province and year dummy variables are omitted to economize on space. Panel-corrected standard errors are in parentheses.
***: $p < 0.01$; **: $p < 0.05$, *: $p < 0.1$ (two-tailed tests).

The results with regard to the effect of the degree of central political control over the provincial governments on economic growth in the provinces are presented in Table A6.2. Following Models 15–16 in Table 6.2, I estimate the 1995–2004 subsample by either including

(Model 30) or excluding (Model 31) the *Revenue Remittance* variable. In Model 32, I follow Model 17 in Table 6.2 to estimate the full sample covering the period of 1979–2004. Once again, the results for *Political Control* are largely similar to those in Table 6.2 in terms of magnitude and statistical significance. Its coefficient is negative and highly significant (at 0.05 or 0.01).

7

Globalization, Single-Party Rule, and China's Transitions

7.1 INTRODUCTION

So far, I have sought to provide one explanation along the territorial dimension for the broader puzzle posed in Chapter 1 – the resilience of national rule by the CCP-led Chinese central government in the face of the mounting challenges from the country's embrace of economic reform and the global markets. In particular, I have focused on the regionally selective exercise of political control over the subnational governments by the political center via the sole governing political party. Although helping the center ward off the centrifugal tendencies menacing its national rule so far, such territorially targeted exercise of political control by the Chinese political center has also engendered mixed economic consequences at the provincial level.

The empirical evidence for this book mainly comes from one country. Can our argument be relevant to the settings of other countries? What implications does the research have for the broader comparative political economy scholarship on domestic territorial politics of economic globalization and the cross-national literature on the macroeconomic consequences of political decentralization? What light can the focus of this book on the central-provincial political relations in China shed on the role of CCP single-party rule in contouring China's path of economic transition during this period, and more tentatively, in shaping the trajectory of the country's future political transition?

In the remainder of this concluding chapter, I first stress the need to incorporate the incentives of and institutional resources available to the national politicians in studying domestic territorial conflicts under rising global market integration. I then briefly suggest other possible cases – specifically contemporary Vietnam and the former Soviet Union – where my argument might be fruitfully applied in future research. I also discuss the hitherto neglected utility of employing subnational-level data to measure and empirically test the macroeconomic effects of political decentralization. Next I turn to assess the overall role of authoritarian single-party rule – the most centralized of the Rikerian political (party) system – in China's ongoing economic transition to a market-based economy, and speculate on the implications for china's future transition to political democracy.

7.2 BROADER IMPLICATIONS

7.2.1 Economic Globalization and Centralized Political Parties

The study of "authority migration" has gained new prominence in political science in recent years.[1] Focusing on the powerful centrifugal forces unleashed by global market integration from below, some prominent economists have predicted that the winner subnational regions thriving in the global markets and demanding greater fiscal and ultimately political autonomy will overawe the central governments of the existing states (for example, Alesina and Spolaore 1997; Bolton et al. 1996). There is no denying that a perspective privileging the demands of the winner regions for greater autonomy might be more valid in settings where the political center has been institutionally disadvantaged in the first place. Nevertheless, an approach prophesizing the inevitable implosion of the national-level political authority under the fissiparous pressures of economic openness may be a little oversweeping and the blanket pronouncement of the universal demise of the political center premature.

Several decades into the latest phase of economic globalization, the resilience of the national-level political authority seems to have been largely underestimated. Few countries have disintegrated because of an opening to the global markets. Fiscal powers, the fulcrum of the conflicts between the center and the subnational regions, seem to be more centralized in the more globalized economies. In this volume, I have highlighted the crucial importance of the incentives of and institutional resources for national-level political actors. In countries where centralized political

---

[1] For example, see the various contributions at the symposium on "Authority Migration: Defining an Emerging Research Agenda," in the July 2004 issue of the disciplinary journal *PS: Political Science & Politics*.

parties rule both the national and regional tiers of government and the national offices of the governing parties play a key role in selecting subnational government personnel, national political leaders are equipped for, as well as interested in, wielding a tighter political grip over the subnational governments of the winner regions in the global markets. Our empirical evidence from China during the 1978–2005 period shows that the national leaders via the ruling CCP did indeed seek to exercise a greater degree of political control over the subnational governments in those provinces that thrived on foreign trade and exports.

My emphasis on the national-level political actors' incentives and institutional resources broadly echoes the call by Kahler and Lake (2003a, 27) for more attention to "actor incentives and existing institutional rules" in studying patterns of domestic as well as international "authority transition" under globalization. Unfortunately, at this preliminary stage of comparative data collection on political party centralization (Rodden and Wibbels 2002, 509), I have only tested the argument on China through a subnational research design. More work might be directed at collecting similar party organizational data and subnational foreign trade, export, and other economic data in other countries governed by centralized political parties.

Future research might start with the comprehensive list of effective authoritarian single-party regimes carefully compiled by Geddes (1999a) for the 1950–99 period. By definition, one political party rules all the subnational regions in single-party states. For the most part, the political center in authoritarian single-party regimes wields a greater degree of political control over its copartisans governing the subnational regions than do its counterparts elsewhere. In general, the single ruling party thus constitutes the most centralized political party along the two Rikerian dimensions (Riker 1964). As economic globalization exacerbates interregional disparity and fuels centrifugal pressures from below, we should expect national political leaders in these states to seek a tighter political grip over the subnational governments in the winner regions. Exercise of more stringent political control will facilitate the extraction of resources from the winner regions, redress the rising interregional disparity stoking regional discontent, and help maintain territorial integrity and national rule by the political center. Two cases are particularly fascinating in this regard.

7.2.1.1 *Vietnam*

One attractive case for comparison with China in future research is contemporary Vietnam. Like China, since its reunification Vietnam has been ruled by a single political party – the Vietnamese Communist Party. Like its Chinese counterpart, the central government of Vietnam jumped aboard the globalization bandwagon to flee the rising "opportunity costs of closure" amidst the country's economic transition to a market economy under Doi Moi (renovation) launched in the late 1980s (Duiker 1995, 159–161; Vuving 2006, 811). Like the CCP national leadership, the national leaders of the Communist Party of Vietnam have so far managed to avoid the fate of their Eastern European and Soviet counterparts and have been able to hold onto their power and keep the country together. More interesting for our purposes, the territorial politics of economic openness in Vietnam has also grown increasingly salient during this period. Nevertheless, national rule by the Communist Party center in Vietnam has endured despite the centrifugal forces unleashed from below by the country's increasing integration with the global markets.

Above all, uneven regional participation in the global markets seemed to have also created (at least relative) winners and losers among the Vietnamese provinces.[2] The coastal provinces were much more exposed to the global markets. In Table 7.1, I first report summary data on the ability to attract foreign direct investment (FDI) for the coastal and inland provinces of Vietnam, consistent with our earlier presentation of Chinese provincial data. I also divide the data into two roughly equal periods to gauge possible cross-year changes. To be sure, over the years, the role of foreign capital in the provincial economies surged for all provinces, both along the coast and in the inland. Yet in both periods, the coastal provinces witnessed significantly greater FDI inflows relative to the size of their economies. The average share of FDI stock in provincial GDP for the coastal provinces was 8.9 percent during 1990–96 and 29.5 percent during 1997–2003, compared with only 3.5 percent and 19 percent, respectively, for the inland provinces.

The coastal provinces seemed to have also fared better than the inland provinces. It is true that economic growth was only slightly faster along the coast during both periods. The average growth rate of per capita GDP for the coastal provinces was 6.4 percent during 1990–96 and 15.1 percent during 1997–2003, compared with 4.95 and 13.2 percent,

---

[2] Unless otherwise noted, I draw extensively on the work of Malesky (2008) and his data for discussions in this part. I am grateful for his generosity in sharing the data and for the many clarifications to help me make sense of them. Following his original study, here I use Vietnamese data on FDI, rather than trade or exports, to measure the degree of provincial exposure to the global markets.

TABLE 7.1. *Economic Openness, Provincial Autonomy Seeking, and Central Political Control in Vietnam, 1990–2004*

	FDI		Autonomy		Political Control	
	1990–96***	1997–2003***	1990–96***	1997–2003***	1991–97**	1998–2004***
Coast	8.94	29.50	4.10	11.08	1.29	1.40
Inland	3.48	18.99	1.96	6.04	1.10	1.00

Note: Data are the period averages for the coastal and inland provinces. *FDI* is the percentage share of the stock of foreign direct investment in provincial GDP. *Autonomy* is the stock of provincial violations of central policy directives cited in a sample of state-owned national newspapers. *Political Control* is the bureaucratic integration score of provincial party secretaries coded according to rules similar to those for the Chinese data, on a four-point scale (1 for a localist, 2 for an outsider, 3 for a centralist, and 4 for a concurrent centralist). The provinces coded as "coastal" are Ba Ria-Vung Tau, Bac Lieu (since 1997), Ben Tre, Binh Dinh, Binh Thuan (since 1993), Ca Mau (since 1997), Da Nang (since 1997), Dong Nai, Ha Noi, Ha Tinh (since 1993), Hai Phong, Ho Chi Minh City, Khanh Hoa (since 1991), Kien Giang, Long An, Nam Dinh (since 1997), Nghe An (since 1993), Ninh Binh (since 1993), Phu Yen (since 1991), Quang Binh (since 1991), Quang Nam (since 1997), Quang Ngai (since 1991), Quang Ninh, Quang Tri (since 1991), Soc Trang (since 1993), Thai Binh, Thanh Hoa, Tien Giang, Tra Vinh (since 1991), Thua Thien-Hue (since 1991), Vinh Long (since 1993), Nam Ha (1993–1996), Quang Nam-Da Nang (1990–1996), and Minh Hai (1990–1996). With the exception of Ha Noi (the national capital), which is coded as "coastal" for consistency with the coding convention for the Chinese data, coding of the coastal and inland status of the provinces follows the political maps (for 1992 and 2001) produced by the United States Central Intelligence Agency. The maps are available through the Perry-Castañeda Library Map Collection of the University of Texas, Austin at http://www.lib.utexas.edu/maps/vietnam.html, accessed on April 19, 2009. As in China, the number of provinces in Vietnam has increased over the years as new provinces were created out of existing provincial boundaries and old provinces were often renamed during this period (Malesky 2009).

***: $p < 0.01$ in two-group mean comparison tests for the coastal and inland provinces (two-tailed tests with unequal variances); **: $p < 0.05$; *: $p < 0.1$.

Source: Malesky (2008).

respectively, for the inland provinces. Nevertheless, the gap in the levels of wealth between the two regional cohorts further widened over the years. Average per capita GDP for the coastal provinces rose from 2.84 to 5.21 million of constant 1994 Vietnam dong (VND) across the two periods, while that for the inland provinces grew from 1.69 to only about 2.82 million.[3] Not surprisingly, the coastal provinces were much less reliant on fiscal transfers from the central government than were their inland counterparts. In 2002, for example, the vast majority (eleven out of the fifteen) of the surplus provinces that did not receive any central fiscal subsidies were located along the coast. In fact, the central government was heavily dependent on these provinces for fiscal contributions that could finance its interregional redistribution and poverty alleviation programs (Malesky 2008, 103–104).

Consistent with the predictions of the prevailing economic theories, the winner provinces of Vietnam along the coast seemed also more prone to policy intransigence toward the center than their inland counterparts. Emboldened by their more abundant fiscal resources, the coastal provincial governments were more inclined to seek economic policy autonomy through pursuit of "fence-breaking" activities, often in open violation of the explicit policy directives of the central government. For example, Malesky has conducted careful content analysis of state-owned newspapers for reported instances of provincial governments being singled out for public criticism over alleged violations of central economic policy directives. He finds that the Vietnamese central government tended to reprimand more frequently the provincial governments overseeing greater inflows of FDI in their jurisdictions.

Provincial "fence breaking" was surely on the rise for all provinces as the country opened up to the global markets during these years. Again, according to Table 7.1, the average value of *Autonomy* (measuring the extent of publicly cited provincial autonomy-seeking activities that contravened central policy edicts) increased even for the inland provinces, from about 1.96 during 1990–96 to 6.04 during 1997–2003.[4]

---

[3] Somehow, the differences in per capita GDP growth between the coastal and inland provinces fail to attain statistical significance at the conventional levels during the two periods. However, the differences in per capita GDP levels are highly significant (at 0.01).

[4] Malesky (2008) uses a dummy variable indicating whether autonomy-seeking behavior occurred in a province/year during the period of 1990–2000 in his original analysis. Instead, here I use a continuous variant of the measure, from the same dataset, on the "stock," or the cumulative "amount of autonomous incidents" for the provinces because of its greater variation and longer year coverage.

The respective figures for the coastal cohort in the two periods, however, were much larger, at about 4.1 and 11.08, respectively. That is, the frequency of public denunciation by the central government for violating central policies was much higher for the coastal provincial governments than for their inland counterparts throughout the years. Although the tendency for all provincial governments to pursue unsanctioned policy experiments might have grown over the years, this suggests that those overseeing the coastal provinces were much more likely to "fence-break" than were their inland counterparts.

To be sure, autonomy-seeking activities in the various economic policy realms often did not entail outright fiscal belligerence toward the center, such as refusal to contribute to the central coffers. For Malesky (2008, 106), they mainly involved "investment incentives, land use rights, legal reform, administrative policies, micro-economic policies, infrastructure, trade policies, environmental policies, labor policies, taxes, investment zones, credit funds, treatment of foreigners," and so on. Nevertheless, provincial "fence-breaking" in order to attract FDI inflows was primarily motivated by the urge of the provincial governments to increase their own revenue.[5] Such activities as tax evasion or granting of unauthorized tax exemptions could hurt the center's fiscal standing. Because the provincial governments along the coast were more likely to buck central economic rules, the Vietnamese case seems also to point to rising fiscal conflicts between the center and the winner regions in the age of economic openness.

Public reproach, however, could equally indicate willingness of the center to clamp down on perceived policy infractions by delinquent provincial governments. It may well be that provincial governments presiding over jurisdictions that benefited more from a link to the global markets did become more unruly in the eyes of the central government. In consequence, however, these provincial governments might have also incurred greater central interest in ensuring their policy compliance. Still, the existing research has shed little light on whether the national leaders of Vietnam, in response, resorted to exercising tighter political control over these provincial governments by installing, through the sole-governing Communist Party, pro-center agents in their top government post.

There is some evidence that the political center of Vietnam could have pursued a similar strategy of regionally targeted political control. In the remainder of Table 7.1, I present the provincial average values of *Political Control*, measured as the bureaucratic integration score of the provincial

---

[5] See, for instance, the discussion along these lines in Malesky (2008, 101–102).

party secretaries for the coastal and inland provinces during the period of 1991–2004.[6] Like the Chinese data, the variable is coded according to the career trajectories of the provincial party secretaries in Vietnam. Indeed, as we can see, the political center seemed to have sought a tighter political grip over the coastal provincial governments than over those in the inland provinces throughout these years.

During the 1991–97 period, the average bureaucratic integration score of the provincial party chiefs along the coast was about 1.3, compared with 1.1 for those in the inland provinces in the same period. It further rose to over 1.4 during the period of 1998–2004, while that for their inland counterparts actually declined somewhat to only about 1.0. In other words, across the two periods, it became less likely for the coastal provinces to be ruled by a localist provincial party secretary, but the opposite seemed true for the inland provinces.[7] Our earlier discussions have shown that provincial governments along the coast tended to preside over jurisdictions that were faring better under economic openness with greater FDI inflows and higher levels of wealth. They were also more inclined to seek economic policy autonomy in the absence of prior central imprimaturs. In response, the Vietnamese national leadership seemed to have resorted to exercising tighter political control precisely over these provincial governments by dispatching the more loyal and sympathetic agents to rule these localities.

The patterns of provincial-level data from Vietnam examined here are only indicative. More future research is clearly in order, as space constraints will not allow us to delve further into the data in this book. Rigorous regression analysis will be essential to helping us ascertain the direction and quantify the magnitude of the effect of FDI-induced provincial autonomy-seeking behavior on the degree of political control they incurred from the center. If the regionally differential exercise of central political control was aimed at facilitating provincial compliance with central resource extraction, as I have argued in the case of China,

---

[6] The *Autonomy* data cover 1990–2003. A lag of one year is adopted because we are interested in getting a sense of whether the Vietnamese center responded to provincial policy intransigence by exercising of tighter political control over their provincial governments.

[7] It is interesting to note the generally lower bureaucratic integration score for Vietnamese provincial party secretaries than that for their Chinese counterparts. In post-1986 Vietnam, the average provincial party secretary was slightly more than a localist, whereas in post-1978 China, an outsider was more the norm. The average score for all Vietnamese provincial party chiefs during 1990–2004 was 1.21, while the Chinese average during 1978–2005 was 2.15.

such control could also have empirically testable consequences for central revenue extraction from the provinces and in turn provincial economic growth in Vietnam. For all the caveats, prima facie, the story from contemporary Vietnam seems in keeping with the argument of this book predicting the exercise of tighter central political control, via centralized governing political parties, over the subnational governments that oversee the more unruly winner regions in the age of economic globalization. It is also broadly consistent with our provincial-level evidence from post-1978 China.

7.2.1.2 *The Former Soviet Union*
Although the case of Vietnam is interesting, it is important to point out that the country is much smaller than China in terms of geographic size. Thus, the nature of territorial challenges unleashed by the embrace of the global markets and the task of exercising territorially targeted political control that confronts the Vietnamese national leadership might be qualitatively different from those of China. In this context, a more befitting comparative case might be the former Soviet Union, another continental size country ruled by one most-centralized Soviet Communist Party. More important, its territorial collapse when its former constituent republics declared independence in the early 1990s could conceivably contradict the argument pursued in this book. In fact, the former Soviet case seems more consonant with the predictions of the prevailing economic theories as the more export-oriented Baltic states more closely linked to Western Europe first initiated separatist demands before the other republics jumped on the separatist bandwagon (Bunce 1999; Treisman 1999). Why did the former Soviet national leadership in not Moscow not act like their Chinese counterparts and resort to tighter political control, via the single ruling Soviet Communist Party, over the subnational governments in its more economically resourceful but politically restive Union Republics?

The sudden disintegration of the Soviet Union, to be sure, caught many social scientists by surprise. However, it is not clear that the direct cause of the Soviet implosion was a high level of exposure to the global markets. In fact, the Soviet economy as a whole had been quite autarkic. Even on the eve of its collapse, at the national aggregate level, total Soviet foreign trade (imports plus exports) actually contributed to a relatively small share of the Soviet economy, only about 15 percent of GDP in 1989, when it was last observed in the *Penn World Table* (Heston et al. October 2002). In comparison, this was far lower than the share in China (about 48 percent for 2000 when last observed by the same source) or Vietnam (95 percent for 1997) for that matter, but Communist Party national rule in the latter two countries has so far survived.

Globalization, however, might have had indirect consequences that eventually paved the way for Soviet disintegration. Reacting to the recent "renaissance" in the study of "ideas" in world politics, especially regarding the end of the Cold War, Brooks and Wohlforth (2000) cogently argue that the "material incentives" confronting the Soviet elites in the early to mid-1980s might better explain Soviet foreign policy retrenchment and the initiation of "engagement with the West" by the top Soviet leadership. Such "material incentives" were primarily dictated by both systemic Soviet economic decline and the rising opportunity costs of being isolated from the ongoing economic globalization. These incentives transformed the foreign as well as domestic policy outlook of the Soviet leaders, especially those of Communist Party General Secretary Mikhail Gorbachev, ultimately leading to the demise of the Soviet Union. "Glasnost" and "perestroika," launched by Gorbachev at home, which gradually phased out the hitherto dominant role of the Communist Party in Soviet politics – a more direct cause of the Soviet collapse – might have come about due to the eager, though belated, desire of Soviet leaders to partake of the benefits of the ongoing global market integration.

It is entirely possible that the scaling back of the Soviet foreign military commitment in the late 1980s resulted from perceptions by the Moscow leadership of the serious decline in the material capacity of the Soviet Union. The Soviet elites might have correctly determined that the West had gained an unmistakable edge by embracing the recent round of global market integration sweeping across the world. However, such perceptions of foreign threats and domestic economic weaknesses due to closure, and the consequent peaceful turn in foreign policy, did not have to lead to the atrophy of Communist Party rule. After all, similar conclusions of domestic economic weaknesses might have driven the Chinese leadership to rapprochement with the West and to the embrace of the global markets, as discussed earlier in Chapter 3. Largely the same material causes seemed to have motivated the Vietnamese economic reforms and opening in the late 1980s, as noted earlier in this chapter.

An equally plausible explanation is that the former Soviet Union fell apart exactly because it did *not* open itself to the global markets early enough to capture the economic gains required to reverse the economic decline and to resurrect dying Communist Party legitimacy in the costly global power contest with its Cold War nemesis. Indeed, in terms of its relative timing, market liberalization and opening up to the West came fairly late to the Soviet Union (Huang 1994). "Glasnost" and "perestroika" were not formally introduced until the mid-1980s (Colton 1986), more than sixty years after the founding of the Union of Soviet Socialist Republics (USSR). In China, it took the CCP leadership three decades after establishing their rule on the Chinese mainland to turn to reform and opening. The Vietnamese leadership waited for only about ten years after the end of the Vietnam War and the reunification of the country before embarking on Doi Moi in 1986 (Duiker 1995). Had the Soviet leaders acted sooner, the secular economic decline plaguing the country and ultimately dooming the political union might have been averted without severely weakening Communist rule. The history of the end of the Cold War would have had to be rewritten.

Nevertheless, the Soviet case, where national disintegration was preceded by the weakening of the sole governing political party, is consistent with my emphasis on how centralized political parties can help the political center respond effectively to the centrifugal challenges of rising economic globalization through the exercise of regionally selective political control. Regardless of the actual reasons, Gorbachev's decision to degrade further the role of the Communist Party in Soviet politics and to introduce direct local elections into the republics might have deprived the Soviet political center of the major institutional tool at its disposal to hold the leaders of the republics in line and to keep the Soviet Union together. Filippov et al. (2004, 93–94) offer the following perceptive observation:

> For seventy years, then, the Communist Party was the essential coordinating force in the USSR, holding its diverse territories and peoples together.... Thus, according to accounts provided by party officials themselves, the crucial decision in weakening the party's role was the change in personnel policy under Gorbachev whereby centralized nominations from *nomenklatura* lists were slowly replaced by the direct election of officials .... Democracy replaced the political dependence on Moscow of regional party bosses and directed their attention instead to local party elites. ... [I]n response to the challenge of electoral competition, they [the regional party bosses] began to request more independence from Moscow.[8]

This line of argument differs from the notion that the Soviet Union collapsed due to the failure of the Kremlin to engage in "fiscal pacification" of the restive subnational regions (Treisman 1999). The latter notion,

---

[8] A similar assessment is also made by Solnick (1996, 229).

however, is probably more applicable after the loosening of the grip of the Communist Party center over the careers of the subnational elite. Weakened personnel powers at the subnational level must have undermined the fiscal extractive capacity of Moscow amidst growing difficulty of revenue extraction. This could have helped instigate fiscal assertiveness and intransigency from the richer republics, spawn widespread regional discontent elsewhere, aggravate other centrifugal tendencies in the Soviet polity, and ultimately contribute to its collapse.

The argument also departs from the emphasis of Bunce (1999) on the role of constitutional federalism – defined along the lines of the *national* groups in its various constituent republics – in the disintegration of the former Soviet Union as well as Czechoslovakia and Yugoslavia.[9] Under this latter view, the relative stability on the territorial front (though still problematic at times) of the current Russian Federation that practices the same "nationally framed federalism" certainly is puzzling. My focus on the national governing party, however, would point to the centripetal pull of an increasingly centralized United Russia Party led by Putin in contemporary Russia (Konitzer and Wegren 2006). Indeed, even according to Bunce (1999, Chapters 2 and 5), decline of national-level political authority in the former USSR could well have started in the 1970s. The nomenklatura hold of the Soviet central leadership over the subnational republican leadership began to fray under Brezhnev's policy of "stability in cadres" that provided secure tenure for regional officials in exchange for their political support. Gorbachev's move thus might have further enervated, if only fatally, the personnel powers and ability to exercise political control at the subnational level by the Soviet national leadership.

As I will discuss further next, the integrative role played by the ruling Communist Party in keeping the country together might also pose pitfalls and dilemmas for China's future political transition and democratization, which might directly imperil the monopoly personnel control over the provincial leadership by the center. Nonetheless, the notion and evidence of weakening party institutions partially responsible for the Soviet collapse will only strengthen the argument of this book. The resilient political strength of the Chinese Communist Party center and

---

[9] It might also be important to note that these three states were composed of major constituent units that had enjoyed relatively recent independence experiences before being cobbled together into their not-always-voluntary collective political existence in the aftermath of World War II.

its continued monopoly personnel powers at the provincial level have helped the national political leadership maintain political predominance over the provincial governments and thus hold the country together despite China's embrace of economic globalization.

7.2.2 Political Decentralization

Meanwhile, future data collection at the subnational level within other single-party states in order to gauge the degree of political control by the center over the subnational governments of the different regions will also contribute to the better measurement of the degree of political decentralization and improve empirical efforts to study its macroeconomic effects. Indeed, cross-national research has been beset by conceptual and measurement complexities regarding a country's degree of political decentralization (Rodden 2004).

The conventional coding scheme to capture the degree of political decentralization adopts a constitutional litmus test. Political systems under an explicit federalist constitution are coded as politically decentralized. However, such an approach might be too crude. In contrast, Riker's notion of political decentralization revolves around the extent of governing political party decentralization. For Riker (1964, 129–131), more decentralized governing political party systems make more decentralized political systems. A more centralized political (party) system operates when (1) the political party of the national chief executive rules a larger share of the subnational governments; and (2) the political party of the national chief executive exercises a greater degree of political control over its copartisans running the subnational governments, for instance, through personnel powers over nomination or appointment of candidates. Under these criteria, an effective authoritarian single ruling party constitutes the most centralized party system in which one political party whose national leaders are capable of wielding such subnational-level personnel powers rules the entire country.

To study the macroeconomic consequences of political decentralization, ideally, we need cross-national data that bear upon both of these partisan dimensions for all possible countries in all possible years. However, this is too overwhelming a task for existing data collection endeavors. Pioneering cross-national research that capitalizes on the Rikerian conceptualization of political party decentralization (Rodden and Wibbels 2002; Wibbels 2005) primarily focuses on dimension (1), which mostly captures the ability of the central government to coordinate policymaking with subnational governments. Riker's dimension (2), which gauges the ability of the central government to secure policy compliance from below, has been largely neglected in the existing literature. This second dimension has been the focus in my book.

A subnational research design to examine regional variation within a country under single-party rule is especially useful for studying the effect of the Rikerian dimension (2) of political party decentralization. If one single political party rules both the central government and all the subnational governments, in effect, we have already held constant (and controlled for) Riker's first partisan dimension of political decentralization. This allows us to zero in on the macroeconomic effects of political control by the central government over the subnational governments and the related ability of the central government to solicit subnational policy compliance through the single ruling political party.

In the case of China, the political center via the single ruling CCP in theory wields substantial political control over all provincial governments by virtue of its monopoly nomenklatura powers at the provincial level. However, the fact that the national leaders assign to the various provincial governments different types of leading officials predisposed to varying degrees of policy compliance with the central government also implies that the center effectively exercises varying degrees of political control over the different regional governments. These subnational governments in turn should enjoy varying degrees of de facto political decentralization. The varying likelihood of compliance with central policy preferences by the different types of top provincial cadres is entirely consistent with Riker's partisan dimension (2) on political decentralization – central political control over the subnational governments and the ability of the central government to extract policy compliance from below via the national governing political party.

The perceived vices of concentration of political power at the national level in tempting possible fiscal predation from above (Weingast 1995), or the putative virtues of a strong political center in remedying subnational-level "collective action" problems in providing national-level public goods for economic development (Bardhan 2000; Prud'homme 1995; Rodden and Rose-Ackerman 1997), can then be tested with subnational data. In Chapter 6, I argue that the central government's commitment to the protection of local property rights should be less credible for Chinese provinces that were overseen by the more tightly controlled provincial governments more compliant with central extractive demands. Unsurprisingly, these provinces also tended to be subject to greater fiscal extraction by the center and to witness slower economic growth, other things being held constant. A subnational approach thus helps us situate the MPF argument, when applied to the context of post-1978 China, at a more appropriate (provincial) level than was originally intended by the approach's foremost advocates or has been commonly envisioned by their critics.

In the meantime, Chinese provincial governments under a tighter political grip by the center, those enjoying a lower degree of de facto political decentralization, tended to follow more closely central policy injunctions against local public investment fervor that could endanger macroeconomic stability (Huang 1996). Indeed, these provincial governments also presided over lower inflation in their jurisdictions (Huang and Sheng 2009). Similar subnational data collected from other single-party states will also allow us to examine the macroeconomic consequences of political decentralization at the subnational level. They will not necessarily supplant the more cross-national research, but can offer a feasible way to test the macroeconomic effects of political decentralization when cross-national data bearing on both dimensions of Rikerian political party decentralization are still largely unavailable.

7.3 SINGLE-PARTY RULE AND CHINA'S TRANSITIONS

7.3.1 Economic Transition

Discussions of the mixed macroeconomic effects of the regionally differential exercise of central political control, via the institutions of the single ruling CCP, lead naturally to the possible implications of single-party rule for China's ongoing economic transition from socialist planning to a modern market. After all, throughout this period, it was single-party rule under the CCP that endowed the political center in China with the requisite institutional wherewithal to wield selective control over the provincial governments. Exercise of tighter political control via the sole governing CCP might have dampened local public investment urges and inflationary pressures, especially in the targeted provinces. Thus, it might have helped China avert the hyperinflation that plagued many other developing countries and contributed to the presence of a relatively stable macroeconomic environment for domestic economic restructuring.

Such benevolent effects on macroeconomic stability, however, must be weighed against the potentially baneful effects upon local economic growth due to the predatory nature of central political coercion that inheres in a center-dominated single-party state, especially for the subnational regions overseen by provincial governments subject to tighter central political control (Chapter 6). This assessment differs from the implications from the recent argument by Blanchard and Shleifer (2001). For them, one major factor behind China's relatively successful economic transition, compared with that of post-Soviet Russia, is the remarkable growth of the nonstate sector made possible in part by the political supremacy of the Chinese central government. At least before recentralization set in under Putin, post-Soviet Russia was deprived of the presence of a centralized ruling political party. Due to the resultant weakness of the national-level political authority, capture of regional governments by rent-seeking vested interests – inefficient regional state firms – blocked the market entry of the more efficient nonstate firms, even if the Russian central government might have been interested in promoting the latter's development and the further liberalization of the regional economies. This seems to have stalled economic liberalization and led to the stagnation of the Russian economy in the years following the Soviet collapse.[10]

At the subnational level, this implies that the exercise of tighter political control by the center over the regional governments might constrain such rent seeking by helping the regional governments overcome the "capture" and resistance by the inefficient but powerful regional state firms. In China, if the center had favored the more vibrant nonstate sector driving economic dynamism while the provincial governments had been more susceptible to capturing by the inefficient state industries in their jurisdictions, we should expect the nonstate sector to thrive better and the economy to grow faster in localities overseen by the more compliant, tightly controlled provincial governments. Our empirical analysis of Chinese provincial-level data in Chapter 6 does not seem to bear out this conjecture about economic growth, even though a larger nonstate industrial sector itself was growth-conducive. In fact, consistent with the thesis on the central government's "credible commitment" to protection of local property rights, we find that tighter central political control over the provincial governments facilitated central fiscal extraction from the provinces and could have hurt provincial economic growth. The relationship

---

[10] This line of argument is consistent with the "partial reform equilibrium" thesis of Hellman (1998) applied to the subnational level. Regional state firms might have benefited from the initial phases of economic liberalization, but later sought to prevent the further progress of economic reform and to block the entry of nonstate firms in order to protect their newly acquired advantages. For an excellent discussion of the predatory nature of the Russian regional governments, see also Zhuravskaya (2000).

between central political control and nonstate sector development, however, has not been directly tested in this book. A hypothesis positing the nonstate-sector-friendly role of central political control in China thus awaits future empirical testing.

Nevertheless, some positive light might still be shed on the seemingly growth-hindering effect of the more stringent central political control exercised over the subnational governments via the ruling single party. A greater degree of political control might have been targeted by the center toward the subnational governments ruling the winner regions in the global markets to help extract resources and to meet the mounting imperative for interregional redistribution. Although tighter political control and the consequent heavier fiscal extraction by the center might have retarded economic growth in those targeted subnational regions, it could also have facilitated central fiscal redistribution. This could have helped mitigate some of the worst momentums in rising interregional disparity in China. After all, the yawning economic schism among the subnational regions was partly responsible for the breakup of the former socialist state of Yugoslavia (Pleština 1992). In this sense, tighter central political control via the ruling CCP over selected provincial governments might have helped China achieve more balanced regional economic development than otherwise would have been possible, contributing to the general political stability required for a relatively smooth economic transition.

This notion of a possibly salutary function in the country's economic transition served by the regionally selective exercise of control by a politically predominant center under CCP single-party rule has been echoed in a number of recent works on contemporary Chinese political economy. Several contributors to an important volume, for instance, stress the vital importance of the CCP monopoly nomenklatura powers wielded by the center over the top provincial leadership in "holding China together" (Naughton and Yang 2004b), despite popular predictions to the contrary. For one thing, absent sufficient political strength, the center certainly would not have been able to muster the requisite fiscal resources to fund the "Western Development Program" aimed at reducing the growing economic gap between the coastal and the inland provinces (Naughton 2004). Similarly, the political supremacy of the Chinese central government imparted by a centralized ruling single party must have been instrumental in helping the national leaders overcome possible resistance from vested interests in order to (re)construct the regulatory and other state capacities befitting a modern market system (Yang 2004; Zheng 2004a).

Although explicitly highlighting the importance of the nomenklatura powers monopolized by the center via the sole governing CCP, what these studies do not show is exactly *how* such powers have been used. Fiscal extraction for redistribution to the inland provinces that were faring less well during this period, economic restructuring to dismantle old practices and antiquated bureaucracies, and regulatory state building might all have met with fierce resistance from vested interests – for instance, those provinces, economic sectors, or functional ministries of the central government standing to lose. After all, no reform is easy (Fernandez and Rodrik 1991). This book has emphasized how tighter central political control via the institutions of the single ruling party tended to be targeted toward the provincial government leadership of the winner provinces in the global markets. The goal was to facilitate provincial government compliance with central revenue extraction for interregional redistribution and to help the political center maintain its national rule in this era of rising economic openness and regional disparity. Future research might examine the use of the nomenklatura powers by the Chinese political center in other realms against the backdrop of the country's market transition at home and its embrace of markets abroad.

7.3.2 Political Transition

In this book I argue that the national political leaders in China have resorted to the institutional tools at their disposal within the ruling CCP to tackle the territorial challenges from the embrace of the global markets. The argument is also broadly consistent with a nascent literature in comparative politics positing the relative longevity of single-party authoritarianism, compared with their counterparts under military rule or personalist dictatorship. Most of these studies have emphasized how autocrats in single-party regimes seem to be more effective in co-opting and controlling rival political forces from the civil society (Dickson 2003, 2008; Huntington and Moore 1970) or potential adversaries from within the ruling regime (Brownlee 2007; Gandhi 2008; Geddes 1999b; Haber 2006; Magaloni 2008). Research focusing on the state-society dichotomy or internal elite rivalry within authoritarian regimes, however, has neglected the territorial dimension of the challenges to authoritarian rule, especially salient in the age of globalization.

Different subnational regions faring differently in the global markets can exhibit different propensities for intransigence and pose different threats to national unity on which the political survival of the national autocrats hinges. Thus, the authoritarian political center can engage in regionally targeted control by appointing different types of leading regional officials, as was pursued by the Chinese national leaders during the period in this study. That is, CCP single-party rule has endowed the center with the requisite institutional powers for such regionally selective exercise of political control and helped keep China together despite the fissiparous challenges unleashed from below by the country's embrace of the global markets.[11] By shunning so far truly meaningful political contestation for public office, however, the same single ruling political party that has prolonged the political survival of the Chinese national leaders has also helped preserve CCP national authoritarian rule.[12] How will this bode for the country's political transition and democratization? Conversely, if democratization by definition undermines CCP single-party rule, how will the likely prospect of a transition to democracy affect the center's ability to tame the centrifugal forces unleashed by a widening window to the global markets and to maintain territorial integrity in the years to come?

To be sure, greater political liberalization may eventually be necessitated by the imperative to combat the unprecedented rampancy of corruption among CCP officials at all levels (Lü 2000; Manion 2004; Sun 2004). Corruption can surely pose grave threats to, as much as it has been encouraged by, CCP single-party rule. Recent calls by the highest CCP leadership to gradually introduce greater "within-party democracy" (*dangnei minzhu*) and to hold elections that feature a greater number of bona fide candidates than the number of available local positions are encouraging to all those aspiring for more political liberalization in the Chinese polity. Indeed, in his report to the Sixteenth Party Congress in late 2002, outgoing CCP chief Jiang Zemin exalted "within-party democracy" as the very "life of the party," while his successor, the current general secretary of the CCP Hu Jintao made similar calls for "furthering within-party democracy" in his report to the Seventeenth Party Congress in the fall of 2007.[13]

---

[11] In this context, I have examined how the Chinese national leaders pursued such regional co-optation and control by selecting some provincial leaders to be members of the Politburo of the CCP Central Committee during the 1978–2005 period elsewhere (Sheng 2009a).

[12] For a minimalist definition of democracy that chiefly revolves around the role of "contested elections for public office," see Przeworski et al. (2000, Chapter 1).

[13] This is according to http://news.xinhuanet.com/newscenter/2002-11/17/content_632308.htm, accessed on November 27, 2006, and http://news.xinhuanet.com/newscenter/2007-10/24/content_6938568_11.htm, accessed on April 11, 2008. This is encouraging because Taiwan's democratization might have started with the single-ruling Nationalist Party (Kuomintang) first introducing elements of democracy into its own ranks in the 1980s (Cheng 1989).

Public nominations, campaign speeches, and even live, televised debates among candidates for lower-level offices started to appear, for instance, in Jiangsu province in 2004.[14] At the township level, some localities in Guangxi, for example, have begun to experiment with choosing the party secretaries via "public nominations" and even "direct elections."[15] Such localized experimentation, if successful, might later expand to other localities and eventually be introduced nationwide, like other reform policy initiatives during this period (Heilmann 2008). Someday, it might also move to encompass higher-level political offices.

Furthermore, a fledgling, if still crude, sense of political "representation" seems to have already been creeping into the territorial realm. Shares of incumbent provincial officials in the alternate membership of the CCP Central Committee were positively related to the provincial population sizes during the 1978–2002 period (Sheng 2007a). The alternate membership category is the least powerful type of membership within the CCP Central Committee due to the lack of voting power for the alternate members at the party plenums (Jing Shan 1991, 170). Still, this seems to point to the germination of some form of population-based "representation" for the provinces at the national level. After all, the CCP Central Committee remains the de facto national "representative" political institution in a one-party state where the national legislature performs mostly rubber-stamp functions.

Nevertheless, we cannot be too sanguine. For one thing, due to its nonvoting nature, alternate membership on the CCP Central Committee might denote mere "symbolic representation" aimed at ensuring tighter central control over the represented provincial governments (Sheng 2005a).[16] As I show in Chapter 5, the Chinese political center was actively pulling the levers of the personnel powers by assigning to the top

---

[14] Gu Zhaonong, "Gongtui gongxuan futingji ganbu: Jiangsu shouci xianchang zhibo yanjiang dabian guocheng [Public Nomination and Election of Vice-Chiefs at the Provincial Departmental Level: Live Coverage of Campaign Speeches and Debates for the First Time in Jiangsu]," available at http://www.people.com.cn/GB/shizheng/14562/2812038. html, accessed on September 28, 2004.

[15] Long Songlin, Wang Mian, and Gu Yuanjiang, "Ezhi 'taipingguan' he 'quanli xunzu' wanji: Guangxi tianlin xian gongtui zhixuan zheng dangweishuji diaocha [Containing the Wicked Diseases of 'Becoming Do-Nothing Officials' and 'Engaging in Rent-Seeking through Power': An investigation of the Public Nominations and Direct Elections of Township Party Secretaries in Tianlin County, Guangxi Autonomous Region]," available at http://news.xinhuanet.com/newscenter/2008-08/17/content_9432402.htm, accessed on August 18, 2008.

[16] I draw on Donaldson (1972) and Solinger (1977) for the notion of "symbolic representation" here.

leadership post of the winner provinces in the global markets provincial party secretaries with pro-center career trajectories. Insofar as Chinese politics is a top-down process and the political center has little interest in relinquishing the ultimate personnel powers at the provincial level, continued central political supremacy under CCP single-party rule cannot be regarded as supportive of any meaningful shift within the Chinese polity toward greater democracy. If democratization means that provincial leaders are held accountable to lower-level electorates, any calls for greater democratization from below will be difficult to implement under the current institutional arrangements privileging the political center.

Conversely, democratization will also pose challenges to the center's continued ability to keep China together in the future. If democratization and the end of single-party rule will eventually deprive the political center of its institutional monopoly powers via the single ruling CCP to manage the careers of the provincial government leadership, the country might confront the real perils of breaking up in the face of the centrifugal forces unleashed by growing global market integration and unbalanced regional development. After all, democratization seems to have already been associated with the disintegration of the former Soviet Union, Yugoslavia, and Czechoslovakia (Filippov et al. 2004; Treisman 1999). As noted, indeed, a number of other scholars have regarded central monopoly personnel powers over the provincial governments as one key unifying force for maintaining the country's political stability and territorial integrity (for example, Goodman 1994, 4; Huang 1995b; Naughton and Yang 2004a, 11; Yang 1994, 86). By weakening the personnel powers that are now monopolized by the party center – the very centripetal pull holding the country together – democratization might spell disconcerting consequences in the territorial realm as well as for the general macroeconomic stability required for a smooth transition to the market.

Although the prospect of democracy in China has attracted much attention in recent years,[17] surprisingly much less ink has been spilled to explore the possible implications of the country's eventual democratization for China's territorial integrity. Thus, Gilley's recent (2004) discussion in this context, though largely speculative in nature and overly single-minded in his embrace of the putative virtues of a liberal democracy

---

[17] For instance, no less apt a publication as the *Journal of Democracy* has devoted two special issues in recent years, in January 1998 and January 2003, respectively, to debating China's future democratization. See also Nathan (1997), Zhao (2000), and Zheng (2004b).

for China with little apparent concern for its possibly destabilizing consequences, seems to be a welcome departure. Valiantly predicting the likely course China will actually traverse on its path to democracy, Gilley (2004, 169–172) readily admits that in the process, secession by certain regions is a real possibility.

Such prognostications are essentially in consonance with the diagnosis of the immediate cause for the Soviet demise as lying in Gorbachev's decision to introduce competitive local elections that weakened the personnel powers held by the Soviet Communist Party center over the leaders of the republics (Filippov et al. 2004, 93–94). For Gilley, however, only the inland border provinces populated by the ethnic minorities such as Tibet and Xinjiang present the gravest potential to break away from the rest of China. Instead, our examination of the leading economic theories on economic globalization and national political disintegration highlights the additional perils posed by the more globalized, prosperous provinces along China's coast.

Indeed, consistent with the findings of Wang (2004), our preliminary evidence in Chapter 6 suggests that ethnic minority regions in China might have been wooed to stay in the political union with the other provinces through generous fiscal subsidies from the central government. Moreover, despite the occasional agitations for even political independence by indigenous ethnic groups from below, so far, no top provincial government officials ruling these ethnic minority regions have openly challenged the central government. In contrast, we have noted earlier the cases of Ye Xuanping in Guangdong and Shen Daren in Jiangsu defying the fiscal centralization efforts initiated by Beijing. These cases suggest a different and perhaps no less dangerous territorial menace toward the national leadership – the new bellicosity of the subnational governments ruling these winner provinces in the global markets. The intransigence of the subnational governments in the rich coastal provinces toward the center's extractive demands would not only directly undermine the authority and legitimacy of the Chinese national leaders. Their fiscal belligerence would also further weaken the ability of the central government to engage in fiscal appeasement of the ethnic minority regions and aggravate the latter's separatist tendencies.

Taking the lessons from the former Soviet Union to heart, the Chinese political center might want to put up the fiercest possible resistance toward any perceived movement toward democratization that seeks to force it to end single-party rule and to relinquish its political grip over the provincial governments. This does not imply that political transition toward future democracy is unlikely in China. History is full of uncertainties and surprises. Furthermore, it is beyond the scope of this book to determine whether democracy or national territorial unity and political stability hold a higher intrinsic value when they come into possible conflict with each other.

This one point, however, might be less controversial. The Chinese political center under the CCP, or any future successor entity controlling the national government, will have to find effective ways of continuing to hold the allegiance of candidates for provincial and lower-level political offices once competitive local elections are introduced. Otherwise, the advent of democracy in the age of economic globalization and regional disparity could inject more instability into the territorial realm of Chinese politics. Maintaining some degree of political control over subnational copartisans who run the provincial governments while still ensuring the political accountability of the regional officials to the local electorates might be a difficult balancing act for future successor political parties vying for power through democratic contestations in China. Some form of institutional guarantees along these lines, in the meantime, will certainly reduce potential opposition to political transition from the CCP national leaders in the first place.

7.4 CONCLUSION

Short of another monumental catastrophe or economic crisis plunging the nations of the world back into the dark, gloomy years of mutual "beggar-thy-neighbor" policies and trade barriers of the interwar period of the last century (Kindleberger 1973), most probably, global market integration will remain with us in the foreseeable future, despite the ebb and flow of modern cyclical capitalism. Some states will be more susceptible than others to their powerful sweep as the forces of the global markets continue to leave their imprint upon the political contours worldwide, both domestic and across national borders. Political authority in some states will "migrate" more easily away from their traditional locus in the national capital toward lower-level constituent units than in others. In this book, I suggest that the path of such downward "authority migration" will be less smooth in states that are governed by centralized political parties empowering the political center to mount more effective resistance.

Regardless of the direction in which the future trajectory of economic globalization will take, however, the political institutions that govern domestic intergovernmental relations will continue to matter for macroeconomic outcomes. Tradeoffs and dilemmas will continue to be unavoidable. Political institutions that privilege the center will enable it to secure greater subnational policy compliance and help mitigate "collective action" problems among subnational units. Political institutions that endow too much power in the hands of national-level politicians and facilitate fiscal extraction from below will also tempt unwarranted central government predation upon and expropriation of local wealth, increase the risk of distorting local incentives, and hinder local economic dynamism, especially in those regions bearing the brunt of the exercise of such national political prowess.

Amidst China's recent embrace of the global markets during the period of 1978–2005, the political center was largely able to fend off the fissiparous forces unleashed in the process by resorting to the institutional resources imparted by the sole governing CCP. It sought to exert tighter political control over the provincial governments that rule the winner subnational regions in order to ease resource extraction, carry out interregional redistribution, and above all, keep itself in existence. Central political predominance under CCP single-party rule not only helped provide a more stable macroeconomic and political environment for the country's ongoing economic transition. It might also have been detrimental to economic growth in those subnational regions that were ruled by the more stringently controlled provincial governments and more susceptible to the center's extractive reach. An effective central political grip over the provincial governments, however, might be undermined by the prospect of the country's political transition. To forestall such a threat, national-level politicians might have more incentives to delay the advent of political democracy, especially if democratization means the end of single-party rule and the drastic weakening of the sway of central political powers in the provinces.

References

Achen, Christopher H. 2000. "Why Lagged Dependent Variables Can Suppress the Explanatory Power of Other Independent Variables." Paper presented at the Annual Meeting of the Political Methodology Section of the American Political Science Association, UCLA.

Adserà, Alícia, and Carles Boix. 2002. "Trade, Democracy, and the Size of the Public Sector: The Political Underpinnings of Openness." *International Organization* 56 (2):229–62.

Alchian, Armen A., and Harold Demsetz. 1972. "Production, Information Costs, and Economic Organization." *American Economic Review* 62 (5):777–95.

Alesina, Alberto, and Enrico Spolaore. 1997. "On the Number and Size of Nations." *Quarterly Journal of Economics* 112 (4):1027–56.

2003. *The Size of Nations*. Cambridge: MIT Press.

Alesina, Alberto, Enrico Spolaore, and Romain Wacziarg. 2000. "Economic Integration and Political Disintegration." *American Economic Review* 90 (5):1276–96.

Amsden, Alice H. 1989. *Asia's Next Giant: South Korea and Late Industrialization*. New York: Oxford University Press.

An Xiumei, and Yang Yuanwei. 2008. "Fenshui Zhi Caizheng Tizhi Gaige He Caizheng Jiandu [Fiscal Reform through the Tax Sharing System and Fiscal Monitoring]." *Caizheng Jiandu [Fiscal Monitoring]* (4):16–21.

Ansolabehere, Stephen, Alan Gerber, and James Snyder. 2002. "Equal Votes, Equal Money: Court-Ordered Redistricting and Public Expenditures in the American States." *American Political Science Review* 96 (4):767–77.

Bahl, Roy W. 1999. *Fiscal Policy in China: Taxation and Intergovernmental Fiscal Relations*. South San Francisco: The 1990 Institute.

Bao, Shuming, Gene Hsin Chang, Jeffrey D. Sachs, and Wing Thye Woo. 2002. "Geographic Factors and China's Regional Development under Market Reforms, 1978–1998." *China Economic Review* 13 (1):89–111.

Bardhan, Pranab K. 2000. "Understanding Underdevelopment: Challenges for Institutional Economics from the Point of View of Poor Countries." *Journal of Institutional and Theoretical Economics* 156 (1):216–35.

Barnett, A. Doak (with a contribution by Ezra F. Vogel). 1967. *Cadres, Bureaucracy, and Political Power in Communist China*. New York: Columbia University Press.

Barro, Robert J. 1991. "Economic Growth in a Cross Section of Countries." *Quarterly Journal of Economics* 106 (2):407–43.

1996. "Democracy and Growth." *Journal of Economic Growth* 1 (1):1–27.

Bartke, Wolfgang. 1997. *Who Was Who in the People's Republic of China*. 2 vols. München: K.G. Saur.

Bates, Robert H. 1981. *Markets and States in Tropical Africa: The Political Basis of Agricultural Policies*. Berkeley: University of California Press.

Baum, Richard. 1994. *Burying Mao: Chinese Politics in the Age of Deng Xiaoping*. Princeton: Princeton University Press.

1997. "The Road to Tiananmen: Chinese Politics in the 1980s." In *The Politics of China: The Eras of Mao and Deng*, ed. R. MacFarquhar. New York: Cambridge University Press.

Beck, Nathaniel. 2001. "Time-Series-Cross-Section Data: What Have We Learned in the Past Few Years?" *Annual Review of Political Science* 4:271–93.

Beck, Nathaniel, and Jonathan N. Katz. 1995. "What to Do (and Not to Do) with Time-Series Cross-Section Data." *American Political Science Review* 89 (3):634–47.

1996. "Nuisance vs. Substance: Specifying and Estimating Time-Series-Cross-Section Models." *Political Analysis* 6:1–36.

2001. "Throwing out the Baby with the Bath Water: A Comment on Green, Kim, and Yoon." *International Organization* 55 (2):487–95.

Beck, Nathaniel, Jonathan N. Katz, and Richard Tucker. 1998. "Taking Time Seriously: Time-Series-Cross-Section Analysis with a Binary Dependent Variable." *American Journal of Political Science* 42 (4):1260–88.

Beck, Thorsten, George Clarke, Alberto Groff, Philip Keefer, and Patrick Walsh. 2001. "New Tools and New Tests in Comparative Political Economy: The Database of Political Institutions." *World Bank Economic Review* 15 (1):165–76

Beijing Shi Tongji Ju [Beijing Bureau of Statistics]. 2005. *Beijing Tongji Nianjian 2005 [Beijing Statistical Yearbook 2005]*. Beijing: Zhongguo tongji chubanshe.

Bennett, Gordon. 1973. "Military Regions and Provincial Party Secretaries: One Outcome of China's Cultural Revolution." *The China Quarterly* (54):294–357.

Berger, Suzanne. 2000. "Globalization and Politics." *Annual Review of Political Science* 3:43–62.

Bernstein, Thomas P., and Xiaobo Lü. 2003. *Taxation without Representation in Contemporary Rural China*. New York: Cambridge University Press.

Blanchard, Olivier, and Andrei Shleifer. 2001. "Federalism with and without Political Centralization: China Versus Russia." *IMF Staff Papers* 48 (Special Issue):171–9.

Bloom, David E., and Jeffrey D. Sachs. 1998. "Geography, Demography, and Economic Growth in Africa." *Brookings Papers on Economic Activity* (2):207–95.

Bo, Zhiyue. 2007. *China's Elite Politics: Political Transition and Power Balancing.* Hackensack: World Scientific.

Bolton, Patrick, and Gérard Roland. 1997. "The Breakup of Nations: A Political Economy Analysis." *Quarterly Journal of Economics* 112 (4):1057–90.

Bolton, Patrick, Gérard Roland, and Enrico Spolaore. 1996. "Economic Theories of the Break-up and Integration of Nations." *European Economic Review* 40 (3–5):697–705.

Bordo, Michael, Barry Eichengreen, and Douglas Irwin. 1999. "Is Globalization Today Really Different from Globalization a Hundred Years Ago?" *Brookings Trade Forum, 1999*:1–50.

Bovingdon, Gardner. 2002. "The Not-So-Silent Majority: Uyghur Resistance to Han Rule in Xinjiang." *Modern China* 28 (1):39–78.

Branstetter, Lee, and Nicholas Lardy. 2008. "China's Embrace of Globalization." In *China's Great Economic Transformation*, ed. L. Brandt and T. G. Rawski. New York: Cambridge University Press.

Brooker, Paul. 2000. *Non-Democratic Regimes: Theory, Government and Politics.* New York: St. Martin's Press.

Brooks, Stephen G., and William C. Wohlforth. 2000. "Power, Globalization, and the End of the Cold War: Reevaluating a Landmark Case for Ideas." *International Security* 25 (3):5–53.

Brownlee, Jason. 2007. *Authoritarianism in an Age of Democratization.* New York: Cambridge University Press.

Bunce, Valerie. 1999. *Subversive Institutions: The Design and the Destruction of Socialism and the State.* New York: Cambridge University Press.

Burns, John P. 1994. "Strengthening Central CCP Control of Leadership Selection: The 1990 Nomenklatura." *The China Quarterly* (138):458–91.

Cai, Hongbin, and Daniel Treisman. 2006. "Did Government Decentralization Cause China's Economic Miracle?" *World Politics* 58 (4):505–35.

Caizhengbu Difangsi [Department of Local Affairs of China Ministry of Finance]. 1996. *Difang Caizheng Tongji Ziliao 1995 [Statistical Materials on Local Finance 1995].* Beijing: Xinhua chubanshe.

1998. *Difang Caizheng Tongji Ziliao 1996 [Statistical Materials on Local Finance 1996].* Beijing: Zhongguo caizheng jingji chubanshe.

Caizhengbu Guokusi [Department of State Treasury of China Ministry of Finance], and Caizhengbu Yusuansi [Department of Budget of China Ministry of Finance]. 2002. *Difang Caizheng Tongji Ziliao 2001 [Statistical Materials on Local Finance 2001].* Beijing: Zhongguo caizheng jingji chubanshe.

2003. *Difang Caizheng Tongji Ziliao 2002 [Statistical Materials on Local Finance 2002].* Beijing: Zhongguo caizheng jingji chubanshe.

2005. *Difang Caizheng Tongji Ziliao 2003 [Statistical Materials on Local Finance 2003].* Beijing: Zhongguo caizheng jingji chubanshe.

2006. *Difang Caizheng Tongji Ziliao 2004 [Statistical Materials on Local Finance 2004].* Beijing: Zhongguo caizheng jingji chubanshe.

Caizhengbu Yusuansi [Department of Budget of China Ministry of Finance]. 1998. *Difang Caizheng Tongji Ziliao 1997 [Statistical Materials on Local Finance 1997].* Beijing: Xinhua chubanshe.

1999. *Difang Caizheng Tongji Ziliao 1998 [Statistical Materials on Local Finance 1998]*. Beijing: Zhongguo caizheng jingji chubanshe.

2001a. *Difang Caizheng Tongji Ziliao 1999 [Statistical Materials on Local Finance 1999]*. Beijing: Zhongguo caizheng jingji chubanshe.

2001b. *Difang Caizheng Tongji Ziliao 2000 [Statistical Materials on Local Finance 2000]*. Beijing: Zhongguo caizheng jingji chubanshe.

Cameron, David R. 1978. "The Expansion of the Public Economy: A Comparative Analysis." *American Political Science Review* 72 (4):1243–61.

Camões, Pedro Jorge Sobral. 2003. Political and Fiscal Decentralization in Western Europe: The Dynamics of Institutional Development and Change. Ph.D. Dissertation, Government and International Studies, University of South Carolina, Columbia, SC.

Castles, Francis G. 1999. "Decentralization and the Post-War Political Economy." *European Journal of Political Research* 36 (1):27–53.

Chan, Hon S. 2004. "Cadre Personnel Management in China: The *Nomenklatura* System, 1990–1998." *The China Quarterly* (179):703–34.

Chang, Gordon G. 2001. *The Coming Collapse of China*. 1st ed. New York: Random House.

Chang, Maria Hsia. 1992. "China's Future: Regionalism, Federation, or Disintegration." *Studies in Comparative Communism* 25 (3):211–27.

Chang Yimin. 1999. "Shirun 'Renwushui' De Wenti Yu Duice [A Preliminary Discussion of the Problems Associated With 'Tax Quotas' And Possible Solutions]." *Jiangxi Caizheng Shuiwu Zhuanke Xuexiao Xuebao [Journal of Jiangxi School of Finance and Taxation]* (2):14–7.

Cheibub, José Antonio, and Jennifer Gandhi. 2004. "Classifying Political Regimes: A Six Fold Classification of Democracies and Dictatorships." Unpublished manuscript, Department of Political Science, Yale University.

Chen, Baizhu, and Yi Feng. 2000. "Determinants of Economic Growth in China: Private Enterprise, Education, and Openness." *China Economic Review* 11 (1):1–15.

Chen, Chung, Lawrence Chang, and Yimin Zhang. 1995. "The Role of Foreign Direct Investment in China Post-1978 Economic Development." *World Development* 23 (4):691–703.

Cheng, Tun-Jen. 1989. "Democratizing the Quasi-Leninist Regime in Taiwan." *World Politics* 41 (4):471–99.

Cheung, Peter Tsan-yin. 1994. "The Case of Guangdong in Central-Provincial Relations." In *Changing Central-Local Relations in China: Reform and State Capacity*, ed. Jia Hao and Lin Zhimin. Boulder: Westview.

China Ministry of Commerce. 2004–2005. *Zhongguo Shangwu Nianjian [China Commerce Yearbook]*. Zhong wen ban. ed. Beijing: Zhongguo shangwu chubanshe.

China Ministry of Foreign Trade and Economic Cooperation. 1987–2003. *Zhongguo Duiwai Jingji Maoyi Nianjian [Almanac of China's Foreign Economic Relations and Trade]*. Xianggang: Huarun maoyi zixun youxian gongsi.

Cho, Young Nam. 2009. *Local People's Congresses in China: Development and Transition*. New York: Cambridge University Press.

Chung, Jae Ho. 1994. "Beijing Confronting the Provinces: The 1994 Tax-Sharing Reform and Its Implications for Central-Provincial Relations in China." *China Information* 9 (2–3):1–23.

———. 2000. *Central Control and Local Discretion in China: Leadership and Implementation During Post-Mao Decollectivization.* New York: Oxford University Press.

Chung, Jae Ho, Hongyi Lai, and Ming Xia. 2006. "Mounting Challenges to Governance in China: Surveying Collective Protestors, Religious Sects and Criminal Organizations." *The China Journal* (56):1–31.

Colton, Timothy J. 1986. *The Dilemma of Reform in the Soviet Union.* Rev. and expanded ed. New York: Council on Foreign Relations.

Correlates of War 2 Project. 2003. "State System Membership List, V2002.1. Online, http://www.correlatesofwar.org/."

Dacosta, Maria, and Wayne Carroll. 2001. "Township and Village Enterprises, Openness and Regional Economic Growth in China." *Post-Communist Economies* 13 (2):229–41.

Dayal-Gulati, Anuradha, and Aasim M. Husain. 2002. "Centripetal Forces in China's Economic Takeoff." *IMF Staff Papers* 49 (3):364–94.

Delfs, Robert. 1991. "Saying No to Peking: Centre's Hold Weakened by Provincial Autonomy." *Far Eastern Economic Review*, April 4, 21–4.

Démurger, Sylvie. 2000. *Economic Opening and Growth in China.* Paris: Development Centre of the Organisation for Economic Cooperation and Development (OECD).

Démurger, Sylvie, Jeffrey D. Sachs, Wing Thye Woo, Shuming Bao, and Gene Chang. 2002a. "The Relative Contributions of Location and Preferential Policies in China's Regional Development: Being in the Right Place and Having the Right Incentives." *China Economic Review* 13 (4):444–65.

Démurger, Sylvie, Jeffrey D. Sachs, Wing Thye Woo, Shuming Bao, Gene Chang, and Andrew Mellinger. 2002b. "Geography, Economic Policy, and Regional Development in China." *Asian Economic Papers* 1 (1):146–97.

Deng Xiaoping. 1993 [1984]. "Women De Hongwei Mubiao He Genben Zhengce [Our Grand Goals and Basic Policies]." In *Deng Xiaoping Wenxuan Vol. 3 [Selected Works of Deng Xiaoping Vol. 3].* Beijing: Renmin chubanshe.

———. 1993 [1992]. "Zai Wuchang, Shenzhen, Zhuhai, Shanghai Dengdi De Tanhua Yaodian [Key Points of Talks Given in Wuchang, Shenzhen, Zhuhai, Shanghai, and Other Localities]." In *Deng Xiaoping Wenxuan Vol. 3 [Selected Works of Deng Xiaoping Vol. 3].* Beijing: Renmin chubanshe.

Diaz-Cayeros, Alberto. 2005. "The Centralization of Fiscal Authority: An Empirical Investigation." Paper presented at the Yale University Comparative Politics Workshop.

———. 2006. *Federalism, Fiscal Authority, and Centralization in Latin America.* New York: Cambridge University Press.

Dickson, Bruce J. 2003. *Red Capitalists in China: The Party, Private Entrepreneurs, and Prospects for Political Change.* New York: Cambridge University Press.

———. 2008. *Wealth into Power: The Communist Party's Embrace of China's Private Sector.* New York: Cambridge University Press.

Dittmer, Lowell, and Yu-shan Wu. 1995. "The Modernization of Factionalism in Chinese Politics." *World Politics* 47 (4):467–94.

Donaldson, Robert H. 1972. "The 1971 Soviet Central Committee: An Assessment of the New Elite." *World Politics* 24 (3):382–409.

Donnithorne, Audrey. 1972. "China's Cellular Economy: Some Economic Trends since the Cultural Revolution." *The China Quarterly* (52):605–19.

Duiker, William J. 1995. *Vietnam: Revolution in Transition.* 2nd ed. Boulder: Westview.

Eggertsson, Thrainn. 1990. *Economic Behavior and Institutions.* New York: Cambridge University Press.

Elazar, Daniel J. 1995. "From Statism to Federalism: A Paradigm Shift." *Publius: the Journal of Federalism* 25 (2):5–18.

Europa Publications Limited. 1980. *The Europa World Year Book.* 21st ed. 2 vols. London: Europa Publications Limited.

1999. *The Europa World Year Book.* 40th ed. 2 vols. Vol. 2. London: Europa Publications Limited.

Ewing, Richard Daniel. 2003. "Hu Jintao: The Making of a Chinese General Secretary." *The China Quarterly* (173):17–34.

Feder, Gershon. 1983. "On Exports and Economic Growth." *Journal of Development Economics* 12 (1–2):59–73.

Fernandez, Raquel, and Dani Rodrik. 1991. "Resistance to Reform: Status-Quo Bias in the Presence of Individual-Specific Uncertainty." *American Economic Review* 81 (5):1146–55.

Fewsmith, Joseph. 1997. "Reaction, Resurgence, and Succession: Chinese Politics since Tiananmen." In *The Politics of China: The Eras of Mao and Deng*, ed. R. MacFarquhar. New York: Cambridge University Press.

Filippov, Mikhail, Peter C. Ordeshook, and Olga Shvetsova. 2004. *Designing Federalism: A Theory of Self-Sustainable Federal Institutions.* New York: Cambridge University Press.

Fong, Leslie. 2004. "Leadership Dispute over China Growth; Premier Wen Has Heated Debate with Shanghai Party Secretary over Stringent Measures to Cool Economy." *The Strait Times* (Singapore), July 10.

Frankel, Jeffrey A., and David Romer. 1999. "Does Trade Cause Growth?" *American Economic Review* 89 (3):379–99.

Freeman, Richard B. 1995. "Are Your Wages Set in Beijing?" *Journal of Economic Perspectives* 9 (3):15–32.

Frieden, Jeffry A. 1991a. *Debt, Development, and Democracy: Modern Political Economy and Latin America, 1965–1985.* Princeton: Princeton University Press.

1991b. "Invested Interests: The Politics of National Economic Policies in a World of Global Finance." *International Organization* 45 (4):425–51.

Frieden, Jeffry A., and Ronald Rogowski. 1996. "The Impact of the International Economy on National Policies: An Analytical Overview." In *Internationalization and Domestic Politics*, ed. R. O. Keohane and H. V. Milner. New York: Cambridge University Press.

Friedman, Edward. 1993. "China's North-South Split and the Forces of Disintegration." *Current History* 92 (575):270–4.

Fu, Jun. 2000. *Institutions and Investments: Foreign Direct Investment in China During the Reform Era.* Ann Arbor: The University of Michigan Press.

Fujita, Masahisa, and Dapeng Hu. 2001. "Regional Disparity in China 1985–1994: The Effects of Globalization and Economic Liberalization." *Annals of Regional Science* 35 (1):3–37.

Gallagher, Mary Elizabeth. 2005. *Contagious Capitalism: Globalization and the Politics of Labor in China.* Princeton: Princeton University Press.

Gandhi, Jennifer. 2008. *Political Institutions under Dictatorship.* New York: Cambridge University Press.

Gao Binhuai. 1990. "Wanshan Waimao Chengbao Jingyingzhi De Sikao [Thoughts on Improving the Foreign Trade Contracting System]." *Guoji Maoyi Wenti [Issues in International Trade]* (12):18–21.

Garman, Christopher, Stephan Haggard, and Eliza Willis. 2001. "Fiscal Decentralization: A Political Theory with Latin American Cases." *World Politics* 53 (2):205–36.

Garrett, Geoffrey. 1998a. "Global Markets and National Politics: Collision Course or Virtuous Circle?" *International Organization* 52 (4):149–76.

1998b. *Partisan Politics in the Global Economy.* New York: Cambridge University Press.

2000. "The Causes of Globalization." *Comparative Political Studies* 33 (6–7):941–91.

Garrett, Geoffrey, and Peter Lange. 1996. "Internationalization, Institutions and Political Change." In *Internationalization and Domestic Politics*, ed. R. O. Keohane and H. V. Milner. New York: Cambridge University Press.

Garrett, Geoffrey, and Jonathan Rodden. 2003. "Globalization and Fiscal Decentralization." In *Governance in a Global Economy: Political Authority in Transition*, ed. M. Kahler and D. A. Lake. Princeton: Princeton University Press.

Geddes, Barbara. 1999a. "Authoritarian Breakdown: Empirical Test of a Game Theoretic Argument." Paper presented at the Annual Meeting of the American Political Science Association, Atlanta, GA.

1999b. "What Do We Know About Democratization after Twenty Years?" *Annual Review of Political Science* 2:115–44.

Gilley, Bruce. 2004. *China's Democratic Future: How It Will Happen and Where It Will Lead.* New York: Columbia University Press.

Godwin, Paul H. B. 1976. "The PLA and Political Control in China's Provinces: A Structural Analysis." *Comparative Politics* 9 (1):1–20.

Goldstein, Carl. 1993. "South China: Resisting the Centre." *Far Eastern Economic Review*, September 2, 42.

Goldstone, Jack A. 1995. "The Coming Chinese Collapse." *Foreign Policy* (99):35–52.

Goodman, David S. G. 1984. "Provincial Party First Secretaries in National Politics: A Categoric or a Political Group?" In *Groups and Politics in the People's Republic of China*, ed. D. S. G. Goodman. Cardiff, U.K.: University College Cardiff Press.

1986. *Centre and Province in the People's Republic of China: Sichuan and Guizhou, 1955–1965.* New York: Cambridge University Press.

1994. "The Politics of Regionalism: Economic Development, Conflict and Negotiation." In *China Deconstructs: Politics, Trade and Regionalism*, ed. D. S. G. Goodman and G. Segal. London: Routledge.

Goodman, David S. G., and Feng Chongyi. 1994. "Guangdong: Greater Hong Kong and the New Regionalist Future." In *China Deconstructs: Politics, Trade and Regionalism*, ed. D. S. G. Goodman and G. Segal. London: Routledge.

Goodman, David S. G., and Gerald Segal, eds. 1994. *China Deconstructs: Politics, Trade and Regionalism*. London: Routledge.

Green, Donald P., Soo Yeon Kim, and David H. Yoon. 2001. "Dirty Pool." *International Organization* 55 (2):441–68.

Greene, William H. 2000. *Econometric Analysis*. 4th ed. Upper Saddle River, N.J.: Prentice Hall.

Guillén, Mauro F. 2001. "Is Globalization Civilizing, Destructive or Feeble? A Critique of Five Key Debates in the Social Science Literature." *Annual Review of Sociology* 27:235–60.

Guo Kesha, and Li Haijian. 1995. "Zhongguo Duiwai Kaifang Diqu Chayi Yanjiu [A Study of Regional Disparity under China's Opening]." *Zhongguo Gongye Jingji [China Industrial Economy]* (8):61–8.

Guojia Shuiwu Zongju [State Tax Administration]. 2002. "Guanyu Suodeshui Shouru Fenxiang Tizhi Gaigehou Shuishou Zhengguan Fanwei De Tongzhi [Circular on Jurisdiction of Collection after Reform of Income Tax Sharing]." *Zhongguo Shuiwu [China Taxation]* (4):32–3.

Guojia Tongji Ju [National Bureau of Statistics]. 1982. *Zhongguo Tongji Nianjian 1981 [China Statistical Yearbook 1981]*. Beijing: Zhongguo tongji chubanshe.

———. 1995. *Zhongguo Tongji Nianjian 1995 [China Statistical Yearbook 1995]*. Beijing: Zhongguo tongji chubanshe.

———. 1996. *Zhongguo Tongji Nianjian 1996 [China Statistical Yearbook 1996]*. Beijing: Zhongguo tongji chubanshe.

———. 1998–2005. *Zhongguo Chengshi Tongji Nianjian [China City Statistical Yearbook] (Individual Issue for Each Year)*. Beijing: Zhongguo tongji chubanshe.

———. 1999a. *Xin Zhongguo Wushinian Tongji Ziliao Huibian [Comprehensive Statistical Data and Materials on 50 Years of New China]*. Beijing: Zhongguo tongji chubanshe.

———. 1999b. *Zhongguo Tongji Nianjian 1999 [China Statistical Yearbook 1999]*. Beijing: Zhongguo tongji chubanshe.

———. 2000. *Zhongguo Tongji Nianjian 2000 [China Statistical Yearbook 2000]*. Beijing: Zhongguo tongji chubanshe.

———. 2002. *Zhongguo Tongji Nianjian 2002 [China Statistical Yearbook 2002]*. Beijing: Zhongguo tongji chubanshe.

———. 2005. *Zhongguo Tongji Nianjian 2005 [China Statistical Yearbook 2005]*. Beijing: Zhongguo tongji chubanshe.

Guowuyuan [State Council]. 2002. "Guowuyuan Guanyu Yinfa Suodeshui Shouru Fenxiang Gaige Fang'an De Tongzhi [Circular on Issuing the Plan to Reform Income Tax Sharing]." *Guowuyuan Gongbao [Gazette of the State Council of the People's Republic of China]* (4):21–2.

Haber, Stephen. 2006. "Authoritarian Government." In *The Oxford Handbook of Political Economy*, ed. B. R. Weingast and D. Wittman. New York: Oxford University Press.

Hankla, Charles R. 2008. "Parties and Patronage: Analysis of Trade and Industrial Policy in India." *Comparative Politics* 41 (1):41–60.

Harasymiw, Bohdan. 1969. "Nomenklatura: The Soviet Communist Party's Leadership Recruitment System." *Canadian Journal of Political Science* 2 (4):493–512.

Harding, Harry. 1987. *China's Second Revolution: Reform after Mao.* Washington, D.C.: Brookings Institution.

———. 1994. "Comment." In *How China Opened Its Door: The Political Success of the PRC's Foreign Trade and Investment Reforms* by S. Shirk. Washington, D.C.: The Brookings Institution.

Hays, Jude C. 2009. *Globalization and the New Politics of Embedded Liberalism.* New York: Oxford University Press.

He Husheng, Li Yaodong, and Xiang Changfu. 1993. *Zhonghua Renmin Gongheguo Zhiguanzhi [Annals of the Official Posts and Their Occupants in the People's Republic of China].* Beijing: Zhongguo shehui chubanshe.

Heilmann, Sebastian. 2008. "Policy Experimentation in China's Economic Rise." *Studies in Comparative International Development* 43 (1):1–26.

Hellman, Joel S. 1998. "Winners Take All: The Politics of Partial Reform in Postcommunist Transitions." *World Politics* 50 (2):203–34.

Hernández-Rodríguez, Rogelio. 2003. "The Renovation of Old Institutions: State Governors and the Political Transition in Mexico." *Latin American Politics and Society* 45 (4):97–128.

Heston, Alan, Robert Summers, and Bettina Aten. October 2002. "Penn World Table Version 6.1. Center for International Comparisons at the University of Pennsylvania (CICUP)."

Hiscox, Michael J. 2002. *International Trade and Political Conflict: Commerce, Coalitions, and Mobility.* Princeton: Princeton University Press.

———. 2003. "Political Integration and Disintegration in the Global Economy." In *Governance in a Global Economy: Political Authority in Transition*, ed. M. Kahler and D. A. Lake. Princeton: Princeton University Press.

Horiuchi, Yasaku, and Jun Saito. 2003. "Reapportionment and Redistribution: Consequences of Electoral Reform in Japan." *American Journal of Political Science* 47 (4):669–82.

Horowitz, Shale. 2004. "Restarting Globalization after World War II: Structure, Coalitions, and the Cold War." *Comparative Political Studies* 37 (2):127–51.

Howell, Jude. 1993. *China Opens Its Doors: The Politics of Economic Transition.* Boulder: Lynne Rienner Publishers.

Hu, Zuliu F., and Mohsin S. Khan. 1997. "Why Is China Growing So Fast?" *IMF Staff Papers* 44 (1):103–31.

Huang, Jing. 2000. *Factionalism in Chinese Communist Politics.* New York: Cambridge University Press.

Huang, Yasheng. 1990. "Web of Interests and Patterns of Behavior of Chinese Local Economic Bureaucracies and Enterprises During Reforms." *The China Quarterly* (123):431–58.

1994. "Information, Bureaucracy, and Economic Reforms in China and the Soviet Union." *World Politics* 47 (1):102–34.

1995a. "Administrative Monitoring in China: Institutions and Processes." *The China Quarterly* (143):828–43.

1995b. "Why China Will Not Collapse." *Foreign Policy* (99):54–68.

1996. *Inflation and Investment Controls in China: The Political Economy of Central-Local Relations During the Reform Era.* New York: Cambridge University Press.

2002. "Managing Chinese Bureaucrats: An Institutional Economics Perspective." *Political Studies* 50 (1):61–79.

2003. *Selling China: Foreign Direct Investment During the Reform Era.* New York: Cambridge University Press.

Huang, Yasheng, and Yumin Sheng. 2009. "Political Decentralization and Inflation: Sub-National Evidence from China." *British Journal of Political Science* 39 (2):389–412.

Huntington, Samuel P., and Clement H. Moore, eds. 1970. *Authoritarian Politics in Modern Society: The Dynamics of Established One-Party Systems.* New York: Basic Books.

Iversen, Torben, and Thomas R. Cusack. 2000. "The Causes of Welfare State Expansion: Deindustrialization or Globalization?" *World Politics* 52 (3):313–49.

Janda, Kenneth. 1980. *Political Parties: A Cross-National Survey.* New York: Free Press.

Jeanneney, Sylviane Guillaumont, and Ping Hua. 2004. "Why Do More Open Chinese Provinces Have Bigger Governments?" *Review of International Economics* 12 (3):525–42.

Jensen, Michael C., and William H. Meckling. 1976. "Theory of the Firm: Managerial Behavior, Agency Costs and Ownership Structure." *Journal of Financial Economics* 3 (4):305–60.

Jia Hao, and Lin Zhimin, eds. 1994. *Changing Central-Local Relations in China: Reform and State Capacity.* Boulder: Westview.

Jie Wenxiu. 1993. "Gaige Waihui Guanli Tizhi, Cujin Duiwai Jingmao Fazhan [Reforming the Foreign Exchange Management System, Furthering the Development of Foreign Economics and Trade]." *Guoji Maoyi [Journal of International Trade]* (1):14–5, 48.

Jin, Hehui, Yingyi Qian, and Barry Weingast. 2005. "Regional Decentralization and Fiscal Incentives: Federalism, Chinese Style." *Journal of Public Economics* 89 (9–10):1719–42.

Jing Shan, ed. 1991. *Zhongguo Gongchandang Zhishi Daquan [A Comprehensive Knowledge Book on the Communist Party of China].* Harbin: Harbin chubanshe.

Kahler, Miles, and David A. Lake. 2003a. "Globalization and Governance." In *Governance in a Global Economy: Political Authority in Transition*, ed. M. Kahler and D. A. Lake. Princeton: Princeton University Press.

eds. 2003b. *Governance in a Global Economy: Political Authority in Transition.* Princeton: Princeton University Press.

Kanbur, Ravi, and Xiaobo Zhang. 2005. "Fifty Years of Regional Inequality in China: A Journey through Revolution, Reform and Openness." *Review of Development Economics* 9 (1):87–106.

Karmel, Solomon M. 1995. "Ethnic Tension and the Struggle for Order: China's Policies in Tibet." *Pacific Affairs* 68 (4):485–508.

Katz, Richard S., and Peter Mair. 1992. *Party Organizations: A Data Handbook on Party Organizations in Western Democracies, 1960–90*. London: Sage.

Kaufman, Robert, and Alex Segura-Ubiergo. 2001. "Globalization, Democratization and Social Spending in Latin America: A Time-Series Cross-Section Analysis, 1973–97." *World Politics* 53 (4):553–87.

Kaye, Lincoln. 1995. "The Grip Slips." *Far Eastern Economic Review*, May 11, 18–20.

Keefer, Philip. 2005. "DPI 2004 – Database of Political Institutions: Changes and Variable Definitions." Working Paper, Development Research Group, The World Bank.

Keohane, Robert, and Joseph Nye, Jr. 2000. "Globalization: What's New? What's Not? (and So What)?" *Foreign Policy* (118):104–19.

Keohane, Robert O., and Helen V. Milner, eds. 1996. *Internationalization and Domestic Politics*. New York: Cambridge University Press.

Kim, Byung-Yeon, Suk Jin Kim, and Keun Lee. 2007. "Assessing the Economic Performance of North Korea, 1954–1989: Estimates and Growth Accounting Analysis." *Journal of Comparative Economics* 35 (3):564–82.

Kim, Heung-Kyu. 2002. The Political Capacity of Beijing Still Matters: Political Leadership and Institutionalization of Fiscal Systems During the Period of Economic Decentralization in China, 1979–1997. Ph.D. Dissertation, Political Science, University of Michigan, Ann Arbor.

Kindleberger, Charles P. 1973. *The World in Depression, 1929–1939*. Berkeley: University of California Press.

King, Gary. 1991. "'Truth' Is Stranger Than Prediction, More Questionable Than Causal Inference." *American Journal of Political Science* 35 (4):1047–53.

King, Gary, Robert O. Keohane, and Sidney Verba. 1994. *Designing Social Inquiry: Scientific Inference in Qualitative Research*. Princeton: Princeton University Press.

King, Gary, Michael Tomz, and Jason Wittenberg. 2000. "Making the Most of Statistical Analyses: Improving Interpretation and Presentation." *American Journal of Political Science* 44 (2):347–61.

Konitzer, Andrew, and Stephen K. Wegren. 2006. "Federalism and Political Recentralization in the Russian Federation: United Russia as the Party of Power." *Publius: The Journal of Federalism* 36 (4):503–22.

Lam, Willy Wo-Lap. 1999. *The Era of Jiang Zemin*. Singapore; New York: Prentice Hall.

Lampton, David M. 1987. "Chinese Politics: The Bargaining Treadmill." *Issues & Studies* 23 (3):11–41.

——— 1992. "A Plum for a Peach: Bargaining, Interest, and Bureaucratic Politics in China." In *Bureaucracy, Politics, and Decision Making in Post-Mao China*, ed. K. G. Lieberthal and D. M. Lampton. Berkeley: University of California Press.

Landry, Pierre F. 2008. *Decentralized Authoritarianism in China: The Communist Party's Control of Local Elites in the Post-Mao Era.* New York: Cambridge University Press.

Lardy, Nicholas R. 1978. *Economic Growth and Distribution in China.* New York: Cambridge University Press.

  1992. *Foreign Trade and Economic Reform in China, 1978–1990.* New York: Cambridge University Press.

  1998. *China's Unfinished Economic Revolution.* Washington, D.C.: Brookings Institution.

  2002. *Integrating China into the Global Economy.* Washington, D.C.: Brookings Institution Press.

Lau, Lawrence, Yingyi Qian, and Gérard Roland. 2000. "Reform without Losers: An Interpretation of China's Dual-Track Approach to Transition." *Journal of Political Economy* 108 (1):120–43.

Layne, Christopher. 2009. "The Waning of U.S. Hegemony – Myth or Reality?: A Review Essay." *International Security* 34 (1):147–72.

Lee, Dongmin. 2006. "Chinese Civil-Military Relations: The Divestiture of People's Liberation Army Business Holdings." *Armed Forces & Society* 32 (3):437–53.

Lee, Hong Yung. 1991. *From Revolutionary Cadres to Party Technocrats in Socialist China.* Berkeley: University of California Press.

Levi, Margaret. 1988. *Of Rule and Revenue.* Berkeley: University of California Press.

Levi, Margaret, and David Olson. 2000. "The Battles in Seattle." *Politics & Society* 28 (3):309–29.

Lewis, John Wilson. 1963. *Leadership in Communist China.* Ithaca: Cornell University Press.

Li, Cheng. 2001. *China's Leaders: The New Generation.* Lanham: Rowman & Littlefield Publishers.

  2002. "The 'Shanghai Gang': Force for Stability or Cause for Conflict?" *China Leadership Monitor* (2), available at http://www.hoover.org/publications/clm/issues/2906851.html.

Li Lanqing. 1991. "Guanyu Woguo Duiwai Jingmao Gongzuo De Ruogan Wenti [On Several Issues in Our Country's Foreign Trade Work]." *Guoji Maoyi [Journal of International Trade]* (9):4–9.

  ed. 1995. *Zhongguo Liyong Waizi Jichu Zhishi [Basic Knowledge on China's Utilization of Foreign Investment].* Beijing: Jingji guanli chubanshe.

Liao Gailong, Luo Zhufeng, and Fan Yuan. 1994. *Zhongguo Renmin Dacidian: Xianren Dangzhengjun Lingdao Renwujuan [Who's Who in China: Current Leaders].* Beijing: Waiwen chubanshe.

Lieberthal, Kenneth G. 1992. "Introduction: The 'Fragmented Authoritarianism' Model and Its Limitations." In *Bureaucracy, Politics, and Decision Making in Post-Mao China,* ed. K. G. Lieberthal and D. M. Lampton. Berkeley: University of California Press.

  2003. *Governing China: From Revolution through Reform.* 2nd ed. New York: W. W. Norton.

Lieberthal, Kenneth G. (with James Tong and Sai-cheung Yeung). 1978. *Central Documents and Politburo Politics in China*. Ann Arbor: Center for Chinese Studies, University of Michigan.

Lieberthal, Kenneth, and Michel Oksenberg. 1988. *Policy Making in China: Leaders, Structures, and Processes*. Princeton: Princeton University Press.

Lin, Justin Yifu, Fang Cai, and Zhou Li. 1996. *The China Miracle: Development Strategy and Economic Reform*. Hong Kong: Published for the Hong Kong Centre for Economic Research and the International Center for Economic Growth by the Chinese University Press.

Lin, Justin Yifu, and Zhiqiang Liu. 2000. "Fiscal Decentralization and Economic Growth in China." *Economic Development and Cultural Change* 49 (1):1–21.

Lin, Shuanglin. 2000. "Foreign Trade and China's Economic Development: A Time-Series Analysis." *Journal of Economic Development* 25 (1):145–54.

Lindblom, Charles Edward. 1977. *Politics and Markets: The World's Political Economic Systems*. New York: Basic Books.

Liu, Ling. 2008. "Local Government and Big Business in the People's Republic of China – Case Study Evidence from Shandong Province." *Asia Pacific Business Review* 14 (4):473–89.

Liu, Xiaming, Haiyan Song, and Peter Romilly. 1997. "An Empirical Investigation of the Causal Relationship between Openness and Economic Growth in China." *Applied Economics* 29 (12):1679–86.

Liu Xiangdong. 1993. "Zhongguo De Waimao Tizhi Gaige [Reform of China's Foreign Trade System]." *Guoji Maoyi Wenti [Issues in International Trade]* (8):2–4.

Long, Simon. 1994. "Regionalism in Fujian." In *China Deconstructs: Politics, Trade and Regionalism*, ed. D. S. G. Goodman and G. Segal. London: Routledge.

Lu Libin. 1989. "Zubu Wanshan Waimao Chengbao Jingying Zerenzhi [Gradually Improving the Foreign Trade Contracting System]." *Guoji Maoyi Wenti [Issues in International Trade]* (4):20–2.

Lü, Xiaobo. 2000. *Cadres and Corruption: The Organizational Involution of the Chinese Communist Party*. Stanford: Stanford University Press.

Magaloni, Beatriz. 2008. "Credible Power-Sharing and the Longevity of Authoritarian Rule." *Comparative Political Studies* 41 (4–5):715–41.

Malesky, Edmund. 2008. "Straight Ahead on Red: How Foreign Direct Investment Empowers Subnational Leaders." *Journal of Politics* 70 (1):97–119.

2009. "Gerrymandering–Vietnamese Style: Escaping the Partial Reform Equilibrium in a Nondemocratic Regime." *Journal of Politics* 71 (1):132–59.

Manion, Melanie. 1985. "The Cadre Management System, Post-Mao: The Appointment, Promotion, Transfer and Removal of Party and State Leaders." *The China Quarterly* (102):203–33.

1993. *Retirement of Revolutionaries in China: Public Policies, Social Norms, Private Interests*. Princeton: Princeton University Press.

2004. *Corruption by Design: Building Clean Government in Mainland China and Hong Kong*. Cambridge: Harvard University Press.

Marshall, Monty G., and Keith Jaggers. 2002. "Polity IV Project." Dataset Users' Manual, Integrated Network for Societal Conflict Research (INSCR) Program, Center for International Development and Conflict Management (CIDCM), University of Maryland, College Park, MD.

Mayhew, David R. 1974. *Congress: The Electoral Connection*. New Haven: Yale University Press.

McCubbins, Mathew D., Roger G. Noll, and Barry R. Weingast. 1989. "Structure and Process, Politics and Policy: Administrative Arrangements and the Political Control of Agencies." *Virginia Law Review* 75 (2):431–82.

McCubbins, Mathew D., and Thomas Schwartz. 1984. "Congressional Oversight Overlooked: Police Patrols Versus Fire Alarms." *American Journal of Political Science* 2 (1):165–79.

Meadwell, Hudson, and Pierre Martin. 1996. "Economic Integration and the Politics of Independence." *Nations and Nationalism* 2 (1):67–87.

Mertha, Andrew C. 2005. "China's 'Soft' Centralization: Shifting *Tiao/Kuai* Authority Relations." *The China Quarterly* (184):791–810.

Moe, Terry M. 1984. "The New Economics of Organization." *American Journal of Political Science* 28 (4):739–77.

Montinola, Gabriella, Yingyi Qian, and Barry R. Weingast. 1995. "Federalism, Chinese Style: The Political Basis for Economic Success in China." *World Politics* 48 (1):50–81.

Nathan, Andrew J. 1973. "A Factionalism Model for CCP Politics." *The China Quarterly* (53):33–66.

Nathan, Andrew J. (with contributions by Tianjian Shi and Helena V. S. Ho). 1997. *China's Transition*. New York: Columbia University Press.

Naughton, Barry. 1995. *Growing Out of the Plan: Chinese Economic Reform, 1978–1993*. New York: Cambridge University Press.

1996. "China's Emergence and Prospects as a Trading Nation." *Brookings Papers on Economic Activity* (2):273–337.

Naughton, Barry J. 2004. "The Western Development Program." In *Holding China Together: Diversity and National Integration in the Post-Deng Era*, ed. B. J. Naughton and D. L. Yang. New York: Cambridge University Press.

Naughton, Barry J., and Dali L. Yang. 2004a. "Holding China Together: Introduction." In *Holding China Together: Diversity and National Integration in the Post-Deng Era*, ed. B. J. Naughton and D. L. Yang. New York: Cambridge University Press.

2004b. *Holding China Together: Diversity and National Integration in the Post-Deng Era*. New York: Cambridge University Press.

Niskanen, William A. 1975. "Bureaucrats and Politicians." *Journal of Law and Economics* 18 (3):617–43.

North, Douglass Cecil, and Barry R. Weingast. 1989. "Constitutions and Commitment: The Evolution of Institutions Governing Public Choice in 17th-Century England." *Journal of Economic History* 49 (4):803–32.

O'Brien, Kevin J. 1990. *Reform without Liberalization: China's National People's Congress and the Politics of Institutional Change*. New York: Cambridge University Press.

Oi, Jean C. 1999. *Rural China Takes Off: Institutional Foundations of Economic Reform*. Berkeley: University of California Press.

Oksenberg, Michel, and James Tong. 1991. "The Evolution of Central-Provincial Fiscal Relations in China, 1971–1984: The Formal System." *The China Quarterly* (125):1–32.

Olson, Mancur. 1971. *The Logic of Collective Action: Public Goods and the Theory of Groups*. Cambridge: Harvard University Press.

   1993. "Dictatorship, Democracy, and Development." *American Political Science Review* 87 (3):567–76.

   1996. "Distinguished Lecture on Economics in Government: Big Bills Left on the Sidewalk: Why Some Nations Are Rich, and Others Poor." *Journal of Economic Perspectives* 10 (2):3–24.

Park, Jong H., and Penelope B. Prime. 1997. "Export Performance and Growth in China: A Cross-Provincial Analysis." *Applied Economics* 29 (10):1353–63.

Pearson, Margaret M. 1991. *Joint Ventures in the People's Republic of China: The Control of Foreign Direct Investment under Socialism*. Princeton: Princeton University Press.

People's Bank of China Research and Statistics Department. 1988. *Chinese Financial Statistics 1952–1987*. Beijing: Chinese Financial Publishing House.

Pleština, Dijana. 1992. *Regional Development in Communist Yugoslavia: Success, Failure, and Consequences*. Boulder: Westview.

Prud 'homme, Rémy. 1995. "The Dangers of Decentralization." *The World Bank Research Observer* 10 (2):201–20.

Przeworski, Adam, Michael E. Alvarez, José Antonio Cheibub, and Fernando Limongi. 2000. *Democracy and Development: Political Institutions and Material Well-Being in the World, 1950–1990*. New York: Cambridge University Press.

Pu Xingzu. 1990. *Dangdai Zhongguo Zhengzhi Zhidu [The Political System of Contemporary China]*. Shanghai: Shanghai renmin chubanshe.

Pye, Lucian W. 1990. "China: Erratic State, Frustrated Society." *Foreign Affairs* 69 (4):56–74.

   1992. *The Spirit of Chinese Politics*. Cambridge: Harvard University Press.

Qian, Yingyi, and Barry R. Weingast. 1997. "Federalism as a Commitment to Preserving Market Incentives." *Journal of Economic Perspectives* 11 (4):83–92.

Radelet, Steven, Jeffrey Sachs, and Jong-Wha Lee. 2001. "The Determinants and Prospects of Economic Growth in Asia." *International Economic Journal* 15 (3):1–29.

Ramseyer, J. Mark, and Frances McCall Rosenbluth. 1995. *The Politics of Oligarchy: Institutional Choice in Imperial Japan*. New York: Cambridge University Press.

Richardson, J. David. 1995. "Income Inequality and Trade: How to Think and What to Conclude." *Journal of Economic Perspectives* 9 (3):33–55.

Rigby, T. H. 1982. "Foreword." In *The Soviet Politburo*, by John Löwenhardt. rev. ed. New York: St. Martin's Press.

Riker, William H. 1964. *Federalism: Origin, Operation, Significance*. Boston and Toronto: Little, Brown and Company.

Rivera-Batiz, Luis, and Paul M. Romer. 1991. "Economic-Integration and Endogenous Growth." *Quarterly Journal of Economics* 106 (2):531–55.

Rodden, Jonathan. 2002. "Strength in Numbers? Representation and Redistribution in the European Union." *European Union Politics* 3 (2):151–75.

2004. "Comparative Federalism and Decentralization: On Meaning and Measurement." *Comparative Politics* 36 (4):481–500.

Rodden, Jonathan, and Susan Rose-Ackerman. 1997. "Does Federalism Preserve Markets?" *Virginia Law Review* 83 (7):1521–72.

Rodden, Jonathan, and Erik Wibbels. 2002. "Beyond the Fiction of Federalism: Macroeconomic Management in Multitiered Systems." *World Politics* 54 (4):494–531.

Rodrik, Dani. 1998. "Why Do More Open Economies Have Bigger Governments?" *Journal of Political Economy* 106 (5):997–1032.

Rogowski, Ronald. 1989. *Commerce and Coalitions: How Trade Affects Domestic Political Alignments*. Princeton: Princeton University Press.

Rothschild, Emma. 1999. "Globalization and the Return of History." *Foreign Policy* (115):106–16.

Sachs, Jeffrey, and Xavier Sala-i-Martin. 1992. "Fiscal Federalism and Optimum Currency Areas: Evidence for Europe from the United States." In *Establishing a Central Bank: Issues in Europe and Lessons from the US*, ed. M. B. Canzoneri, P. R. Masson, and V. Grilli. New York: Cambridge University Press.

Sachs, Jeffrey D., and Andrew Warner. 1995. "Economic Reform and the Process of Global Integration." *Brookings Papers on Economic Activity* (1):1–95.

Salem, Ellen. 1988. "Things Fall Apart, the Centre Cannot Hold." *Far Eastern Economic Review*, October 27, 38.

Schroeder, Paul E. 1992. "Territorial Actors as Competitors for Power: The Case of Hubei and Wuhan." In *Bureaucracy, Politics, and Decision Making in Post-Mao China*, ed. K. G. Lieberthal and D. M. Lampton. Berkeley: University of California Press.

Shambaugh, David L. 2003. *Modernizing China's Military: Progress, Problems, and Prospects*. Berkeley: University of California Press.

Shan, Jordan, Gary Tian, and Fiona Sun. 1999. "Causality between FDI and Economic Growth." In *Foreign Direct Investment and Economic Growth in China*, ed. Y. Wu. Northampton, MA: Edward Elgar.

Shen Xueming, and Zheng Jianying, eds. 2001. *Zhonggong Diyijie Zhi Shiwujie Zhongyang Weiyuan [Members of the 1st -15th Central Committees of the Chinese Communist Party]*. Beijing: Zhongyang wenxian chubanshe.

Sheng Tongji Ju [Provincial Bureaus of Statistics]. 2000–2005. *Provincial Statistical Yearbooks 2000–2005 (Individual Issue for Each Province in Each Year)*. Beijing: Zhongguo tongji chubanshe.

Sheng, Yumin. 2002. "Synergistic Globalization: The Political Economy of China's GATT/WTO Accession." In *New Directions in Chinese Politics for the New Millennium*, ed. G. Liu and W. Chen. Lewiston, N.Y.: Edwin Mellen Press.

2005a. "Central-Provincial Relations at the CCP Central Committees: Institutions, Measurement and Empirical Trends, 1978–2002." *The China Quarterly* (182):338–55.

2005b. Governing Globalization at Home: The Political Economy of China's Central-Provincial Relations, 1977–2002. Ph.D. Dissertation, Political Science, Yale University, New Haven, CT.

2007a. "The Determinants of Provincial Presence at the CCP Central Committees, 1978–2002: An Empirical Investigation." *Journal of Contemporary China* 16 (51):215–37.

2007b. "Global Market Integration and Central Political Control: Foreign Trade and Intergovernmental Relations in China." *Comparative Political Studies* 40 (4):405–34.

2009a. "Authoritarian Co-optation, the Territorial Dimension: Provincial Political Representation in Post-Mao China." *Studies in Comparative International Development* 44 (1):71–93.

2009b. "How Globalized Are Chinese Provinces?" *EAI Background Brief No. 423*, East Asian Institute, National University of Singapore.

Shepsle, Kenneth A., and Mark S. Bonchek. 1997. *Analyzing Politics: Rationality, Behavior, and Institutions.* 1st ed. New York: W. W. Norton.

Shi Yupeng, and Zhou Li' an. 2007. "Diqu Fangquan Yu Jingji Xiaolü: Yi Jihua Danlie Weili [Economic Decentralization and Efficiency: The Case of Cities Separately Listed under the Plan]." *Jingji Yanjiu [Economic Research]* (1):17–28.

Shih, Victor C. 2008. *Factions and Finance in China: Elite Conflict and Inflation.* New York: Cambridge University Press.

Shirk, Susan L. 1990. "'Playing to the Provinces': Deng Xiaoping's Political Strategy of Economic Reform." *Studies in Comparative Communism* 23 (3–4):227–58.

1993. *The Political Logic of Economic Reform in China.* Berkeley: University of California Press.

1994. *How China Opened Its Door: The Political Success of the PRC's Foreign Trade and Investment Reforms.* Washington, D.C.: Brookings Institution.

1996. "Internationalization and China's Economic Reforms." In *Internationalization and Domestic Politics*, ed. R. O. Keohane and H. V. Milner. New York: Cambridge University Press.

Shue, Vivienne. 1988. *The Reach of the State: Sketches of the Chinese Body Politic.* Stanford: Stanford University Press.

Sichuan Sheng Tongji Ju [Sichuan Provincial Bureau of Statistics]. 1991–1996. *Sichuan Tongji Nianjian 1991–1996 [Sichuan Statistical Yearbook 1991–1996].* Beijing: Zhongguo tongji chubanshe.

Snyder, Richard. 2001. "Scaling Down: The Subnational Comparative Method." *Studies in Comparative International Development* 36 (1):93–110.

Solinger, Dorothy J. 1977. *Regional Government and Political Integration in Southwest China, 1949–1954.* Berkeley: University of California Press.

1992. "Urban Entrepreneurs and the State: The Merger of State and Society." In *State and Society in China: The Consequences of Reform*, ed. A. L. Rosenbaum. Boulder: Westview Press.

1996. "Despite Decentralization: Disadvantages, Dependence, and Ongoing Central Power in the Inland – the Case of Wuhan." *The China Quarterly* (145):1–34.

2009. *States' Gains, Labor's Losses: China, France, and Mexico Choose Global Liaisons, 1980–2000.* Ithaca: Cornell University Press.

Solnick, Steven L. 1996. "The Breakdown of Hierarchies in the Soviet Union and China: A Neoinstitutional Perspective." *World Politics* 48 (2):209–38.

Sorens, Jason. 2004. "Globalization, Autonomy, and the Politics of Secession." *Electoral Studies* 23 (4):727–52.

Spence, Jonathan D. 1990. *The Search for Modern China.* 1st ed. New York: Norton.

Stavis, Benedict. 1989. "The Political Economy of Inflation in China." *Studies in Comparative Communism* 22 (2–3):235–50.

Stolper, Wolfgang F., and Paul A. Samuelson. 1941. "Protection and Real Wages." *Review of Economic Studies* 9 (1):58–73.

Su, Fubing, and Dali L. Yang. 2000. "Political Institutions, Provincial Interests, and Resource Allocation in Reformist China." *Journal of Contemporary China* 9 (24):215–30.

Sun, Haishun, and Ashok Parikh. 2001. "Exports, Inward Foreign Direct Investment (FDI) and Regional Economic Growth in China." *Regional Studies* 35 (3):187–96.

Sun, Yan. 2004. *Corruption and Market in Contemporary China.* Ithaca: Cornell University Press.

Tao, Ran, and Dali L. Yang. 2008. "The Revenue Imperative and the Role of Local Government in China's Transition and Growth." Paper presented at the Conference on China's Economic Transformation, University of Chicago Gleacher Center, July 14–18.

Tao, Yi-feng. 2001. "The Evolution of Central-Provincial Relations in Post-Mao China, 1978–98: An Event History Analysis of Provincial Leader Turnover." *Issues & Studies* 37 (4):90–120.

Thorlakson, Lori. 2009. "Patterns of Party Integration, Influence and Autonomy in Seven Federations." *Party Politics* 15 (2):157–77.

Toffler, Alvin, and Heidi Toffler. 1993. *War and Anti-War: Survival at the Dawn of the Twenty-First Century.* 1st ed. Boston: Little, Brown.

Tomz, Michael, Jason Wittenberg, and Gary King. 2003. Clarify: Software for Interpreting and Presenting Statistical Results (Version 2.1), Stanford University, University of Wisconsin, and Harvard University, available at http://gking.harvard.edu/.

Treisman, Daniel. 1999. *After the Deluge: Regional Crises and Political Consolidation in Russia.* Ann Arbor: University of Michigan Press.

2000. "Decentralization and Inflation: Commitment, Collective Action, or Continuity?" *American Political Science Review* 94 (4):837–57.

Tsai, Kellee S. 2004. "Off Balance: The Unintended Consequences of Fiscal Federalism in China." *Journal of Chinese Political Science* 9 (2):1–26.

2007. *Capitalism without Democracy: The Private Sector in Contemporary China.* Ithaca: Cornell University Press.

Tsou, Tang. 1976. "Prolegomenon to the Study of Informal Small Groups in CCP Politics." *The China Quarterly* (65):98–114.

1995. "Chinese Politics at the Top: Factionalism or Informal Politics? Balance-of-Power Politics or a Game to Win All?" *The China Journal* (34):95–156.

Tsui, Kai-yuen, and Youqiang Wang. 2004. "Between Separate Stoves and a Single Menu: Fiscal Decentralization in China." *The China Quarterly* (177):71–90.

Unger, Jonathan, and Lowell Dittmer, eds. 2002. *The Nature of Chinese Politics: From Mao to Jiang*. Armonk: M. E. Sharpe.

van Houten, Pieter. 2003. "Globalization and Demands for Regional Autonomy in Europe." In *Governance in a Global Economy: Political Authority in Transition*, ed. M. Kahler and D. A. Lake. Princeton: Princeton University Press.

2009. "Multi-Level Relations in Political Parties: A Delegation Approach." *Party Politics* 15 (2):137–56.

Vogel, Ezra F. 2005. "Chen Yun: His Life." *Journal of Contemporary China* 14 (45):741–59.

Vogel, Ezra F. (with a contribution by John Kamm). 1989. *One Step Ahead in China: Guangdong under Reform*. Cambridge: Harvard University Press.

Vuving, Alexander L. 2006. "Strategy and Evolution of Vietnam's China Policy: A Changing Mixture of Pathways." *Asian Survey* 46 (6):805–24.

Wade, Robert. 1990. *Governing the Market: Economic Theory and the Role of Government in East Asian Industrialization*. Princeton: Princeton University Press.

2004. "Is Globalization Reducing Poverty and Inequality?" *World Development* 32 (4):567–89.

Walder, Andrew G. 1991. "Workers, Managers, and the State: The Reform Era and the Political Crisis of 1989." *The China Quarterly* (127):467–92.

1992. "Local Bargaining Relationships and Urban Industrial Finance." In *Bureaucracy, Politics, and Decision Making in Post-Mao China*, ed. K. G. Lieberthal and D. M. Lampton. Berkeley: University of California Press.

1995a. "Local Governments as Industrial Firms: An Organizational Analysis of China's Transitional Economy." *American Journal of Sociology* 101 (2):263–301.

1995b. "The Quiet Revolution from Within: Economic Reform as a Source of Political Decline." In *The Waning of the Communist State: Economic Origins of Political Decline in China and Hungary*, ed. A. G. Walder. Berkeley: University of California Press.

Waldron, Arthur. 1990. "Warlordism Versus Federalism: The Revival of a Debate." *The China Quarterly* (121):116–28.

Wan, Guanghua, Ming Lu, and Zhao Chen. 2007. "Globalization and Regional Income Inequality: Empirical Evidence from within China." *Review of Income and Wealth* 53 (1):35–59.

Wang, Hongying. 2001. *Weak State, Strong Networks: The Institutional Dynamics of Foreign Direct Investment in China*. New York: Oxford University Press.

Wang Jianying. 1994. *Zhongguo Gongchandang Zuzhishi Ziliao Huibian: Lingdao Jigou Yange He Chengyuan Minglu [A Compilation of Materials on the Organizational History of the Chinese Communist Party: The Evolution of the Leadership Structure and a Name List of Its Leaders]*. Beijing: Zhonggong zhongyang dangxiao chubanshe.

Wang, Shaoguang. 1995. "The Rise of the Regions: Fiscal Reform and the Decline of Central State Capacity in China." In *The Waning of the Communist*

State: Economic Origins of Political Decline in China and Hungary, ed. A. G. Walder. Berkeley: University of California Press.

———. 1997. "China's 1994 Fiscal Reform: An Initial Assessment." *Asian Survey* 37 (9):801–16.

———. 2002. "Defective Institutions and Their Consequences: Lesson from China, 1980–1993." *Communist and Post-Communist Studies* 35 (2):133–54.

———. 2004. "For National Unity: The Political Logic of Fiscal Transfer in China." In *Nationalism, Democracy and National Integration in China*, ed. L. H. Liew and S. Wang. New York: RoutledgeCurzon.

———. 2006. "Uneven Economic Development." In *Critical Issues in Contemporary China*, ed. C. Tubilewicz. London: Routledge.

Wang Shaoguang, and Hu Angang. 1993. *Zhongguo Guojia Nengli Baogao [A Study of China's State Capacity]*. Shenyang: Liaoning renmin chubanshe.

Wang, Shaoguang, and Angang Hu. 1999. *The Political Economy of Uneven Development: The Case of China*. Armonk: M. E. Sharpe.

Wang Zutang. 1992. *Zhongguo Renmin Dacidian: Dangdai Renwujuan [Who's Who in China: Contemporary]*. Shanghai: Shanghai cishu chubanshe.

Wedeman, Andrew. 1999. "Agency and Fiscal Dependence in Central-Provincial Relations in China." *Journal of Contemporary China* 8 (20):103–22.

———. 2001. "Incompetence, Noise, and Fear in Central-Local Relations in China." *Studies in Comparative International Development* 35 (4):59–83.

———. 2003. *From Mao to the Market: Rent Seeking, Local Protectionism and Marketization in China, 1984–1993*. New York: Cambridge University Press.

Wei Xiumei. 1992. *Qingdai Zhi Huibi Zhidu [Rule of Avoidance During the Qing Dynasty]*. Taibei: Zhongyang yanjiuyuan jindaishi yanjiusuo.

Weingast, Barry R. 1984. "The Congressional Bureaucratic System: A Principal-Agent Perspective (with Applications to the SEC)." *Public Choice* 44 (1):147–91.

———. 1995. "The Economic Role of Political Institutions: Market-Preserving Federalism and Economic Development." *Journal of Law, Economics, and Organization* 11 (1):1–31.

White, Lynn T. 1989. *Shanghai Shanghaied?: Uneven Taxes in Reform China*. Hong Kong: Centre of Asian Studies, University of Hong Kong.

Whiting, Susan H. 2001. *Power and Wealth in Rural China: The Political Economy of Institutional Change*. New York: Cambridge University Press.

Wibbels, Erik. 2005. *Federalism and the Market: Intergovernmental Conflict and Economic Reform in the Developing World*. New York: Cambridge University Press.

Willerton, John, and William Reisinger. 1991. "Troubleshooters, Political Machines, and Moscow's Regional Control." *Slavic Review* 50 (2):347–58.

Willis, Eliza, Christopher da C. B. Garman, and Stephan Haggard. 1999. "The Politics of Decentralization in Latin America." *Latin American Research Review* 34 (1):7–56.

Womack, Brantly, and Guangzhi Zhao. 1994. "The Many Worlds of China's Provinces: Foreign Trade and Diversification." In *China Deconstructs: Politics, Trade and Regionalism*, ed. D. S. G. Goodman and G. Segal. London: Routledge.

Wong, Christine P. W. 1991. "Central-Local Relations in an Era of Fiscal Decline: The Paradox of Fiscal Decentralization in Post-Mao China." *The China Quarterly* (128):691–715.

1992. "Fiscal Reform and Local Industrialization: The Problematic Sequencing of Reform in Post-Mao China." *Modern China* 18 (2):197–227.

ed. 1997. *Financing Local Government in the People's Republic of China.* Hong Kong and New York: Oxford University Press.

Wong, Christine P. W., Christopher Heady, and Wing T. Woo. 1995. *Fiscal Management and Economic Reform in the People's Republic of China.* Hong Kong: Oxford University Press.

World Bank. 1990. *China: Revenue Mobilization and Tax Policy.* Washington, D.C.: World Bank.

1994. *China: Foreign Trade Reform.* Washington, D.C.: World Bank.

2003. *World Development Indicators 2003 CD-ROM.* Washington, D.C.: World Bank.

2008. *World Development Indicators 2008.* Washington, D.C.: World Bank.

Wu Zesong. 1988. "Jinyibu Jiaqiang Waimao Caikuai Gongzuo, Wanshan Waimao Chengbao Jingying Zerenzhi [On Further Strengthening the Work of Foreign Trade Financing and Accounting, and Improving the Foreign Trade Contracting Responsibility System]." *Guoji Maoyi Wenti [Issues in International Trade]* (11):9–13.

Xia, Ming. 2000. *The Dual Developmental State: Developmental Strategy and Institutional Arrangements for China's Transition.* Aldershot: Ashgate.

2008. *The People's Congresses and Governance in China: Toward a Network Mode of Governance.* New York: Routledge.

Xu, Chenggang. 2009. "The Institutional Foundations of China's Reforms and Development." Unpublished Manuscript, School of Economics and Finance, University of Hong Kong.

Yang Bing, and Jiao Wei. 2001. "Guo Di Shui Jigou Fenshe Cunzaide Wenti Ji Duice [Problems and Remedies Regarding the Establishment of Separate National and Local Tax Administration]." *Shuiwu yu jingji [Taxation and Economy]* (6):28–30.

Yang, Dali L. 1990. "Patterns of China's Regional Development Strategy." *The China Quarterly* (122):230–57.

1991. "China Adjusts to the World Economy: The Political Economy of China's Coastal Development Strategy." *Pacific Affairs* 64 (1):42–64.

1994. "Reform and the Restructuring of Central-Local Relations." In *China Deconstructs: Politics, Trade and Regionalism,* ed. D. S. G. Goodman and G. Segal. London: Routledge.

1996. "Governing China's Transition to the Market: Institutional Incentives, Politicians' Choices, and Unintended Outcomes." *World Politics* 48 (3):424–52.

2004. *Remaking the Chinese Leviathan: Market Transition and the Politics of Governance in China.* Stanford: Stanford University Press.

2006. "Economic Transformation and Its Political Discontents in China: Authoritarianism, Unequal Growth, and the Dilemmas of Political Development." *Annual Review of Political Science* 9:143–64.

Yang, Dali L., and Houkai Wei. 1996. "Rising Sectionalism in China?" *Journal of International Affairs* 49 (2):456–76.

Yep, Ray. 2008. "Enhancing the Redistributive Capacity of the Chinese State? Impact of Fiscal Reforms on County Finance." *The Pacific Review* 21 (2):231–55.

Yu, Qiao. 1998. "Capital Investment, International Trade and Economic Growth in China: Evidence in the 1980–90s." *China Economic Review* 9 (1):73–84.

Yue, Changjun, and Ping Hua. 2002. "Does Comparative Advantage Explain Export Patterns in China?" *China Economic Review* 13 (2–3):276–96.

Zhang Amei, and Zou Gang. 1994. "Foreign Trade Decentralization and Its Impact on Central-Local Relations." In *Changing Central-Local Relations in China: Reform and State Capacity*, ed. Jia Hao and Lin Zhimin. Boulder: Westview.

Zhang, Jianmin. 2002. The Dynamics of Economic Reform Process in China: The Case of Reforms of Foreign Exchange Regimes. Ph.D. Dissertation, Political Science, Washington University, St. Louis, MO.

Zhang, Jie, and Gustav Kristensen. 2001. "The Paradox of Unequal Regional Investment and Equal Regional Economic Growth in China." *Annals of Regional Science* 35 (4):637–55.

Zhang, Le-Yin. 1999. "Chinese Central-Provincial Fiscal Relationships, Budgetary Decline and the Impact of the 1994 Fiscal Reform: An Evaluation." *The China Quarterly* (157):115–41.

Zhang, Tao, and Heng-fu Zou. 1998. "Fiscal Decentralization, Public Spending, and Economic Growth in China." *Journal of Public Economics* 67 (2):221–40.

Zhang, Zhichao. 2001. "China's Exchange Rate Reform and Exports." *Economics of Planning* 34 (1–2):89–112.

Zhao Dexin, ed. 1989. *Zhonghua Renmin Gongheguo Jingjishi (1967–1984) [An Economic History of the People's Republic of China (1967–1984)]*. Zhengzhou: Henan renmin chubanshe.

Zhao Jinping, ed. 2001. *Liyong Waizi Yu Zhongguo Jingji Zengzhang [Foreign Capital Utilization and China's Economic Growth]*. Beijing: Renmin chubanshe.

Zhao Lei, and Zheng Yan. 2006. "Zhongzubu Qianbuzhang Zhiyan Gaoguan Guanli: Duihua Zhang Quanjing [Former Head of Central Department of Organization Talking Candidly About Management of High-Ranking Officials: A Conversation with Zhang Quanjing]." *Nanfang Zhoumo* [Southern Weekend], November 9, A1–2.

Zhao, Suisheng. 1990. "The Feeble Political Capacity of a Strong One-Party Regime: An Institutional Approach toward the Formulation and Implementation of Economic Policy in Post-Mao Mainland China (Part Two)." *Issues & Studies* 26 (2):35–74.

ed. 2000. *China and Democracy: The Prospect for a Democratic China*. New York: Routledge.

Zhao Yining. 2003. "Fenshuizhi Juece Beijing Huifang [Playback of the Background for the Making of the Tax Sharing System]." *Liaowang Xinwen Zhoukan [Liaowang News Weekly]* 37:20–9.

Zhao Yongqing. 1998. "1997 Nian Woguo Duiwai Jingji Maoyi Tizhi Gaige Shuping [On Our Country's Foreign Trade Reform in 1997]." *Jingji Yanjiu Cankao [Reference on Economic Research]* (12):2–20.

Zhao Ziyang. 2009. *Gaige Licheng [The Secret Journal of Zhao Ziyang]*. Hong Kong: New Century Press.

Zheng, Yongnian. 1994. "Perforated Sovereignty: Provincial Dynamism and China's Foreign Trade." *The Pacific Review* 7 (3):309–21.

2004a. *Globalization and State Transformation in China*. New York: Cambridge University Press.

2004b. *Will China Become Democratic?: Elite, Class and Regime Transition*. Singapore: Eastern University Press.

2007. *De Facto Federalism in China: Reforms and Dynamics of Central-Local Relations*. Hackensack: World Scientific.

Zhonggong Zhongyang [Central Committee of the Chinese Communist Party]. 1996[1995]. "Dangzheng Lingdao Ganbu Xuanba Renyong Gongzuo Zanxing Tiaoli [Provisional Rules for the Selection and Use of Party/ Government Leading Officials]." In *Renshi Gongzuo Wenjian Xuanbian [Selected Documents on Personnel Work]*, ed. Laodong renshi bu [Ministry of Labor and Personnel]. Beijing: Laodong renshi chubanshe.

2002. Dangzheng Lingdao Ganbu Xuanba Renyong Gongzuo Tiaoli [Rules for the Selection and Use of Party/Government Leading Officials], available at http://past.people.com.cn/GB/shizheng/252/8665/8666/20020723/782504. html, accessed on July 3, 2006.

Zhonggong Zhongyang Zuzhibu [Department of Organization of the CCP Central Committee]. 1984[1980]-a. "Guanyu Chongxin Banfa 'Zhonggong Zhongyang Guanli De Ganbu Zhiwu Mingcheng Biao' De Tongzhi [Circular on Reissuing the 'List of Centrally Managed Cadre Positions']." In *Renshi Gongzuo Wenjian Xuanbian [Selected Documents on Personnel Work]*, ed. Laodong renshi bu [Ministry of Labor and Personnel] 4: 158–64. Beijing: Laodong renshi chubanshe.

1984[1980]-b. "Zhongyang Zuzhibu Guanyu Zhixing 'Zhonggong Zhongyang Guanli De Ganbu Zhiwu Mingcheng Biao' Zhong Jige Juti Wenti De Tongzhi [Circular of the Department of Organization of the CCP Central Committee on Several Concrete Problems in Implementing the 'List of Centrally Managed Cadre Positions']." In *Renshi Gongzuo Wenjian Xuanbian [Selected Documents on Personnel Work]*, ed. Laodong renshi bu [Ministry of Labor and Personnel] 4: 165–70. Beijing: Laodong renshi chubanshe.

1986[1983]-a. "Guanyu Gaige Ganbu Guanli Tizhi Ruogan Wenti De Guiding [Rules Regarding Several Issues in Reforming the Cadre Management System]." In *Renshi Gongzuo Wenjian Xuanbian [Selected Documents on Personnel Work]*, ed. Laodong renshi bu [Ministry of Labor and Personnel] 6: 115–21. Beijing: Laodong renshi chubanshe.

1986[1983]-b. "Guanyu Lingdao Banzi 'Sihua' Jianshe De Banian Guihua [The Eight-Year Plan on the 'Four Modernizations' in Leadership Structures]." In *Renshi Gongzuo Wenjian Xuanbian [Selected Documents on Personnel Work]*, ed. Laodong renshi bu [Ministry of Labor and Personnel] 6: 107–14. Beijing: Laodong renshi chubanshe.

1991[1990]. "Guanyu Xiuding 'Zhonggong Zhongyang Guanli De Ganbu Zhiwu Mingcheng Biao' De Tongzhi [Circular on Revising and Compiling the 'List of Centrally Managed Cadre Positions']." In *Renshi Gongzuo Wenjian Xuanbian [Selected Documents on Personnel Work]*, ed. Laodong renshi bu [Ministry of Labor and Personnel] 13: 35–53. Beijing: Laodong renshi chubanshe.

1992[1991]. "Guanyu Zuohao Sheng, Zizhiqu, Zhixiashi Ganbu Bei'an Gongzuo De Tongzhi [On Improving the Work of Reporting for the Records Regarding Cadres of the Provinces/Municipalities/Autonomous Regions]." In *Renshi Gongzuo Wenjian Xuanbian [Selected Documents on Personnel Work]*, ed. Laodong renshi bu [Ministry of Labor and Personnel] 14: 53–5. Beijing: Laodong renshi chubanshe.

1999[1994]. "Circular on Resolutely Preventing or Rectifying Unsound Practices in the Work of Cadre Selection and Appointment." *Chinese Law and Government* 32 (1):38–43.

Zhonggong Zhongyang Zuzhibu [Department of Organization of the CCP Central Committee], and Zhonggong Zhongyang Dangshi Yanjiushi [CCP Central Party History Research Office]. 2004. *Zhongguo Gongchandang Lijie Zhongyang Weiyuan Dacidian [Dictionary of the Members of the Central Committees of the Chinese Communist Party]*. Beijing: Zhonggong dangshi chubanshe.

Zhonggong Zhongyang Zuzhibu [Department of Organization of the CCP Central Committee], Zhonggong Zhongyang Dangshi Yanjiushi [CCP Central Party History Research Office], and Zhongyang Dang'anguan [CCP Central Archives], eds. 2000a. *Zhongguo Gongchandang Zuzhishi Ziliao: Guodu Shiqi He Shehui Zhuyi Jianshe Shiqi (1949.10–1965.5) [Materials on the Organizational History of the Chinese Communist Party: The Eras of Transition and Building Socialism (Oct. 1949 – May 1965)]*. 13 vols. Vol. 5. Beijing: Zhonggong dangshi chubanshe.

eds. 2000b. *Zhongguo Gongchandang Zuzhishi Ziliao: Shehui Zhuyi Shiye Fazhan Shiqi (1976.10–1997.9) [Materials on the Organizational History of the Chinese Communist Party: The Era of Developing Socialism (Oct. 1976 – Sept. 1997)]*. 13 vols. Vol. 7 (parts I and II). Beijing: Zhonggong dangshi chubanshe.

eds. 2000c. *Zhongguo Gongchandang Zuzhishi Ziliao: Wenhua Dageming Shiqi (1966.6–1976.10) [Materials on the Organizational History of the Chinese Communist Party: The Era of the Cultural Revolution (Jun. 1966 – Oct. 1976)]*. 13 vols. Vol. 6. Beijing: Zhonggong dangshi chubanshe.

Zhongguo Caizheng Nianjian Bianji Weiyuanhui [Editorial Committee of the *Finance Yearbook of China*]. 1992. *Zhongguo Caizheng Nianjian [Finance Yearbook of China]*. Beijing: Zhongguo caizheng zazhishe.

1996. *Zhongguo Caizheng Nianjian [Finance Yearbook of China]*. Beijing: Zhongguo caizheng zazhishe.

1997–2005. *Zhongguo Caizheng Nianjian [Finance Yearbook of China] (Individual Issue for Each Year)*. Beijing: Zhongguo caizheng zazhishe.

2006. *Zhongguo Caizheng Nianjian [Finance Yearbook of China]*. Beijing: Zhongguo caizheng zazhishe.

Zhongguo Xingzheng Guanli Xuehui [China Society of Public Administration], ed. 2002. *Xin Zhongguo Xingzheng Guanli Jianshi (1949–2000) [A Synoptic History of Public Administration in New China (1949–2000)]*. Beijing: Renmin chubanshe.

Zhuravskaya, Ekaterina V. 2000. "Incentives to Provide Local Public Goods: Fiscal Federalism, Russian Style." *Journal of Public Economics* 76 (3):337–68.

Zoco, Edurne. 2004. "A Review of the World Bank Data Base on Political Institutions." *APSA-CP* 15 (2):32–4.

Zweig, David. 2002. *Internationalizing China: Domestic Interests and Global Linkages*. Ithaca: Cornell University Press.

Index

Achen, Christopher H., 155, 172
Adserà, Alícia, 22 fn. 3
Alchian, Armen A., 41, 118
Alesina, Alberto, 3, 4, 6 fn. 6, 22, 23, 30, 47, 144, 222
Alvarez, Michael E., 26 fn. 10, 214, 239 fn. 12
Amsden, Alice H., 54, 204
An Xiumei, 83, 89, 89 fn. 27, 190, 191
Anhui, 58, 67, 71, 85, 87, 132–33
Ansolabehere, Stephen, 86
Aten, Bettina, 229
authoritarianism. *See* single-party rule
authority migration, 2, 222, 223, 243
autonomous regions, ethnic minority
  bureaucratic integration in, 158, 163–64
  central political control of, 153, 157, 162
  vs. coastal provinces, 242
  ethnic unrest in, 73, 153, 163–64, 191
  foreign exchange earnings and, 55, 57, 58
  native sons in, 134, 178
  preferential policies and, 165, 168, 169, 171, 172, 173
  secession potential of, 242
  subsidies to, 87–88, 191, 193
autonomy, demands for
  central political control and, 20–21, 228–29
  from coastal provinces, 8, 73–75, 92, 242
  federal structure and, 32–33
  fiscal, 22, 31, 74–75, 148

globalization and, 5, 8, 16, 22, 24–25, 40, 145, 242
  redistribution and, 31–32
  in USSR, 229
  in Vietnam, 226–27, 228–29
  by winner regions, 21, 25, 27, 30–31, 46, 144

Bahl, Roy W., 82 fn. 20, 85 fn. 24
Bao, Shuming, 59, 60, 61, 61 fn. 11, 65 fn. 12, 165, 166
Bardhan, Pranab K., 234
Barnett, A. Doak, 114
Barro, Robert J., 204, 214
Bartke, Wolfgang, 138
Bates, Robert H., 152, 161
Baum, Richard, 54, 75, 93 fn. 29, 102 fn. 2, 103, 109
Beck, Nathaniel, 27, 153, 154, 171, 205
Beck, Thorsten, 48
Beijing
  bureaucratic integration in, 132, 135–36
  as centrally administered municipality, 98, 153, 178
  economic growth of, 71
  foreign exchange retention of, 58
  globalization of, 67
  redistribution and, 87
Bennett, Gordon, 103
Berger, Suzanne, 5 fn. 5
Bernstein, Thomas P., 1, 152, 162
Blanchard, Olivier, 236
Bloom, David E., 65 fn. 12

Ma Wanli, 140
Macao, 63–64, 69
Magaloni, Beatriz, 16, 238
Mair, Peter, 38
Malaysia, 69
Malesky, Edmund, 40 fn. 27, 224 fn. 2,
    225, 226, 226 fn. 4, 227, 227 fn. 5
Manion, Melanie, 10, 104, 106 fn. 7, 131,
    239
Mao Zedong, 63, 102–03
Marshall, Monty G., 48, 48 fn. 33
Martin, Pierre, 25, 33
Mayhew, David R., 17
McCubbins, Mathew D., 39, 41
Meadwell, Hudson, 25, 33
Meckling, William H., 41, 118
Mellinger, Andrew, 59, 60, 61, 61 fn. 11,
    165, 166
Mertha, Andrew C., 198 fn. 11
Mexico, 36, 42
military, PRC, 102–03, 106
Milner, Helen, V., 5, 5 fn. 5
Moe, Terry M., 39, 41
Montinola, Gabriella, 11, 12, 44, 76, 195,
    196
Moore, Clement H., 16, 238
municipalities, centrally administered
    (CAM), 98, 140, 142, 153, 158, 178,
    205
  central political control of, 157, 162
  provincial party secretaries and, 176–77

NAFTA (North American Free Trade
    Agreement), 23
Nanjing, 140, 152
Nathan, Andrew J., 108, 241 fn. 17
National Congress Party (India), 34
Nationalist Party (Kuomintang), 239
natural resources, regional, 2, 8, 14, 30
  of coastal provinces, 50, 92, 166,
    167–68
  foreign trade and, 56
  globalization and, 163, 164
  preferential policies and, 65, 172, 174
Naughton, Barry, J., 3, 10, 54, 56, 59 fn.
    10, 90, 95 fn. 34, 115 fn. 17, 144, 191,
    196, 205, 237, 241
Ningbo, 140, 152, 161, 180
Ningxia
  bureaucratic integration in, 133
  economic growth of, 71

ethnic minorities in, 153
globalization of, 68
redistribution and, 84, 88
revenues of, 57, 58, 191
Niskanen, William A., 39
Noll, Roger G., 39
nomenklatura system. *See* personnel
    authority
North, Douglass Cecil, 11, 44, 182, 195,
    202
North Korea, 9
Nye, Joseph, Jr., 5 fn. 4

O'Brien, Kevin J., 104 fn. 5
Oi, Jean C., 12, 17, 44, 74 fn. 14, 75, 80,
    82 fn. 20, 89 fn. 26, 115, 118, 185
Oksenberg, Michel, 81 fn. 18, 82,
    82 fn. 20, 111, 85 fn. 24, 111, 116,
    117, 118, 165
Olson, David, 22
Olson, Mancur, 11, 43, 195
Open Coastal Belt, 60
Open River Cities (Yangtze River), 60–61
Ordeshook, Peter C., 231, 241, 242
overseas Chinese, 63–64, 65

Pakistan, 33, 34
Parikh, Ashok, 66
Park, Jong H., 204, 214
Partido Revolucionario Institucional (PRI),
    36
Pearson, Margaret M., 7, 144
people's congresses, 104
People's Liberation Army (PLA), 102–03
personnel authority (nomenklatura system)
  of CCP, 7, 10, 13, 15, 101, 105–06,
    107–08, 110, 111, 112, 149,
    232–33, 234, 238
  central control of, 7, 10, 18, 39, 92–93,
    110–13, 116, 118, 136–37, 149,
    175, 222–23
  centralization of, 33, 34, 110–11, 113,
    232–33
  of centralized political parties, 20, 37, 39
  in Cultural Revolution, 110, 150
  decentralization of, 111–12
  democratization and, 17, 240–41
  of Department of Organization, 106,
    110, 112
  economic growth and, 210–11
  factionalism and, 163